The Asbury Theological Seminary Series in Christian Revitalization Studies

This volume is published in collaboration with the Center for the Study of World Christian Revitalization Movements, a cooperative initiative of Asbury Theological Seminary faculty. Building on the work of the previous Wesleyan/Holiness Studies Center at the Seminary, the Center provides a focus for research in the Wesleyan Holiness and other related Christian renewal movements, including Pietism and Pentecostal movements, which have had a world impact. The research seeks to develop analytical models of these movements, including their biblical and theological assessment. Using an interdisciplinary approach, the Center bridges relevant discourses in several areas in order to gain insights for effective Christian mission globally. It recognizes the need for conducting research that combines insights from the history of evangelical renewal and revival movements with anthropological and religious studies literature on revitalization movements. It also networks with similar or related research and study centers around the world, in addition to sponsoring its own research projects.

This title presents Professor Tony Headley's distinctive and fresh perspective on John Wesley's doctrine of Christian perfection, from the vantage point of what he terms a "relational cognitive-behavioral description of holiness". It is structured by his study of the pattern of Wesley's use of language in terms of a purposeful list. In giving focus to these three dimensions, Headley offers a psychological perspective on his subject which is congruent with the research of the Revitalization Center.

J. Steven O'Malley
General Editor
The Asbury Theological Seminary Studies in Christian Revitalization

Getting It Right: Christian Perfection and Wesley's Purposeful List

Anthony J. Headley

Asbury Theological Seminary Series in
World Christian Revitalization Movements in Pietist/Wesleyan Studies, No. 14

EMETH PRESS
www.emethpress.com

Getting It Right: Christian Perfection and Wesley's Purposeful List

Copyright © 2013 Anthony J. Headley
Printed in the United States of America on acid-free paper

All rights reserved. No part of this book may be reproduced, or stored in a retrieval system or transmitted in any form or by any means, electronic, mechanical, photocopying, recording, scanning or otherwise, except as permitted by the 1976 United States Copyright Act, or with the prior written permission of Emeth Press. Requests for permission should be addressed to: Emeth Press, P. O. Box 23961, Lexington, KY 40523-3961. http://www.emethpress.com.

Library of Congress Cataloging-in-Publication Data

Headley, Anthony J.
  Getting it right : Christian perfection and Wesley's purposeful list / Anthony J. Headley.
       pages cm. -- (Asbury theological seminary series in world Christian revitalization movements in pietist/wesleyan studies)
  Includes bibliographical references.
  ISBN 978-1-60947-053-1 (alk. paper)
  1. Perfection--Religious aspects--Methodist Church. 2. Christianity--Psychology. 3. Wesley, John, 1703-1791. I. Title.
  BT766.H43 2013
  234--dc23
                                              2013008763

Wesley's Photo on Front Cover
This portrait was painted by Henry Edridge in Wesley's eighty-eighth year. Some think this picture was the last to be painted before Wesley's death. Used by permission.

Dedication

To my beloved wife, Adina,
a fellow traveler on the journey

Contents

Acknowledgments / ix

Introduction / xi

Chapter 1   Wesley's Purposeful List and Christian Perfection / 1

Chapter 2   Wesley's Sources for Christian Perfection / 17

Chapter 3   Mapping the Soul: Liberty and the Apprehending Faculties of the Soul / 39

Chapter 4   Mapping the Soul: The Will and the Religious Affections / 65

Chapter 5   Relational Love and Christian Perfection / 89

Chapter 6   Objective, Dispositional Love & Christian Perfection / 111

Chapter 7   Christian Perfection & the Means of Grace / 133

Chapter 8   Getting It Right! / 147

Postscript: Thinking Ahead: The Neuroscience of Wesley's Dispositional Love by Stephen P. Stratton / 171

References   / 179

Acknowledgments

Several influences helped to form and give shape to this book. The initial stimulus for the book derived from my colleague Dr. Steve Stratton asking me to do a lecture on Wesley. Preparing for and completing that lecture led me on a foray into Wesley's concept of Christian perfection. Steve also met with me on several occasions as we discussed various concepts that appear in the book. Of course, he also wrote the postscript to this book. For all these I am deeply indebted to him.

I should also expressed gratitude to Asbury Theological Seminary which granted me a sabbatical in which I completed some of the initial chapters of the book. I am also indebted Dr. Larry Wood of Emeth Press for accepting the proposal for this book. Finally, I am most grateful to my wife Adina who spent many long hours reading and proofing this book. She gave valuable service, catching errors that my weary eyes and mind could not. Besides this, she gave valuable encouragement to me about the value of the book. I can only pray that the reader has half the enthusiasm about it as she did. Thanks Adina for your gracious help and encouragement!

Introduction

The idea for this book is of relatively recent vintage. Around March 2010, my colleague Dr. Steve Stratton approached me about doing one of the Theta Phi Forum lectures for the coming fall on the topic of holiness. Theta Phi is the honor society for theological students and professors. As part of its campus activities, Theta Phi sponsors a fall forum and a spring lecture series.

At first, I was rather hesitant to do the lecture but having talked to Steve and conferred further with Theta Phi, I finally agreed. Little did I know that engaging this project would lead me on an exciting journey into John Wesley's concept of Christian perfection. This excitement began with my rereading of Wesley's *A Plain Account of Christian Perfection.* I had read it back in my seminary days and am sure I had read it on other occasions. But now I read it with fresh eyes and deliberate purpose. Perhaps it's because of this new perspective that I encountered a pattern and words I had never observed before. Actually, that is not completely true. I had seen the words before but they simply had not registered on my radar. In this book, I refer to this pattern of words as a purposeful list. I am indebted to my colleague Dr. Fred Long who introduced me to this concept. I will define this term in the initial chapter of the book.

But there were other aspects of the discovery that intrigued me. In my orientation as a psychologist, I largely operate from a cognitive behavioral perspective; however, the approach I use is also grounded in systemic thinking and the importance of interpersonal relationships. Given this orientation, the other aspects that caught my attention were threefold: First, I was intrigued by the significant relational emphasis Wesley incorporated into his expression of Christian perfection. Second, I was surprised by the important role he carved out for right thinking. I don't think I had previously thought about right thinking as being a significant part of holiness. Yet there it was – over and over again. Third, I saw a strong behavioral emphasis in Wesley's exposition; for him, the right heart and right thinking, considered inward holiness, should always give rise to right words and actions.

In time, as part of the development of my lecture for Theta Phi, I arrived at a psychological description of this process laid out by Wesley. I thought about it as a relational cognitive-behavioral description of holiness. In the various chapters of this book, several of these aspects appear in the discussion, even if I do not specifically and consistently use these terms. In addition, in a final postscript, my friend and colleague Dr. Steve Stratton offers pertinent insights into the relational nature of Christian perfection. He possesses unique expertise in attachment theory, relationships and the neuropsychological dynamics of emotion and affection. Given this expertise, I asked him to provide a final postscript that links Wesley's thoughts and my own to current thinking in the area of relationships, particularly the emphasis on love. Hopefully, these efforts will eventuate in a book that presents holiness in an understandable fashion. I also hope it will make holiness both attractive and presently relevant.

Now, a final word about the title! In the spring of 2012, I attended a clergy retreat of my conference. While there, I met a colleague and friend, Professor Sharon Bryson. She asked about the project I had worked on during my recently concluded sabbatical. I told her I had begun work on a book I would title *Getting It Right*. She immediately asked me, "Do you mean that yours is the definitive perspective on Christian Perfection?" I quickly told her that the title derived from Wesley's emphasis on rightness in his explication of Christian perfection; that is, right heart, right thinking, right words and works. Thus, we have the title: *Getting It Right: Christian Perfection and Wesley's Purposeful List.*

Chapter 1

Wesley's Purposeful List and Christian Perfection

The Inward Nature of Christian Experience

"So that whereas the righteousness of the Scribes and Pharisees was external only, it may be said, in some sense, that *the righteousness of a Christian is internal only*." (Wesley 1872n, 414 (italics added)) These words from one of John Wesley's sermons, riveted my attention. The words sounded untrue. They seemed to suggest that righteous behavior mattered little, if any, in the Christian life. Taken out of context, the words seemed to invite careless behavior. In fact, they appeared to exhibit an almost blatant disregard for the ordinances of God and an inherent antinomianism. Of course, Wesley intended a different perspective on his words and this appeared in the statement's context. The words appeared in his fifth discourse on the Sermon on the Mount dated between October 22-26, 1740. (Smith 1982) Here, he noted: "Thus, to do no harm, to do good, to attend the ordinances of God, (the righteousness of a Pharisee,) are all external; whereas, on the contrary, poverty of spirit, mourning, meekness, hunger and thirst after righteousness, the love of our neighbor, and purity of heart, (the righteousness of a Christian,) are all internal. And even peace-making, (or doing good,) and suffering for righteousness' sake, stand entitled to the blessings annexed to them, only as they imply these inward dispositions, as they spring from, exercise, and confirm them." (Wesley 1872n, 414)

Wesley's words communicated a couple of emphases: First, he drew a deliberate contrast between pharisaic religion based on adherence to externals and true Christian faith grounded in internal attitudes of the heart. Second, although he drew this distinction, he did not devalue the external aspects of faith. Instead, he emphasized that external righteousness must be built upon internal dispositions, such as meekness, love of neighbor and purity of heart. As highlighted in the Beatitudes, he knew that suffering for righteousness' sake and peace-making derive their blessedness from the dispositions that underlie them. In sum, the statement demonstrates the significant emphasis he placed on inward dispositions as the essence of Christianity. It also displays the central place he carved out for transformed dispositions in Christians. Moreover, the statement revealed a kind of genius, combining the internal and external dimensions of Christianity in dynamic synthesis. Nevertheless, he emphatically kept the priority on dispositions of the heart. To get Christian faith and holiness right, one needs to understand this trajectory and order.

Wesley's statements also betrayed a hyperbole that emphasized a significant point; in the Christian life, everything begins from the inside out. All right conduct finds its source in right dispositions of the heart. In turn, the transformed heart births transformed behavior. Moreover, even the most righteous actions, like attending to God's ordinances and engaging in acts of mercy and piety, appear valueless in God's sight if they do not proceed from a transformed heart. External behavior may matter, but the source of one's words and actions matters supremely and validates these same behaviors. In fact, in the sentence immediately following the referenced paragraph, Wesley indicated as much, noting: "All his actions and sufferings being as nothing in themselves, being estimated before God only by the tempers from which they spring." (Wesley 1872n, 414) In sum, right tempers of the heart dictate the rightness of actions and their acceptance before God.

Wesley likely drew this stark contrast between external and internal religion as a way to critique his contemporary Anglican religious culture. According to Randy Maddox, in Wesley's day, there existed a tendency to conceptualize holiness in the external language of doing good and avoiding evil while "neglecting the affectional dimension of human life." (Maddox 1994, 178) Over against this thinking, Wesley placed the critical emphasis on inward aspects of faith, "...described in such terms as "the life of God in the [human] soul, a participation of the divine nature, the mind that was in Christ, or the renewal of our heart after the image of [God who] created us." (Maddox 1994, 178) By statements like this, he hoped to provide a legitimate, scripturally based critique and corrective to the prevailing Anglican view and the external religion the clergy pandered. At the same time, he sought to establish a different and scripturally based understanding of the nature of Christian holiness.

In other places, Wesley made similar statements to the one quoted earlier. In his Journal entry for October 9, 1738, he spoke of the transformation that occurs when one became a new creature. There he noted: "First: His Judgments are new: His judgment of *himself*, of *happiness*, of *holiness*... Yet again: His judgment concerning *holiness* is new. He no longer judges it to be an outward thing: To consist either in doing no harm, in doing good, or in using the ordinances of God. *He sees it is the life of God in the soul; the image of God fresh stamped on the heart; an entire renewal of the mind in every temper and thought, after the likeness of Him that created it.*" (Wesley 1872a, 184, (italics added)) In this statement, one discovers some of the language used to communicate the inward dispositions of the Christian life. He saw God re-creating his image in the heart, the center of one's being. Furthermore, he related this transformation to the renewal of one's mind in "temper and thought," that is, in one's inward disposition. He also displayed similar thoughts in *The Spirit of Bondage and Adoption*, dated April 25, 1739, (Smith 1982). He saw that the natural man neither loved nor feared God. Such a man did not live in fear of God's vengeance because he did not understand it. And why didn't he? According to Wesley, it was because: "He imagines the main point is to *do thus*, to be *outwardly* blameless; and sees not that it extends to every temper, desire, thought, motion of the heart" (Wesley 1872i, 171)

A Journey of Discovery: Wesley' Purposeful List

In many of the quotations noted above, one finds initial traces of what I call Wesley's purposeful list. One finds words such as *inward dispositions* and *tempers* that highlight the internal nature of the Christian life. In fact, many examples of the purposeful list that will be laid out in this book give prominent place to words such as *temper* and *affections*. A good example of this appears in Wesley's use of the term *love*, considered a master temper. (Maddox 1994; Wesley 1872e) But in the purposeful list, one also finds emphasis on the word *thought* or similar language. Significantly, in two of the instances highlighted previously, *thought* appeared and connected to *temper*. For example, in the quotation from Wesley's Journal of October 9, 1738, *thought* seems related to *temper*; both appear as expressions of the renewed image of God and the renewed mind in Christians. A similar connection also appears in the quotation from *The Spirit of Bondage and Adoption*. There, Wesley contrasted outward and inward blamelessness. As part of inward blamelessness he identified *temper, desire* and *thought* and concluded with the term *motion of the heart*. (Wesley 1872i)

A further clue to his usage of the word *thought* appears in the sermon, *The Good Steward*. Here, he spoke of an extensive meaning to the word. He noted that God had entrusted humans with a soul made in his image. This soul came with various powers and faculties. He identified these faculties and accompanying affections as: "... understanding, imagination, memory; will, and a train of affections, either included in it, or closely dependent upon it; love and hatred, joy and sorrow, respecting present good and evil; desire and aversion hope and fear, respecting that which is to come." (Wesley 1872b, 161) Then he linked these powers to the Apostle Paul's use of the terms heart and mind: "All these St. Paul seems to include in two words, when he says, "The peace of God shall keep your hearts and minds." Perhaps, indeed, the latter word, νοηματα, might rather be rendered *thoughts;* provided we take that word in its most extensive sense, for every perception of the mind, whether active or passive." (Wesley 1872b, 161-162) From this quotation, it appears evident that he utilized an extensive as well as a narrow sense for the word *thought*. In the broad sense, he saw it in some manner equivalent to perceptions of the mind. Taken together, these observations confirm that like *temper*, *thought* sometimes constituted an inward aspect; both terms represent aspects of having a renewed mind and image. This observation seems important because examples of the purposeful list appear where *thought* is not explicitly present but might be inferred by the presence of words such as mind. But instances exist where *thought* appears an outcome of the inward disposition and in this sense relates to external behavior. This likely pertains to the more narrow sense Wesley inferred. I will return to aspects of this discussion later when I discuss the language used in his purposeful list.

So far, I have beat around the proverbial bush and have largely hinted at, rather than directly define the term *purposeful list.* Furthermore, I have provided minimal examples of its presence in Wesley's writings. Up front, I confess that the term is not my own. In fact, I had never heard the term until I spoke to my colleague Dr. Fred Long at a men's breakfast at our local church. I had just spoken to him about a pattern I observed while reading *A Plain Account of Christian Perfection*. As I described the pattern, he quickly described it as a purposeful list. I don't know if the term originated with him, but it was clear that from biblical studies he was thoroughly familiar with instances in which New Testament authors ordered and sequenced words to communicate a purpose or central emphasis. In such cases, the sequencing and order arose not accidentally or randomly, but from clear determination and intent on the part of the author.

I think I discovered in Wesley's writings this deliberate ordering of terms relative to the Christian life and Christian perfection in particular. This ordering appeared so often that it seems highly implausible that it was accidental. Besides, Wesley consistently betrayed a penchant for studiousness and thoughtful disposition, coupled with a preference for precision. (Baker 1970) This preference also suggests a deliberate purpose to the consistent pattern. Moreover, this ordering in Wesley's writings seems like a kind of *order salutis*, though not in the classic sense of the term; rather, it tracks Christian experience from its internal beginning to its external manifestation in word and work. The order typically began with reference to the internal life using words such as *temper, affection, design, intentions* or similar words. Following this, Wesley focused on thinking (*thought*), often culminating with an emphasis on *word* and *action*. Sometimes, not all the words appeared although the context usually provided hints about the missing pieces. But even when there is a partial list, the order is almost invariably the same. For example, one might find, thinking, word and action, or simply word and action, but most often in this order. This language and order appeared splattered across many pages in *A Plain Account of Christian Perfection*. I see such examples as his purposeful list in the proper sense of the term. Throughout the book, when I refer to the purposeful list, I mostly intend this definition. It is also the pattern to which I give primary attention.

However, I sometimes refer to this form as an expanded list. I do so because Wesley sometimes employed another purposeful listing shorter in form. I refer to this as a compacted list. Here, he also used various terms to communicate the inside out nature of Christian transformation. For example, one might find reference to inward and outward holiness or to holiness of heart and life. Additionally, in the compacted version, he related the inward and outward dimensions of Christian perfection to theological concepts such as sin, obedience and repentance. Thus, while speaking of poverty of spirit in Discourse one, he noted: "Poverty of spirit then, as it implies the first step we take in running the race which is set before us, is a just sense of our inward and outward sins, and of our guilt and helplessness." (Wesley 1872j, 339) In Discourse five, he made the point in relation to obedience. In this case, he stated that the righteousness of a Christian exceeded that of a Pharisee or Scribe because the former fulfilled "the spirit as well as the letter of the law; by inward as well as outward obedience." (Wesley 1872n, 414) He made a similar point in Discourse seven, noting:

> Let every season, either of public or private fasting, be a season of exercising all those holy affections which are implied in a broken and contrite heart. Let it be a season of devout mourning, of godly sorrow for sin; … Yea, and let our sorrowing after a godly sort work in us the same inward and outward *repentance*; the same entire change of heart, renewed after the image of God, in righteousness and true holiness; and the same change of life, till we are holy as He is holy, in all manner of conversation. (Wesley 1872o, 451)

But he made the same point using the idea and language of internal and external holiness. In these instances, he often laid the two aspects of holiness side by side. For instance, he did this in Discourse 2 when speaking about the characteristics of the man of love: "But he "rejoiceth in the truth," wheresoever it is found; in "the truth which is after godliness;" bringing forth its proper fruit, holiness of heart, and holiness of conversation." (Wesley 1872l, 359) We also find reference to the complementarity of holiness of heart and conversation in Discourse ten where he spoke about one being "holy of heart and all manner of conversation." (Wesley 1872k, 495) Furthermore, in speaking about prayer, he wrote: "Therefore, now, at least, "ask, and it shall be given unto you." Ask, that ye may thoroughly experience, and perfectly practice, the whole of that religion which our Lord has here so beautifully described. It shall then be given you, to be holy as he is holy, both in heart and in all manner of conversation." (Wesley 1872k,

495) Elsewhere, he also spoke of being "holy in heart and life." (Wesley 1872m, 386; Wesley 1872k, 494) Through these varied means, he communicated that holiness pertained to both one's inward being as well as to one's life in the world.

My research focused principally on the purposeful list in its expanded form. However, because of the close connection between the two forms, they often occurred together in some of the examples I discovered. I began my research by searching for various instances of the expanded pattern and the related terms. Having noted the pattern in *A Plain Account of Christian Perfection*, I wondered whether it uniquely appeared in this work or whether it also occurred elsewhere. This curiosity prompted a journey of exploration; I began an eager search for the terms in his journal, sermons and other writings. When I discovered instances including the sequence, I carefully read and considered those within the context of the larger work. To my surprise and fascination, I discovered that the purposeful list appeared many other places. Furthermore, I discovered that it did not simply appear in his discussion of Christian perfection. In fact, it seemed to apply to his overall understanding of salvation. As such, one even finds him discussing unregenerate persons with similar language and sequence seen in *A Plain Account of Christian Perfection*. For example, he taught that God holds the ungodly responsible for their outward and inward state just as he does the Christian; not just for words and actions but also the tempers of their heart. Additionally, when speaking of the judgment of the unregenerate, he reprised the language found in the purposeful list, mostly in reversed order: that is, works, word, affections tempers, thoughts or designs. Thus, in *The Great Assize*, he noted: "After the righteous are judged, the King will turn to them upon his left hand; and *they shall also be judged, every man according to his works. But not only their outward works will be brought into the account, but all the evil words which they have ever spoken; yea, all the evil desires, affections, tempers, which have, or have had, a place in their souls; and all the evil thoughts or designs which were ever cherished in their hearts.*" (Wesley 1872c, 256, (italics added))

One also sees this uniform application to the unregenerate and regenerate when Wesley referenced love. He described the unregenerate as loving the world, the flesh and the devil and not loving the creator. (Wesley 1872h; Wesley 1872i) But he applied the same language to the regenerate. Regenerate persons, not yet made perfect, might find themselves, even if for a moment, slipping back into the tendency to love the creature more than the creator and loving pleasure more than God. In contrast, he described the sanctified as settled in their love of God and neighbor. (Wesley 1872g) This parallel language describing one's experience or lack of experience with God highlights the consistent manner in which Wesley understood salvation. Thus, he often described each state of grace using the same language and sequence; he also did so whether referring to Christians or those outside of Christ. Moreover, he differentiated those in Christ and at different stages of grace in this same manner. In addition, he seemed to understand every state of grace in a relational manner; that is, one's state of grace depends on whether one lovingly relates to God or affixes oneself to some other objects that are not God, such as other creatures, pleasure, or the world.

Examples of the Purposeful List in *A Plain Account of Christian Perfection*

Having provided an initial understanding of the purposeful list, I will attempt to clarify it further by providing examples of it in Wesley's works. These will come principally from *A Plain Account of Christian Perfection*. However, I will also provide select examples from elsewhere in his writings. For emphasis, I will highlight important words indicative of the purposeful list and provide comments on the examples chosen. I now turn attention to identifying some of these instances, beginning with examples from Wesley's *A Plain Account of Christian Perfection*.

The first example came from the year 1725. In this instance, Wesley noted: "In the year 1725, being in the twenty-third year of my age, I met with Bishop Taylor's "Rule and Exercises of Holy Living and Dying." In reading several parts of this book, *I was exceedingly affected; that part in particular which relates to purity of intention. Instantly I resolved to dedicate all my life to God, all my thoughts, and words, and actions.*" (Wesley 1872f, 428, (Italics added)) Several elements of this quotation merit comment. First, this language occurred rather early in his ministry. Second, he identified the source that influenced him, namely, Bishop Taylor's book on holy living and dying. Wesley described himself as exceedingly moved by the book, signified by his use of the word "affected." However, this was no ephemeral response; rather, it deeply impacted him in the area dealing with purity of intention. Third, he highlighted words I associate with his purposeful list. He spoke of a resolution to dedicate his life to God. This seems to point to the inward aspect of the list. In close succession came the other parts of the purposeful list, representing the entirety of his life "*...all my thoughts, and words, and actions.*"

A few pages later, Wesley offered another statement reflecting his list: "*Let every affection, and thought, and word, and action, be subordinate to this. Whatever ye desire or fear, whatever ye seek or shun, whatever ye think, speak, or do, be it in order to your happiness in God, the sole end, as well as source, of your being.*" (Wesley 1872f, 430, (Italics added)) In this statement, he introduced another word worth mentioning. This is the word *affection*, also reflective of the inner life of the Christian. I shall not provide a discussion of affection at this time but shall reserve this for chapter four. Suffice it to say, along with *temper,* this term has received great attention in the literature from persons such as Gregory Clapper, Ken Collins and Randy Maddox among others ((Clapper 1987; Clapper 1985a; Clapper 1984;

Collins 2003; Collins 2004; Leffel 2007; Maddox 1994). These authors have debated its nature. Some like Clapper see it as a term somewhat synonymous with the dispositional term *temper* (Clapper 1985a; Clapper 1985b). On the other hand, unlike the tempers, Ken Collins sees affections as more transient. (Collins 1998)

Additionally, in this last referenced quotation from *A Plain Account of Christian Perfection,* several references to thought and thinking occur. Earlier in this chapter I indicated that Wesley sometimes considered *thought* as part of one's inward life. At other times, *thought* clearly seemed to refer to external behavior. This particular instance provides an example of the latter; if one considers the phrase *whatever ye think, speak, or do,* as paralleling the earlier, *thought, word and action,* then Wesley likely intended an external understanding of *thought.* Even if this issues remains in doubt, the presence of the purposeful list is not. Here we have a clear inward term *(affection),* followed by thought and then the clear externals, word and action.

Another example of this phenomenon appears one page later in the *Plain Account.* Here, Wesley wrote:

> 'Desire not to live but to praise his name; let all your thoughts, words, and works tend to his glory.' 'Let your soul be filled with so entire a love to Him, that you may love nothing but for his sake.' 'Have a pure intention of heart, a steadfast regard to his glory in all your actions.' For then, and not till then, is that 'mind in us, which was also in Christ Jesus,' when in every motion of our heart, in every word of our tongue, in every work of our hands, we 'pursue nothing but in relation to him, and in subordination to his pleasure;' when we too neither think, nor speak, nor act, to fulfill 'our own will, but the will of Him that sent us;' when, 'whether we eat or drink, or whatever we do,' we do it all 'to the glory of God.'" (Wesley 1872f, 431)

Several words in this statement point to Wesley's inward focus and reflect the external and internal aspects of the purposeful list. I will first make brief comments on the external aspects present in this statement and later focus most of the attention on the internal elements. In this statement, one finds several external aspects:

"Let your thoughts, words and actions tend to his glory."
"... in every word of our tongue, in every work of our hands..."
"... when we too neither think, nor speak, nor act to fulfill 'our own will, but the will of Him that sent us"

Towards the end of the quotation, he added language which expanded the contemplated actions, namely, "...when, 'whether we eat or drink, or whatever we do,' we do it all 'to the glory of God'." All of these terms place an emphasis on the externals of Christian behavior that spring from internal dynamics of the soul.

Turning to the internal aspects of the purposeful list, one finds words such as *desire.* This is linked with inward dispositions in Wesley's sermon

The Spirit of Bondage and Adoption. (Wesley 1872i) Although one could debate its usage, the verb *desire* in this context seems to point to an internal usage. The quotation also contains a reference to having the mind of Christ. This terms also links to the renewed image of God in persons and as such connotes an internal dimension. Moreover, we have several clear references to internal aspects when Wesley used words such as *love, a pure intention of heart*, and *motion of the heart.* Thus, even if one debates *desire*, it is yet clear that Wesley was placing major focus on the inward life of the Christian. Furthermore, directives such as "Let your soul be filled with so entire a love to Him" and "Have a pure intention of heart," communicated his inward intent.

Wesley also communicated his inward intent by at least two contrasts drawn in the statement. These contrasts revolved around the motivation for behavior. The first seems to make an implicit contrast between bringing glory to God or to self. The second explicitly contrasted a desire to do God's will rather than our own will. The latter idea of submitting to God's will versus doing our own will also seems captured in the phrase: *we 'pursue nothing but in relation to him, and in subordination to his pleasure."* Taken together, two opposing paths appear; we can live dominated by the desire to glorify ourselves or we can live guided by the desire to glorify God. However, this latter style of life only comes through a radical reorientation of our being. The latter contrast also raises a term he used often, namely, *self-will*. This term reflects aspects of the internal dimensions of the purposeful list. Moreover, it clearly constitutes part of the whole package Wesley intended when he speaks of internal dispositions of the heart. I will discuss self-will in some detail in chapter four when discussing the will of the soul.

Before moving on to examples elsewhere in Wesley's writing, I present two additional examples from *A Plain Account of Christian Perfection*. The first example stands as an excellent example of the purposeful list. Here he noted: "The loving God with all our heart, mind, soul, and strength. This implies, that no wrong temper, none contrary to love, remains in the soul; and that all the thoughts, words, and actions, are governed by pure love." (Wesley 1872f, 461) Clear elements of the purposeful list appear here. First, the quotation reiterates the language reflective of the internal disposition of the heart; he used the words *love* and *temper*, which are closely associated; in fact love served as the master temper from which all other tempers flow. For him, love served as the foundational principle for everything in Adam prior to the fall; and not just for thoughts, words and actions, but even as the basis for other tempers. Second, we learn that a temper can be morally wrong when not governed by love. Third, temper also appears as a disposition of the soul. Finally, we find the external aspects of the purposeful list when Wesley identified *thoughts, words* and *actions* governed by pure love.

The final example presented from *A Plain Account of Christian Perfection* involves a poem. The example actually occurred prior to the previously referenced example. However, I chose to place it here because in some respects, it best depicts the deliberate nature of the purposeful list. Wesley indicated the poem reflected the cry of his heart as he returned from America in 1738. As a result, this occurred before Aldersgate or his experience at Fetter's Lane. Here is Wesley's cry:

> O grant that nothing in my soul
> May dwell, but thy pure love alone!
> O may thy love possess me whole,
> My joy, my treasure, and my crown!
> Strange fires far from my heart remove;
> My every act, word, thought, be love! (Wesley 1872f, 431)

One quickly observes that the stanza began with a plea for the pure, holy temper of love to abide in him. Given his description of love as a foundational principle, it makes sense that he began here. Moreover, he visualized it as a love that possessed his entire being. Along with this possession, he concomitantly pleaded for a removal of "strange fires" from his heart. This most likely represents a petition for cleansing associated with Christian perfection. But the final line in the stanza merits special attention. First, we find elements of the purposeful list in the terms *thought, word and act*. However, a difference exists from previous places where this trio occurred; the list comes completely reversed with love coming at the end. How does one explain this significant change in Wesley's normal order? Two explanations readily appear. The first involves poetic effect. Given the presence of *remove* in the penultimate line, it seems clear that *love* comes at the end as a visual and verbal rhyme with the earlier term. Second and more significantly, Wesley likely changed his order to preserve the normal sequence of his purposeful list *in reverse*. Read from right to left, the order is the same as elsewhere. More importantly, this reversed order preserves his notion that love is the foundational principle from which springs all transformed behavior. Thus, we have the revamped order, act, word, thought, and love. (Headley 2010)

Examples of the Purposeful List Elsewhere

So far, I have drawn examples primarily from *A Plain Account of Christian Perfection*. However, the purposeful list appears elsewhere in Wesley. Similar examples appeared in his discourses on the *Sermon on the Mount*. We also find examples in places such as *Brief Thoughts on Christian Perfection, Circumcision of the Heart, On the Church, On Perfection, Repentance in Believers, The Great Assize, The New Birth*, and *The Witness of Our Own Spirit*. For brevity, I will not provide examples from all these, but instead present a few representative ones. However, in other chapters in the book, occasion will arise to cite additional examples.

One could easily argue that Jesus' Sermon of the Mount fundamentally informed Wesley's inside/out understanding of Christian experience reflected in the purposeful list. As we saw in his fifth discourse, he emphasized internal righteousness over against external righteousness. As such, he contrasted external works of piety and mercy with dispositions of spirit such as poverty of spirit, mourning, meekness, love and purity of heart. For him, these latter qualities of the soul constituted the essential nature of a Christian. More importantly, Wesley's perspective reflected the deliberate order Jesus himself enunciated in the Beatitudes; namely, that it was from the inside that all righteous behavior begins. Given this perspective, it should surprise no one that many good examples of the purposeful list appear in his sermons based on the Sermon on the Mount. One great example comes from his eighth sermon in the series. Here, in commenting on the importance of a singular focus on God, he noted:

> "If thine eye be" thus "single," thus fixed on God, "thy whole body shall be full of light." "Thy whole body:' — all that is guided by the intention, as the body is by the eye. *All thou art; all thou doest; thy desires, tempers, affections; thy thoughts and word and actions.* The whole of these "shall be full of light;" full of true divine knowledge. (Wesley 1872p, 454, (Italics added))

Several truths pertaining to and consistent with the purposeful list appear here. First, here too, Wesley saw transformation as objective, deriving from the object on which one focuses. (Collins 1998; Land 1993) This notion was firmly embedded in Jesus' sermon. The eye derives its light from being fixed on God; that is, if an individual focuses with singular intention on the God who is light, He bathes our whole inner being with light. Second, following Jesus, he implied that the object upon which one focuses becomes the very source of transformation. Thus, if one focuses on God as our principle object, this God who is light illuminates and transforms one's inner being, remaking such a person like unto His glorious nature. However, even here, one finds an implicit place for human response; the individual's singularity of intention and focus on God as divine object creates space for inner change to take place.

Third, in this context, one notices Wesley's attempt to define what he meant by the whole body. As implied in the purposeful list, he began with *being* followed by *doing*. By these emphases one might surmise that he viewed being and doing as important dimensions of personhood. As a result, we have the statement: "All thou art; all thou doest...." Based on the construction of the sentence, one can justly argue that the coordinate phrases that immediately follow; namely "thy desires, tempers, affections; thy thoughts and word and actions" were designed to flesh out respectively what he meant by being and doing. In other words, "... thy desires, tempers, affections," fleshed out what Wesley meant by being. Similarly, "... thy thoughts, and words and actions," laid bare his understanding of doing. Thus, these words constitute two clear examples of his inside out perspective on Christian experience; the first appears in a compacted form broadly focused around being and doing. The second comes in expanded form, highlighting the inner dispositions that give rise to thoughts, words and actions.

Two notable examples also appeared in Wesley's sermon entitled *The New Birth*. After describing the ways in which God created us in His image: namely, a natural, political and moral image, he noted: "In this image of God was man made. "God is love:" Accordingly, *man at his creation was full of love; which was the sole principle of all his tempers, thoughts, words, and actions.*" (Wesley 1872d, 84 (Italics added)) Here, as in *A Plain Account of Christian Perfection,* he clearly identified love as the principal characteristic of our original state at creation. A few pages later, in the same sermon, we find another excellent example of the purposeful list:

> "Gospel holiness is no less than the image of God stamped upon the heart; it is no other than the whole mind which was in Christ Jesus it consists of all heavenly affections and tempers mingled together in one. It implies such a continual, thankful love to him who hath not withheld from us his Son, his only Son, as makes it natural and in a manner necessary to us, to love every child of man; as fills us "with bowels of mercies, kindness, gentleness, long-suffering:" *It is such a love of God as teaches us to be blameless in all manner of conversation; as enables us to present our souls and bodies, all we are and all we have, all our thoughts, words and actions,* a continual sacrifice to God, acceptable through Christ Jesus." (Wesley 1872d, 89 (Italics added))

This statement provides several interesting points. First, holiness involves two key elements: the renewed image of God and the mind of Christ. Concomitant with these, Wesley introduced the idea of heavenly affections and tempers. His phrase regarding these two as "mingled together in one," presents an interesting perspective on their relationship. In addition to suggesting their close association in some aspects, it implied that they are relatively indistinguishable from each other. Whether he meant this literally is a matter for further discussion in chapter four.

Second, as noted elsewhere, we see the prominent place he carved out for love in its many aspects. The first aspect of love involves loving response to God. However, our response answers to the initiating love of God for us revealed in the sacrificial giving of His Son. As a result, he saw it as natural and necessary that we would reciprocate this love God showed to us, to others. Furthermore, he saw our love to God as giving birth to holy fruit which transforms our inner nature, and thereby fills us up "... with bowels of mercies, kindness, gentleness, long-suffering:" Additionally, this love informs our conduct and the sacrificial giving of ourselves to God; it instructs us on how to live blamelessly. Moreover, it enables the sacrificial giving of our entire being to God. This language conjures up images of Romans 12:1-2 where Paul called Christians to sacrificially give themselves to God.

Third, after speaking of giving our souls and bodies, Wesley again raised elements of the purposeful list. By this latter statement I suggest that the earlier emphases on the renewed image of God, the mind of Christ, the affections and tempers and love, all represent the inner dimensions of the list. The inner dimension also comes packaged in his emphasis on the soul as the first thing we are enabled to give. We also likely have here compacted and expanded versions of the list; that is, "our souls and bodies" likely parallel the earlier "all thou art, all thou doest," forming the compacted version. In this way of thinking, what follows souls and bodies comprise the expanded version. Thus, "all we are and all we have," might be expressive of our interior being and "all our thoughts, words and actions" might parallel bodies, namely our external behavior. At any rate, we clearly have a detailed example of his purposeful list and its focus on the inside, outside nature of Christian experience.

Although several other examples abound, I provide two more example of this phenomenon in Wesley. The examples come from his sermon, *The Witness of Our Own Spirit.* In the first example, he introduced the concept of conscience in the following words:

> "And according to the meaning wherein it is generally used there, particularly in the Epistles of St. Paul, we may understand by conscience, a faculty or power, implanted by God in every soul that comes into the world, of perceiving what is right or wrong in his own heart or life, in his tempers, thoughts, words, and actions." (Wesley 1872r, 210 (italics added))

In the following pages, he continued his discussion of conscience with this statement:

> "There is required, Thirdly, an agreement of our hearts and lives, of our tempers and conversation, of our thoughts, and words, and works, with that rule, with the written word of God. For, without this, if we have any conscience at all, it can be only in evil conscience. There is, Fourthly, required, an inward perception of this agreement with our rule: And this habitual perception, this inward consciousness itself, is properly a good conscience; or, in the other phrase of the Apostle, "a conscience void of offense, toward God, and toward men." (Wesley 1872r, 211-212)

Wesley's concept of the conscience requires a discussion all of its own. However, I will not discuss this here in any depth, reserving this discussion for chapter three. Suffice it to say that along with understanding, imagination, memory, will and affections, Wesley saw it as a faculty of the soul. (Wesley 1872b) What's more, God gave conscience to every human soul so that they might judge between right and wrong. Additionally, it would appear from the statement that conscience possesses the ability to judge both the rightness of the interior as well as the exterior life. Thus, in the first quotation, Wesley noted that conscience serves the perceptive role of deciphering: "*...what is right or wrong in his own heart or life, in his tempers, thoughts, words, and action.*" In this statement, one also encounters compacted and expanded versions of the purposeful list; heart and life serve as the compacted example whereas and tempers, thoughts, words and actions provide the expanded version. We find a similar case of compacted and expanded lists in the second quotation, where Wesley spoke of "... *an agreement of our hearts and lives, of our tempers and conversation, of our thoughts, and words, and works, with that rule, with the written word of God.*" In this regard, hearts and lives together with tempers and conversation present the compacted version of the inward and outward. The latter emphasis on thoughts, words and works seem to present an expanded version of the outward dimensions of the purposeful list.

Conclusion

What is the principal import of this discussion? First, I intended this chapter to define the term *purposeful list*. As I suggested earlier, this purposeful language and sequence represented a kind of *order salutis*, tracking the inside/outside trajectory of Christian experience. Second, I wanted to demonstrate its presence by citing relevant examples in Wesley's writings. I principally drew from *A Plain Account of Christian Perfection*. Nevertheless, given its presence elsewhere in his writings and sermons, I produced a few examples from the latter and from his journal. Third, I intended this chapter as a way of introducing the basic affectional language appearing in the purposeful list. This language helps present his vision of the soul, or to borrow Ken Collin's language, it helped map out his topography of the soul. (Collins 1998) It will remain for me to revisit this topic when charting the contours of the soul in chapters three and four.

Fourth, I have sought to characterize the purposeful list as presenting Wesley's views on salvation in succinct, abbreviated form, particularly as it relates to Christian perfection. As noted, he grounded Christian experience in fundamental transformations of the internal dispositions of the heart. For him, Christianity involved a religion which principally transformed from the inside beginning with dispositions of the soul such as tempers and affections. This fits well with the comment that for Wesley, the essential goal of the Christian life is the recovery of holy tempers, with love as the master temper. (Land 1993; Maddox 1994; Wesley 1872e; Wesley 1872q) This way of thinking follows in the train of Jesus who depicted all true spiritual change as beginning in the heart. Without it, everything appears but dross in God's eyes. But saying this does not minimize the importance of external righteousness. Rather, it grounds outward holiness on inward holiness. That is, external righteousness finds it impetus in the dispositions of the soul; transformations begun inwardly in the affections and tempers worked to produce righteous behavior involving thinking, speaking and acting. Furthermore, only when behavior truly springs from these transformed dispositions do they win God's approval and blessing. To reprise a quotation from Wesley laid out at the beginning, external righteous behaviors "... stand entitled to the blessings annexed to them, only as they imply these inward dispositions, as they spring from, exercise, and confirm them." (Wesley 1872n, 414) This idea stands as the ultimate intent of Wesley's purposeful list. To understand this sequence and its import for Christian transformation and conduct is to get Christian perfection right.

Chapter 2

Wesley's Sources for Christian Perfection

Wesley's Sources

The right heart constitutes the essence of Christian faith! Moreover, from such a heart flow right thinking, right words and works. This message forms the core of Wesley's view of salvation especially as it pertains to Christian perfection. It also forms the central truth communicated through his purposeful list. Viewed from this perspective, transformation happens from the inside out, beginning with a radical change in the heart. But a transformed inner nature is not simply a private religious experience known solely by the self; rather, inward religion of the heart always makes itself visible in the world. The radically changed heart together with its new desires, tempers and affections transforms outward behavior exemplified in thoughts, words and actions. Furthermore, Wesley believed this inner transformation makes outward behaviors acceptable sacrifices in God's eyes; without it, God regards external behaviors of little value. (Wesley 1872r)

But from whence did Wesley derive this understanding of Christian faith? His writings provided a clue to the answer to this question. On December 11, 1789, in *Farther Thoughts on Separation from the Church*, he provided a glimpse into the sources that informed his doctrines and his liturgy:

> 1. FROM a child I was taught to love and reverence the Scripture, the oracles of God; and, next to these, to esteem the primitive Fathers, the writers of the three first centuries. Next after the primitive church, I esteemed our own, the Church of England, as the most scriptural national Church in the world. I therefore not only assented to all the doctrines, but observed all the rubric in the Liturgy; and that with all possible exactness, even at the peril of my life.

2. In this judgment, and with this spirit, I went to America, strongly attached to the Bible, the primitive church, and the Church of England, from which I would not vary in one jot or little on any account whatever. In this spirit I returned, as regular a Clergyman as any in the three kingdoms; (Wesley 1872c, 337)

In addressing this passage, Outler expanded Wesley's dependence on the fathers to those of the fourth and fifth centuries. (Outler 1980) However, if we allow Wesley himself to dictate to us the sources of his theology and practice, then this quotation stands as a most definitive statement. In it, he identified three major sources that informed him. First, he highlighted the primary role given to the Scriptures. Immediately following the Scriptures, he referenced the role of the primitive church, specifically the writers of the first three centuries. Finally, he gave the last nod to the teachings of the Anglican Church as the final shaper of his theology and practice. What's more, according to him, he took this threefold source to America and returned with the same approach. Given this fact, I believe any discussion of his sources for theology and practice ought to begin with his own statements on the matter. This does not negate a discussion of possible other influences on his thought. Albert Outler evidently detected additional influences when he added the reference to five centuries in Wesley's statement cited early. One suspects Outler made the addition because he detected influence from the Church Fathers of the fourth and fifth centuries. For example, Outler noted the influence of Church Fathers such as Athanasius who hailed from the third through fourth century and Ephraem Syrus from the fourth century. (Outler 1980) Indeed, he saw more; instead of the three primary influences to which Wesley referred, Outler cited five sources Wesley gained through his Oxford education: "Scripture, the classics, the Early Church Fathers, the Reformation and the new world of science." (Outler 1980, 9) However, with these allowances made, one still ought to take Wesley's statements on this matter seriously and at least begin the discussion there.

In this chapter, I propose to discuss some of these influences, particularly the three that Wesley cited. Along with the influence of his Anglican tradition I will make brief mention of the influences from the Catholic tradition which some have cited. (Collins 1998; Lindstrom 1980; Maddox 1994; Outler 1980) In addition, I will discuss these sources primarily in relation to his doctrine of Christian Perfection especially as it puts forth his inward/outward perspective on full salvation. However, although I will give some attention to these traditions as well as the influence of the Church Fathers, I shall give primary attention to the impact of the Scriptures. In the latter regard, I focus principally on the teachings found in the Sermon on the Mount in Matthew's gospel and Wesley's thirteen sermon based on it.

The Influence of the Church Fathers

According to Outler, Wesley demonstrated life-long dependence on the primitive Fathers of the church. Not surprisingly, several authors trace features of his theology to writers of the early church. (Baker 1970; Clapper 1985a; Collins 2004; Lindstrom 1980; Outler 1980) Because Wesley attached great significance to the writings of the early Church Fathers, he provided extracts of their works in his very first volume of the *Christian Library*. These included excerpts from early Fathers such as St. Clement, St. Ignatius and St. Polycarp as well as an abridgement of the *Homilies* of Macarius. (Outler 1980) This keen interest in the Church Fathers likely sprung from several sources. Judging from comments made by writers on Wesley, his father, Samuel Wesley Sr., shaped his love for the Early Church Fathers. (Baker 1970; Edwards 1961; Outler 1980) In this regard, Outler noted Samuel Wesley's words in his *Advice to a Young Clergyman:* ""Most of the Fathers [of the fourth century] are well worth reading, but especially St. Athanasius, and above all, St. Basil. If I were to preach in Greek, St. Chrysostom would be my master." (Outler 1980, 9) Along with these named recommendations from the Fathers, Samuel endorsed critical attention to the first Councils of the church, seeing these as "...Witnesses of the Faith and Exemplars in practice..."(Outler 1980, 9) A second source for his inherent devotion to the Fathers might have derived from his years of study at Oxford. Here, according to Outler, Wesley came under the tutelage of patrologists such as John Clayton. This patrologist influenced him and members of the Holy Club in study of the Church Fathers. (Outler 1980)

Why did Wesley place such stock and confidence in the Church Fathers? Apparently, he revered them because they: "...were closer in time and spiritual insights to the apostles, and hence, to pure Scriptural Christianity." (Outler 1980, 10) As such, they provided him with models and examples of a more primitive and authentic form of the faith. In addition, given his ardent interest in renewing the British church to a purer and more ancient form of Christianity, these sources provided excellent prototypes for doing so. (Outler 1980) Besides these evangelical reasons, Wesley's interest likely sprung from doctrinal concerns; these authors became sources for some of his theological views, including his perspectives on Christian perfection (Collins 2004; Lindstrom 1980; Maddox 1994; Outler 1980) For example, he apparently borrowed his thoughts on original sin from the Church Fathers. (Lindstrom 1980) But the Church Fathers also influenced him in other areas; in fact, Outler noted that Wesley reflected many motifs of the early church and those of eastern Christian spirituality. According to him, these reflections included:

1. A therapeutic view of the *ordo salutis* as contrasted with a forensic one
2. The *telos* of human life in God
3. The person and primal agency of the Holy Spirit in Christian existence
4. Prevenient grace
5. The concordance of grace and free-will
6. The inspiration of scripture and its pneumatological interpretation
7. Salvation as the restoration of the image of God in man
8. Ascesis and discipline in Christian living
9. The distinctions between the 'moments' of justification and sanctification and, therefore, a doctrine of opened-ended perfection in this life. (Outler 1980, 10)

Several of these reflections relate to Wesley's views on Christian perfection. Not surprisingly, Outler saw Christian perfection as one of the particular ways in which the Church Fathers influenced Wesley's views. (Outler 1980) As a result, Outler spoke about Wesley drawing his views on perfection from Clement of Alexandria's seventh book of *Stromateis* that characterized the perfect Christian. He also noted the influence of the writings of Ephraem Syrus on Wesley. (Outler 1980; See also Curnock 1909) One portion of evidence that lends credence to this latter observation comes from the frequent references to Wesley reading from Ephraem Syrus to Sophy Hopkey while in Georgia. (Curnock 1909) Wesley reputedly shared a similar vision of the Christian life with Ephraem Syrus relative to themes like surrender to God out of love and an emphasis on the Holy Spirit's activity in salvation. (Outler 1980) Similarly, Outler believed that Macarius also influenced Wesley. According to him, Wesley knew and extracted material from the *Homilies of Macarius*, and included an abridgement in *A Christian Library*. (Outler 1980)

In *Responsible Grace*, Randy Maddox made frequent reference to the contributions of Macarius (or more precisely to Pseudo Macarius) to Wesley's theology. (Maddox 1994) He traced these contributions to several key areas in Wesley's theology. Significantly, several of the areas he referenced relate to Outler's list mentioned earlier. First, Maddox traced the influence of Macarius and the Eastern Fathers in the notion of uncreated grace. That is, grace was not seen as some impersonal thing created by God; rather, grace came through the gracious presence of the Holy Spirit at work in our lives. (Maddox 1994; Outler 1980) Related to this, Maddox also believed Wesley borrowed Macarius' emphasis on believers' need to perceive the gracious presence of the Spirit in their lives. (Maddox 1994) Second, he saw Macarius' influence in Wesley's understanding of divine grace and human response to the same; Wesley shared a belief in a legitimate human answer to divine grace, but saw that even this response was divinely empowered. Third, Maddox saw additional influence relative to perfection demonstrated in Wesley's abridgement of *The Homilies of Macarius*. However, Ken Collins has provided a caution in this area; though he generally supported the influence of the Eastern Fathers, he denied the impact of Eastern orthodoxy on Wesley's theology. As proof, he noted that Wesley consciously removed references to the Eastern idea of *theosis* when he reproduced sermons from Pseudo Macarius. (Collins 2004)

Taking this caution into account, according to Maddox, what were some of Macarius' additional contributions? Maddox highlighted an image retained in Wesley's abridgement. This image revolved around the idea of Christ as physician; in this capacity, Christ heals us and makes us partakers of his holiness. Additionally, in reference to overcoming sin, he offered that Wesley sometimes made reference to the idea of "rooting out," or "destruction" of inward sin. Wesley might have borrowed from Macarius the notion that Christ does not immediately deliver new believers from sin. This idea served to leave space for growth in grace. (Maddox 1994) Notwithstanding, regarding the emphasis on growth in grace by Maddox, one also ought to remember that Wesley balanced this with an equally strong emphasis on the instantaneous nature of sanctifying grace. This balanced emphasis appears in several places but two brief examples might suffice. In *Brief Thoughts on Christian Perfection*, Wesley noted the following: "As to the manner. I believe this perfection is always wrought in the soul by a simple act of faith; consequently, in an instant. But I believe a gradual work, both preceding and following that instant." (Wesley 1872a 523) Furthermore, in *A Plain Account of Christian Perfection*, he noted:

> "It need not, therefore, be affirmed over and over, and proved by forty texts of Scripture, either that most men are perfected in love at last, that there is a gradual work of God in the soul, or that, generally speaking, it is a long time, even many years, before sin is destroyed. All this we know: But we know likewise, that God may, with man's good leave, 'cut short his work,' in whatever degree he pleases, and do the usual work of many years in a moment. He does so in many instances; and yet there is a gradual work, both before and after that moment: So that one may affirm the work as gradual, another, it is instantaneous, without any manner of contradiction. (Wesley 1872h, 496)

The Influence of Anglican and Catholic Writers

Earlier, I referenced Wesley's statement regarding his reverence for the Church of England as the "most scriptural national church in the world." (Wesley 1872c) Accordingly, he embraced the doctrines and the rubrics related to the liturgy of the church. He likely developed this deep commitment to the Anglican Church from his father. In fact, Samuel Wesley Sr. instilled in each of his sons a deep commitment to the Anglican Church and its orthodoxy, liturgy, sacraments and music. (Edwards 1961) Given this commitment, it seems likely that Anglican writers exerted influence on Wesley. Albert Outler suggested two broad areas in which these writers influenced Wesley. The first relates to the so-called Wesleyan quadrilateral; many Divines like Erasmus and Thomas Cranmer, adhered to a threefold emphasis on Scripture, reason and Christian Antiquity. Outler also traced this emphasis to British writers such as Hooker, Hammond and Beveridge among others. (Outler 1980) Frank Baker, a Wesley historian supported this perspective relative to the latter's use of these three sources. Baker even acknowledged this influence during Wesley's early years as curate for his father at Epworth and Wroot. During this period, Wesley ascribed to the authority of the Church Fathers almost on the level with Scripture, with reason trailing as a distant third. (Baker 1970) This close equation of Scripture and tradition seems to reflect the Roman Catholic Church that had developed these two sources, although they demonstrated a preference for the latter as the final arbitrator. (Outler 1980)

One can affirm Baker's statement on Wesley's sources directly from the latter's own writings. As previously demonstrated from *Farther Thoughts on Separation from the Church*, Wesley highlighted Scripture, the Primitive Fathers and the Church of England. (Wesley 1872c) But elsewhere in his writings, he also pointed to the role of experience. Such an example occurs in his seventh discourse on the Sermon on the Mount. While speaking about how fasting can help prayer, Wesley referenced Scripture, reason and experience. (Wesley 1872s) According to Timothy L. Smith, this sermon dates from between November 1-16, 1747. (Smith 1982) This information points to the early inclusion of experience as one of his sources. Nevertheless, Wesley did not make experience an overriding source of authority. In fact, he constantly brought individual experience under the control of the Bible as interpreted through the Early Church Fathers and reason. (Lindstrom 1980) As such, for him, Scripture always served as the dominant foundation for discerning truth though construed in the light of experience. (Lindstrom 1980)

Given Wesley's inclusion of experience, it seems important to suggest possible influences for this emphasis. In this regard, Baker suggested that Wesley's time in Georgia helped shape his thoughts relative to experience. Baker saw this period as one of experimentation in various facets of the faith. This might have reflected Wesley's efforts to come to his own perspectives, a kind of differentiation in matters of the faith. (Headley 2010) In this period, Wesley apparently embarked on legalistic churchmanship that moved him to harshness and tactlessness, more than in any other period of his life. But he also experimented with the new; this was demonstrated in the incorporation of unauthorized psalms and hymns into *A Collection of Psalms and Hymns*, published in Charleston, South Carolina in 1737. (Baker 1970) As part of this experimentation, Baker indicated a swing from an undue trust in church traditions to an equally heightened emphasis on experience. Wesley's encounter with Moravian spirituality likely influenced this emphasis on experience. The Moravians also likely influenced Wesley in the organization of the societies for Christian fellowship; that is, his division of the societies into bands likely derived from the Moravian pattern. (Baker 1970) However, Wesley apparently did not persist in an over-emphasis on experience. Rather, he would later balance experience and tradition. Another Anglican author influenced this more balanced perspective. The author was Beveridge and the book was *Synodikon.* (Baker 1970)

One often encounters Beveridge's name during Wesley's time in Georgia and not only in his measured emphasis on tradition. Beveridge also influenced Wesley in his views on the celibacy of priests. In *The Elusive Mr. Wesley,* Heitzenrater noted a developmental progression in Wesley's views on this matter. At the beginning of these stages, he believed priests could not marry. However, by the end of this period, he concluded that they could and made his decision to marry. Wesley's reading of Beveridge's *Codex Conciliorum* partly influenced this final opinion. In it, Wesley encountered perspectives contrary to his own beliefs in celibacy. In fact, he discovered that the Council of Nicaea determined quite the opposite. This reading apparently served as a key element leading him to believe he could marry. (Heitzenrater 1984) This same section on Wesley's thoughts about marriage also lends support to the multiple sources on which he relied. The section related to Beveridge highlights the role of the tradition as an arbiter of truth. Following this section Wesley noted how St. Paul awakened him out of "his mystic dream." Here one finds the appeal to Scripture. In the very next section, he drew upon the role of experience when he referred to Dr. Koker's marriage. This experience convinced him (although reluctantly) that he could serve God in a married state with little distraction. (Heitzenrater 1984) We also find a place for reason. In fact, one could argue that the whole section detailing the journey from believing he could not marry, to permitting his marriage was a detailed and well-thought out exercise in reason.

Anglican writers also influenced Wesley's views on Christian perfection. Langford noted that in discussing Christian perfection, Wesley often associated holiness and happiness. (Langford 1980) Langford observed that this association flowed from deep roots in British theology. He also traced this association in British writers from Richard Hooker through English Puritanism. What's more, Langford stated that by maintaining the association, Wesley consciously placed himself within this Anglican tradition but stated it at a deeper level. (Langford 1980) One does not have to search too diligently to find this association. It appears in sermons such as *The Way of the Kingdom* and *On Sin in Believers*. It's especially prevalent in many of his thirteen sermons based on Jesus' Sermon on the Mount. For example, in the fourth discourse, Wesley declared: "Let your light so shine:" — Your lowliness of heart; your gentleness, and meekness of wisdom; your serious, weighty concern for the things of eternity, and sorrow for the sins and miseries of men; your earnest desire of universal holiness, and full happiness in God; your tender good will to all mankind, and fervent love to your supreme Benefactor. (Wesley 1872p, 397) In the eighth discourse, speaking of the light which fills those with a single eye, Wesley declared: "This light, which fills him who has a single eye, implies, Thirdly, happiness, as well as holiness." (Wesley 1872t, 455) Furthermore, in the tenth discourse, he wrote: "In him are included all good things; all wisdom, peace, joy, love; the whole treasures of holiness and happiness; all that God hath prepared for them that love him." (Wesley 1872j, 496) One final example of the association appears in the thirteenth discourse on the Sermon on the Mount. He wrote: "The life I now live; namely, a divine, heavenly life; a life which is hid with Christ in God. I now live, even in the flesh, a life of love; of pure love both to God and man; a life of holiness and happiness; praising God, and doing all things to his glory." (Wesley 1872m, 524) This demonstrated association of holiness and happiness in Wesley's writings bears testimony to the influence of Anglican writers on him as espoused by Langford.

The Influence of William Law

But other Anglican writings influenced Wesley's perspectives. For example, devotional writings and literature made an impression on him. He noted luminaries such as Bishop Taylor and his *Rules and Exercise of Holy Living and Dying*, and William Law's *Serious Call, Christian Perfection"* and *A Practical Treatise Upon Christian Perfection*. (Lindstrom 1980) Along with Thomas A Kempis, these two persons reputedly exerted influence on his view of perfection. As a result, one sees reflections of these authors in his work. (Lindstrom 1980) Furthermore, these authors also reflected aspects of the Catholic tradition especially in their emphasis on intention and imitating Christ. Given his reported major influence on Wesley, William Law deserves special attention. (Collins 2004; Lindstrom 1980; Outler 1980) Law's influence shows up in several areas. First, he placed emphasis on the individual's love for God and neighbor, as did Wesley. Second, perfection in his writings included an emphasis on purity of intention and the imitation of Christ, emphases also evident in Wesley. (Lindstrom 1980) Third, Law often used the same affectional language to describe holiness as Wesley did. In his writings one finds terms such as affections, tempers and passions described in much the same manner. These terms occur in several of his works including *A Serious Call to a Devout and Holy Life*, *The Spirit of Love*, and *The Spirit of Prayer*. In *A Serious Call to A Devout and Holy Life*, one encounters references to affections such as this one: "...offering to God the daily sacrifice of a reasonable life, wise actions, purity of heart, and heavenly affections." (Law 1997a, 35) Another example of his reference to affections from *A Serious Call* occurred in the following statement: "Devotion is nothing else but right apprehensions and right affections towards God. All practices, therefore, that heighten and improve our true apprehensions of God, all ways of life that tend to nourish, raise, and fix our affections upon Him, are to be reckoned so many helps and means to fill us with devotion." (Law 1997a, 154) In this same work, one also finds the linking of tempers and affections: "For as a Christian is not only required to be honest, but to be of a Christian spirit, and make his life an exercise of humility, repentance, and heavenly affection, so all tempers that are contrary to these are as contrary to Christianity, as cheating is contrary to honesty." (Law 1997a, 40)

But Law made many other references to tempers and their place in the Christian life. In *A Serious Call,* he named various tempers of the heart similar to what one observes in Wesley: "For to seek to be saved by patience, meekness, humility, and resignation to God is truly coming to God through Christ; and when these tempers live and abide in you as the spirit and aim of your life, then Christ is in you of a truth and the life that you then lead is not yours but Christ that liveth in you." (Law 1997b, 135) As noted earlier, John Wesley also spoke about tempers when describing holiness. Besides speaking about love as a master temper, he also named other tempers such as meekness and humility as Law did in the quotation above. (Wesley 1872e; Wesley 1872g; Wesley 1872n; Wesley 1872u) Apparently, this connection of holiness and humility also appears elsewhere. One finds these connections in Catholic sources in addition to reference to holy dispositions. (Collins 1998)

But as indicated earlier, such terms appear in other places in Law's besides *A Serious Call to a Devout and Holy Life.* We also find similar language in his book *The Spirit of Love*:

> Now the holiness of the common Christian is not an occasional thing that begins and ends, or is only for such a time, or place, or action, but is the holiness of that which is always alive and stirring in us, namely, of our thoughts, wills, desires, and affections. If therefore these are always alive in us, always driving or governing our lives, if we can have no holiness or goodness but as this life of thought, will, and affection works in us, if we are all called to this inward holiness and goodness, then a perpetual, always-existing operation of the Spirit of God within us is absolutely necessary.(Law 1997b, 46)

In this statement Law referenced holiness and associated it with thought as well as the affectional language used in Wesley. In another place, Law wrote: "Now if our thoughts, wills, and affections need only be now and then holy and good, then indeed the moving and breathing Spirit of God need only now and then govern us. But if our thoughts and affections are to be always holy and good, then the holy and good Spirit of God is to be always operating as a principle of life within us." (Law 1997b, 46-47) In these two places, he made a close association between the will and affection. As will appear in chapter 4, the same connection appears in Wesley's writings; he envisioned the affections as the will exercising itself. (Wesley 1872f; Wesley 1872b) In general, one might say that many of Law's statements indicated here appear worthy of Wesley. Indeed, they seem to stand in line with his affectional language relative to Christian perfection. However, one would be amiss to conclude that Law influenced Wesley pervasively in all matters. Actually, Wesley made a break with William Law's ethical way of holiness describing it as "practical mysticism." (Lindstrom 1980)

Authors such as Gregory Clapper have traced Wesley's affectional language to Jonathan Edwards. (Clapper 1987; Clapper 1985b; Clapper 1984) This conclusion partly makes sense since Wesley actually published an abridgement of Edwards' *A Treatise Concerning Religious Affections*. (Clapper 1985b; Clapper 1984) But Wesley scholars like Albert Outler went further; Outler saw Jonathan Edwards exerting major influence on Wesley. Indeed, he considered Edwards a major source of Wesley's theology, and one of four factors shaping the latter's thought. (Clapper 1985b; Clapper 1984; Outler 1964) But one ought to remember that Edwards published his treatise on religious affections in 1754. In contrast, William Law's *A Serious Call to a Devout and Holy Life* dates back to 1728 or 1729. As noted earlier, in this latter work, one finds some of the affectional language Wesley used. Although not denying Edwards' influence, one wonders whether Law served as an earlier influence relative to the affectional language. Law might have stirred Wesley's early interest in the affectional language related to holiness. Later, Jonathan Edwards might have provided a more thorough description of the holy affections and thus filled out Wesley's understanding of them.

The Influence of the Scriptures on Wesley Thoughts

Although these sources exerted influence on Wesley's thought relative to the salvation process and Christian perfection, in my opinion, Scripture wielded the greatest power. The powerful influence of Scripture in Wesley's life evidently derived from the teachings of his parents. (Baker 1970; Edwards 1961) Wesley's own statement referenced earlier in the chapter reflected his early love for and reverence for Scripture as the very word of God. This statement suggests he gave primary authority to the Scriptures above the Primitive Fathers and the Church of England. (Wesley 1872c) Indeed, it appears these other sources merited the attention he gave them because they supported or reflected the scriptural message.

Writers such as Timothy Smith in a foreword to *Wesley and Sanctification* noted Wesley's deep reliance on Scripture in crafting his theology. (Lindstrom 1980) Smith noted how different aspects of Wesley's theology showed this scriptural grounding; for example, he noted Wesley crafting his New Testament perspective on the moral law and from a scriptural foundation. The scriptural foundation which informed this perspective derived from Paul's teachings in Romans 3:31. From this passage, Wesley apparently gave three sermons that presented his view of the moral law. (Lindstrom 1980) Similarly, Smith focused on Scripture along with the early Church Fathers as the basis for Wesley's perspectives on original sin. (Lindstrom 1980) Similarly, Thomas Langford supported Wesley's scriptural roots. Langford saw Wesley chiefly as a biblical thinker and according to him, Wesley also saw himself in this light. As such, Wesley demonstrated loyalty to Scripture and displayed this commitment in his understanding and discussion of Christian perfection. (Langford 1980) Accordingly, Langford noted the following quotation from Wesley: "When I began to make the scripture my study (about seven-and-twenty years ago), I began to see that Christians are called to *love God with all their heart and to serve him with all their strength;* which is precisely what I apprehended to be meant by the scriptural term perfection." (Langford 1980, 63)

This dependence on Scripture materializes in his sermons and elsewhere. According to Gregory Clapper, Scripture's influence also appears in his notes on the New Testament. (Clapper 1985b; Clapper 1985a) Moreover, Wesley's reliance on Scripture also appears in the language he used to describe Christian perfection. From the Bible, he seized on the varying terms and phrases used to describe Christian perfection. One example appears in *A Plain Account of Christian Perfection:*

> Look at it again; survey it on every side, and that with the closest attention. In one view, it is purity of intention, dedicating all the life to God. It is the giving God all our heart; it is one desire and design ruling all our tempers. It is the devoting, not a part, but all our soul, body, and substance to God. In another view, it is all the mind which was in Christ, enabling us to walk as Christ walked. It is the circumcision of the heart from all filthiness, all inward as well as outward pollution. It is a renewal of the heart in the whole image of God, the full likeness of Him that created it. In yet another, it is the loving God with all our heart, and our neighbor as ourselves. Now, take it in which of these views you please, (for there is no material difference,) and this is the whole and sole perfection, as a train of writings prove to a demonstration, which I have believed and taught for these forty years, from the year 1725 to the year 1765." (Wesley 1872h, 521)

Many Pauline terms prominently appear in the statement reflecting the deep influence the Apostle Paul exerted on Wesley. Paul's influence can also be seen in the texts Wesley chose for preaching on Christian perfection. For example, he based his first sermon on the subject, *Circumcision of the Heart,* on Romans 2:29 *(Circumcision is that of the heart, in the spirit, and not in the letter).* (Clapper 1985a; Collins 1989; Maddox 1994) He preached this sermon in 1733 at the University of St. Mary's Church. Significantly, the language of "the purposeful list" shows up in many sermons based on Pauline texts. As noted in chapter 1, the progression appeared in his sermon *The Witness of Our Own Spirit,* based on II Corinthians 1:12. Speaking on the topic of conscience, Wesley described it as: "... a faculty or power, implanted by God in every soul that comes into the world, of perceiving what is right or wrong in his own heart or life, *in his tempers, thoughts, words, and actions.*" (Wesley 1872v, 210, (italics added))

Elsewhere in the same sermon, he wrote: "There is required, Thirdly, *an agreement of our hearts and lives, of our tempers and conversation, of our thoughts, and words, and works*, with that rule, with the written word of God. For, without this, if we have any conscience at all, it can be only in evil conscience." (Wesley 1872v, 211-212, (italics added)) One sees similar emphases in sermons such as *The Witness of the Spirit, Discourse 11.* (Wesley 1872w)

Although I have placed initial emphasis on the Apostle Paul in Wesley's discussion of Christian perfection, I do not mean to communicate this as the primary or only scriptural source for Wesley's thoughts. Rather, I cited Paul writings as a prime example of the many scriptural sources Wesley drew on. But, he drew from several other places in Scripture for his teachings on holiness. For example, he drew upon the epistles of St. John and his focus on righteousness as well as his image of Christians being babes, young men and fathers. (Wesley 1872o; Wesley 1872p) One also finds reference to the book of Hebrews, specifically Hebrews 6:4. (Wesley 1872p) But in the pages that follow, I focus on the teachings of Jesus himself as a critical source for Wesley's thoughts on Christian perfection. Specifically, I will focus on the Sermon on the Mount as a key source.

The Sermon on the Mount and Christian Perfection

Wesley gave thirteen discourses on the Sermon on the Mount. He gave this keen attention to it because it described for him the way of salvation and the essence of Christian faith. (Wesley 1872m) One can discern his esteem for the Sermon on the Mount from the many superlatives he used to describe it. He employed terms such as "the whole religion," "The sum of all true religion," and "the religion of the heart." (Wesley 1872i; Wesley 1872m; Wesley 1872o; Wesley 1872p; Wesley 1872t) A particularly good example of Wesley's esteem appeared in Discourse three where he noted:

> Behold Christianity in its native form, as delivered by its great Author! This is the genuine religion of Jesus Christ! Such he presents it to him whose eyes are opened. See a picture of God, so far as he is imitable by man! A picture drawn by God's own hand: "Behold, ye despisers, and wonder, and perish!" Or, rather, wonder and adore! Rather cry out, "Is this the religion of Jesus of Nazareth? the religion which I persecuted? Let me no more be found even to fight against God. Lord, what wouldest thou have me to do?" What beauty appears in the whole! How just a symmetry! What exact proportion in every part! How desirable is the happiness here described! How venerable, how lovely the holiness! This is the spirit of religion; the quintessence of it. These are indeed the fundamentals of Christianity. O that we may not be hearers of it only! — "like a man beholding his own face in a glass, who goeth his way, and straightway forgetteth what manner of man he was." Nay, but let us steadily "look into this perfect law of liberty, and continue therein." Let us not rest, until every line thereof is transcribed into our own hearts. Let us

watch, and pray, and believe, and love; and "strive for the mastery," till every part of it shall appear in our soul, graven there by the finger of God; till we are "holy as He which hath called us is holy, perfect as our Father which is in heaven is perfect!" (Wesley 1872o, 380-381)

From this statement, he clearly saw the Sermon on the Mount charting the life of holiness. In it, Jesus depicted holiness as a present reality rather than simply a future possibility. Furthermore, the life of holiness demonstrated in the Sermon on the Mount always began inwardly in attitudes of the heart. However, it also worked itself out in one's outward life. Thus, in his tenth discourse in the series, Wesley provided a statement depicting the inside out nature of the religion of Jesus Christ: "In the fifth chapter, our great Teacher has fully described inward religion in its various branches. He has there laid before us those dispositions of soul which constitute real Christianity; the tempers contained in that "holiness, without which no man shall see the Lord;" the affections which, when flowing from their proper fountain, from a living faith in God through Christ Jesus, are intrinsically and essentially good and acceptable to God. In the sixth he hath shown how all our actions likewise, even those that are indifferent in their own nature, may be made holy, and good, and acceptable to God, by a pure and holy intention. Whatever is done without this, he declares is of no value with God: Whereas, whatever outward works are thus consecrated to God are, in his sight, of great price." (Wesley 1872j, 488)

For Wesley as for Jesus, true religion principally involved an inward experience centered in transformed dispositions. What's more, Wesley saw this need for inward transformation arising from both the Law and the Gospel. As a result, in his fifth discourse on the Sermon on the Mount, he connected the Law to the Gospel by indicating that like the latter, the Law required inward religion. For example, he argued that the Law was both perfect and holy and required love just as the Gospel did. (Wesley 1872q) In speaking further about inward religion, he resorted to the affectional language of *tempers* and *affections*. These dispositions of the soul represented the inner areas that needed the radical transformation real Christianity brought. He saw this as the central message expressed in the Sermon on the Mount. (Wesley 1872q) As a result, Jesus' discourse in Matthew chapter five began with an emphasis on inward qualities such as poverty of spirit. This entailed for Wesley a just sense of both our inward and outward sins. (Wesley 1872i) In terms of one's inward life, poverty of spirit served as the initial step leading in a definitive direction, namely purity of heart. Outwardly, it would give rise to holy actions in the world such as peacemaking. (Wesley 1872q)

In contrast to this emphasis on inward religion, Wesley accurately perceived that many of his contemporary Anglican preachers emphasized outward religion. In fact, they emphasized it to such a degree as to distort and pervert the way of salvation. In contrast, in his discourses on the

Sermon on the Mount, he consistently described outward religion, cut off from inward holiness, in negative language. Such religion was variously described as "the religion of the Pharisees and Scribes," "the way of the false prophets," "the religion of those who say "Lord, Lord," and "the religion of externals" (contrasted with true religion of the heart). (Wesley 1872m; Wesley 1872q) This "religion of the world," emphasized outward acts, namely, doing no harm, doing good and participating in the means of grace. However, it ignored the transformation of one's inward being. (Wesley 1872n) Wesley saw this emphasis as foreign to the religion Jesus preached. He perceived outward religion as powerless without inward religion; it could only move us so far but never bring us to heaven. (Wesley 1872m) In line with Jesus, he saw the righteousness of the Pharisees as incomplete. Instead of endeavoring to keep all of God's commandments, their external righteousness dictated which they would keep and which they would ignore. In contrast, the real Christian did not selectively observe just some parts of God's law. Rather, the real Christian "keeps all his commandments, loves them all, values them above gold and precious stones." (Wesley 1872q, 414)

But Wesley's negative tone in describing outward religion did not mean he saw no place for it in real Christianity. Though emphasizing religion of the heart, he did not devalue outward holiness except when cut off from its inward aspects. Real Christianity involved grappling with inward and outward sins; furthermore, it carried a concern for both inward and outward righteousness. (Wesley 1872r; Wesley 1872u) The root of true religion might begin in the heart. However, it could not stop there. Rather, it must put forth branches which one should understand as one's visible actions in the world; interior transformations in the dispositions of the heart must evidence their presence by actions in the world. (Wesley 1872p) As a result, Wesley stressed the outgrowth of inward religion. This behavioral focus shows itself in the previously mentioned quotation where he spoke about the intent of the sixth chapter of Matthews' gospel. As noted there, true religion brought about holy actions springing from a pure intention. (Wesley 1872t) In fact, without this holy source to produce one's actions in the world, all such behaviors merit little in the kingdom of God. One easily discerns this inside outside emphasis in the Beatitudes. There, in Matthew 5: 3-8, one finds an initial emphasis on internal attitudes of the heart such as poverty of spirit, mourning, meekness, hungering and thirsting after righteousness, mercy and purity of heart. In verse 9, Jesus transitioned from internal attitudes to works of mercy, in this case, peacemaking. Later one also finds reference to acts of piety when Jesus spoke of fasting and prayer.

For Wesley then, the entire Sermon on the Mount demonstrated holiness as both inward and outward. As a result, his thirteen sermons all demonstrated this emphasis. Even in those passages where one would not logically expect this emphasis, he stressed holiness. For example, in

Discourse eleven based on Matthew 7:13-14, he interpreted the imagery of the broad and narrow ways in terms of inward and outward holiness. (Wesley 1872k) Similarly, in Matthew 7: 15-20, he described the false prophets as identified by corrupt fruit, that is unholy works. He then described good fruit in terms of holiness. (Wesley 1872l) In the thirteenth discourse based on Matthew 7: 21-27, he discussed those servants who cry: "Lord, Lord." But, even here, he reprised the emphasis on inward and outward holiness. Specifically, he identified those who cry "Lord, Lord," as participating in outward religion without the presence of an inward knowledge of God and his holiness. This absence of inward religion nullified even the great deeds done in His name. (Wesley 1872m) One sees a similar emphasis when he described the merciful in Matthew, chapter 5. Here, he identified the merciful as those who loved their neighbor as themselves. He then explicated the nature of love in terms of Paul's description in I Corinthians 13. (Wesley 1872n) In fact, throughout his discourses on the Sermon on the Mount, one finds this constant emphasis on holiness in its dual reality. Besides the inward/outward emphasis, Wesley presented this truth in other ways; he made use of affectional language that described the inward aspects of Christian perfection. He also communicated it through the purposeful list in compacted and expanded form. Furthermore, he presented it through frequent reference to biblical terms denoting holiness.

In the thirteen discourses on the Sermon on the Mount, I was struck by the variety of terms used to communicate Christian perfection. I found terms such as holiness, righteousness, having the mind of Christ, having the image of God, right intention or singleness of intention, purity of heart and love. For example, speaking of holiness in discourse two, he described it as the proper fruit of godliness. He also described is as demonstrated in both "... holiness of heart and holiness of conversation." (Wesley 1872n, 359) Elsewhere in Discourse four, he extolled holiness when he wrote: "THE beauty of holiness, of that inward man of the heart which is renewed after the image of God, cannot but strike every eye which God hath opened, — every enlightened understanding. The ornament of a meek, humble, loving spirit, will at least excite the approbation of all those who are capable, in any degree, of discerning spiritual good and evil.... This inward religion bears the shape of God so visibly impressed upon it, that a soul must be wholly immersed in flesh and blood when he can doubt of its divine original." (Wesley 1872p, 382)

Wesley also used the term *righteousness* to denote the perfect life. For him, righteousness was always the gift and work of God. (Wesley 1872u) As a result, in Discourse nine, he bemoaned those who tried to establish their own righteousness through the law, concomitantly refusing to submit to the righteousness of God. Such righteousness could rightly be called their own because it did not come about through the activity of God's Spirit. Given its source, God did not acknowledge or accept it. In contrast to seeking righteousness through one's own efforts, he described true righteousness as finding its source in God's activity: "And what is "righteousness," but the life of God in the soul; the mind which was in Christ Jesus; the image of God stamped upon the heart, now renewed after the likeness of Him that created it? What is it but the love of God, because he first loved us, and the love of all mankind for his sake?" (Wesley 1872i, 340-341) This statement clearly captured several aspects of Christian perfection. Wesley took a similar posture in discourse two where he equated righteousness with having the image of God, the mind of Christ and the love for God and for one's neighbor. However, in this instance, he also used affectional language. He described righteousness as "… every holy and heavenly temper in one," which both springs from and leads to love of God and neighbor." (Wesley 1872d, 352) Similarly, in Discourse nine, he again used righteousness to describe holiness of heart and God's renewal of the soul. But he resorted to an expanded use of affectional language describing this radical change as entailing "… renewal of the soul in all its desires, tempers and affections." (Wesley 1872u, 482)

As indicated in these statements, Wesley consistently thought about holiness as entailing renewal of the human person in the image of God. For him, Christian perfection entailed God stamping his image deep upon the human heart. But he also thought about it as having the mind of Christ embedded in our being so that we think the thoughts of Christ. In chapter 1, I indicated that *thought* could be considered both inward and outward. Nevertheless, it seems clear that when he spoke of having the mind of Christ, he essentially referred to it as an internal attribute of the heart. Besides this term, he also presented Christian perfection as singleness of intention and having right intention. For him, this focus on right intention came embedded in the sixth chapter of Matthew's gospel where Jesus spoke of the single eye from Matthew 6:19-23. (Wesley 1872i) Such rightness of intention ought to govern all actions in the world; even ordinary and everyday actions ought to remain free from the taint of worldly desires and anxieties of life. (Wesley 1872i) Moreover, one can equate singleness of intention with having a single eye; that is, both demonstrate an entire desire for and focus on God. Wesley equated this with desiring to "— to know him with suitable affections, loving him as he hath loved us; to please God in all things; to serve God (as we love him) with all our heart, and mind, and soul, and strength; and to enjoy God in all, and above all things, in time and in eternity." (Wesley 1872t, 454) What's more, this singleness of heart transformed our entire inward nature. It fills us with light (equated with holiness) and affects our entire being. It transforms our inward being described as desires, tempers, and affections. But it also transforms our actions in the world, namely, our thoughts, and words, and actions. (Wesley 1872t) Thus Wesley admonished: "Now let thine eye be singly fixed on Him in whom is no variableness neither shadow of turning!" Now give Him thy heart; now stay thyself on Him: Now be thou holy, as he is holy! Now lay hold on the blessed opportunity of doing his acceptable and perfect will! Now rejoice to "suffer the loss of all things so thou mayest "win Christ!" (Wesley 1872u, 485-486) In the same sermon, he made another similar appeal: "Today, do and suffer his will! Today, give up thyself, thy body, soul, and spirit to God, through Christ Jesus; desiring nothing, but that God may be glorified in all thou art, all thou doest, all thou sufferest; seeking nothing, but to know God, and his Son Jesus Christ, through the eternal Spirit; pursuing nothing, but to love him, to serve him, and to enjoy him at this hour, and to all eternity!" (Wesley 1872u, 486)

But Wesley also placed emphasis on critical terms such as purity of heart and love. He rightly saw that in the Beatitudes, dispositions of the heart such as poverty of spirit found their ultimate goal in purity of heart. In speaking about this, he described the pure in heart in the following language:

> "The pure in heart" are they whose hearts God hath "purified even as He is pure;" who are purified, through faith in the blood of Jesus, from every unholy affection; who, being "cleansed from all filthiness of flesh and spirit, perfect holiness in the" loving "fear of God." They are through the power of his grace, purified from pride, by the deepest poverty of spirit; from anger, from every unkind or turbulent passion, by meekness and gentleness; from every desire but to please and enjoy God, to know and love him more and more, by that hunger and thirst after righteousness which now engrosses their whole soul: So that now they love the Lord their God with all their heart, and with all their soul, and mind, and strength." (Wesley 1872n, 365-366)

One easily detects in this description some of the very dispositions Jesus described in the Beatitudes. Wesley connected purity of heart to poverty of spirit that comes through purification from pride. He also discussed meekness and gentleness that moves us away from anger and various turbulent passions. Additionally, he saw hungering and thirsting after righteousness moving us away from a desire to please only ourselves; instead, it moved us towards a new desire to please and enjoy God. But even though he acknowledged the power derived from having a purified heart, he admitted that not every minister saw it in the same light or emphasized it as absolutely necessary to the life of faith. In fact, false teachers minimized the importance of purity of heart. As a result, he wrote: "But how little has this purity of heart been regarded by the false teachers of all ages! They have taught men barely to sustain from such outward impurities as God hath forbidden by name; but they did not strike at the heart; and by not guarding against, they in effect countenanced, inward corruptions." (Wesley 1872n, 366)

In Wesley's description of purity of heart, one readily sees its connection to love; purity of heart relates to knowing God more and loving him with all our soul and mind and strength. What's more, loving God gets at the very heart of what it means to worship Him in spirit and truth. Thus, in his fourth discourse on the Sermon on the Mount, Wesley wrote:

> "But then I would ask, What is it to worship God, a Spirit, in spirit and in truth? Why, it is to worship him with our spirit; to worship him in that manner which none but spirits are capable of. It is to believe in him, as a wise, just, holy Being, of purer eyes than to behold iniquity; and yet merciful, gracious and long-suffering; forgiving iniquity, and transgression, and sin; casting all our sins behind his back, and accepting us in the Beloved. It is, to love him, to delight in him, to desire him, with all our heart, and mind, and soul, and strength; to imitate him we love, by purifying ourselves even as He is pure; and to obey him whom we love, and in whom we believe, both in thought, and word, and work. Consequently, one branch of the worshipping God in spirit and in truth is, the keeping his outward commandments. To glorify him, therefore, with our bodies, as well as with our spirits; to go through outward work with hearts lifted up to him; to make our daily employment a sacrifice to God; to buy and sell, to eat and drink, to his glory; — this is worshipping God in spirit and in truth, as much as the praying to him in a wilderness."(Wesley 1872p, 393-394)

But he also connected love to God with loving our neighbor as ourselves. In fact, he saw love of God and neighbor as the true end of all that God commands; it was for him the essence of true religion. Thus, he bemoaned those who confused means and end in the following language: "In the same manner have the end and the means of religion been set at variance with each other. Some well-meaning men have seemed to place all religion in attending the Prayers of the Church, in receiving the Lord's supper, in hearing sermons, and reading books of piety; neglecting, mean time, the end of all these, the love of God and their neighbor." (Wesley 1872s, 436) Speaking further to love of neighbor, he noted: "How excellent things are spoken of the love of our neighbor! It is "the fulfilling of the law," "the end of the commandment." Without this, all we have, all we do, all we suffer, is of no value in the sight of God. But it is that love of our neighbor which springs from the love of God: Otherwise itself is nothing worth." (Wesley 1872o, 364) Furthermore, in answering objections to this idea, he wrote: "I answer, It is granted, that the love of God and man, arising from faith unfeigned, is all in all, the fulfilling of the law, the end of every commandment of God. It is true, that without this, whatever we do, whatever we suffer, profits us nothing. But it does not follow, that love is all in such a sense as to supersede either faith or good works. It is "the fulfilling of the law," not by releasing us from, but by constraining us to obey it. It is "the end of the commandment," as every commandment leads to and centers in it. It is allowed, that whatever we do or suffer without love profits us nothing. But withal, whatever we do or suffer in love, though it were only the suffering reproach for Christ, or the giving a cup of cold water in his name, it shall in nowise lose its reward."(Wesley 1872p, 392)

In the latter part of this quotation, love appears verb-like. Love was more than something passively possessed; rather, it acts in the world in deeds such as giving a cup of cold water in his name. Indeed, Wesley saw love demonstrating itself through Christians becoming light in the world. Christians, according to Wesley, should not hide their light; that is, they should not hide their religion and keep it to themselves. He concluded this for two reasons: First, it was impossible to conceal a true Christian faith. Second, to endeavor to do this ran completely counter to God's design. (Wesley 1872p) Thus, Wesley concluded:

> "Neither do men light a candle to put it under a bushel." As if he had said, As men do not light a candle, only to cover and conceal it, so neither does God enlighten any soul with his glorious knowledge and love, to have it covered or concealed, either by prudence, falsely so called, or shame, or voluntary humility; to have it hid, either in a desert, or in the world; either by avoiding men, or in conversing with them." (Wesley 1872p, 390-391)

Elsewhere in the same sermon, he exhorted: "Let your light so shine:" — Your lowliness of heart; your gentleness, and meekness of wisdom; your serious, weighty concern for the things of eternity, and sorrow for the sins and miseries of men; your earnest desire of universal holiness, and full happiness in God; your tender good will to all mankind, and fervent love to your supreme Benefactor. Endeavor not to conceal this light, wherewith God hath enlightened your soul; but let it shine before men, before all with whom you are, in the whole tenor of your conversation. Let it shine still more eminently in your actions, in your doing all possible good to all men; and in your suffering for righteousness' sake, while you "rejoice and are exceeding glad, knowing that great is your reward in heaven." (Wesley 1872p, 397) As seen here, light shows itself both in the inward dispositions of the heart as well as outward acts. Outwardly, the love that is light reveals itself in works of piety and works of mercy.(Wesley 1872p)

Besides the biblical terms Wesley used in his discourses on the Sermon on the Mount to communicate Christian perfection, he used many dispositional concepts. Dispositional terms as *tempers, affections* and *passions* all appear in these discourses. These concepts have all received substantial attention in the literature. (Clapper 1987; Clapper 1985a; Clapper 1985b; Collins 2003; Collins 1998; Collins 1989; Leffel 2007; Maddox 1994; Mann 2006; Strawn 2004) However, Wesley also used other terms possessing affectional qualities that have received little attention. Here I speak of terms such as *desires* and *designs* that often appear in his writings along with the more common affectional language. For example, a good example of *desires* equated with tempers and affections appeared in Discourse nine. Here, Wesley spoke of "...that holiness of heart, that renewal of the soul in all its desires, tempers and affections." (Wesley 1872u, 482) Similarly, it was associated with tempers and affections in Discourse eight where he spoke of the single eye. (Wesley 1872t) It also appeared in Wesley's seventh discourse on the Sermon on the Mount where it was described as unholy and linked with other vile affections. (Wesley 1872s)

But Wesley also associated the term *designs* with inner dispositions. In Discourse nine, while speaking of being conformed to the world, he introduced this term into the mix with other dispositional terms through the following statement: "To *resemble*, to be *conformed* to, the world, is a Third thing we are to understand by serving mammon; to have not only designs, but desires, tempers, affections, suitable to those of the world; to be of an earthly, sensual mind, chained down to the things of earth; to be self-willed, inordinate lovers of ourselves; to think highly of our own attainments; to desire and delight in the praise of men; to fear, shun, and abhor reproach; to be in patient of reproof, easy to be provoked, and swift to return evil for evil." (Wesley 1872u, 476) One likewise finds similar associations of designs with both desires and tempers in Discourse three: "The Spirit which is in the world is directly opposite to the Spirit which is of God. It must therefore needs be, that those who are of the world will be opposite to those who are of God. There is the utmost contrariety between them, in all their opinions, their desires, designs, and tempers." (Wesley 1872o, 374) Clearly then, terms like *desires* and *designs* appear part of his affectional language.

The Purposeful List and Christian Perfection

In the previous chapter, I indicated that Wesley communicated the dual nature of holiness through a compacted and expanded version of his purposeful list. To reiterate, in the latter case, he usually began his list with some right inner disposition (such as temper, affection, desire or design) followed by right thinking, right word and work. But he sometimes produced a shorter form that communicated the inside/outside nature of holiness. Here, he referenced terms such as inward and outward holiness or to holiness of heart and life. Both forms appeared frequently in his discourses on the Sermon on the Mount. In chapter 1, I spoke at some length about the purposeful list especially seen in *A Plain Account of Christian Perfection*. I will not traverse that territory again. Rather, I simply present a few significant examples of the expanded form of the purposeful list in the Sermon on the Mount discourses.

In several places within these discourses, the trio thoughts, words and actions frequently appear. Moreover, Wesley emphasized that these three should be transformed given our holy life in Christ. Furthermore, in these instances, the internal dispositions readily appear within the larger context. In some examples, it seems clear that he intended poverty of spirit as the internal attitude of the right heart: "Poverty of spirit, in this meaning of the word, begins where a sense of guilt and of the wrath of God ends; and is a continual sense of our total dependence on him, for every good thought, or word, or work..." (Wesley 1872i, 342) The same association appeared in discourse five where he highlighted religion of the heart as transforming thoughts, words and works. First, he explicitly named poverty of spirit as the first attitude of the heart, followed by other tempers such as meekness and love for God and humans:

> Let thy religion be the religion of the heart. Be thou poor in spirit; little, and base, and mean, and vile in thy own eyes; amazed and humbled to the dust at the love of God which is in Christ Jesus thy Lord! Be serious. Let the whole stream of thy thoughts, words, and works be such as flows from the deepest conviction that thou standest on the edge of the great gulf, thou and all the children of men, just ready to drop in, either into everlasting glory or everlasting burnings! Be meek: Let thy soul be filled with mildness, gentleness, patience, long-suffering toward all men; at the same time that all which is in thee is athirst for God, the living God, longing to awake up after his likeness, and to be satisfied with it. Be thou a lover of God, and of all mankind.(Wesley 1872q, 416 (italics added))

The association of love and transformation in thinking, speaking and acting also occurs elsewhere. It occurred in discourse ten where Wesley noted: "Believe in him, and thy faith will work by love. Thou wilt love the Lord thy God, because he hath loved thee: Thou wilt love thy neighbor as thyself: And then it will be thy glory and joy, to exert and increase this love; not barely by abstaining from what is contrary thereto, from every unkind thought, word, and action, but by showing all that kindness to every man, which thou wouldest he should show unto thee." (Wesley 1872j, 498)

But as implied earlier, there exist examples where the entire purposeful list comes clearly laid out. Discourse eight, focused around purity of intention, constitutes one such example. It also provided a good example of an initial compacted list focused around inward being and outward doing. But Wesley immediately followed this with a reference to the internal attitudes of the heart which give rise to transformed thoughts, words and works: ""If thine eye be" thus "single," thus fixed on God, "thy whole body shall be full of light." "Thy whole body:' — all that is guided by the intention, as the body is by the eye. All thou art; all thou doest; thy desires, tempers, affections; thy thoughts, and words, and actions. The whole of these "shall be full of light;" full of true divine knowledge." (Wesley 1872t, 454) But other examples exist where the purposeful list comes combined with affectional language. One such example occurs in discourse eleven where he noted: "How wide do those parent-sins extend, from which all the rest derive their being; — that carnal mind which is enmity against God, pride of heart, self-will, and love of the world! Can we fix any bonds to them? Do they not diffuse themselves through all our thoughts, and mingle with all our tempers! Are they not the leaven which leavens, more or less, the whole mass of our affections? May we not, on a close and faithful examination of ourselves, perceive these roots of bitterness continually springing up, infecting all our words, and tainting all our actions?" (Wesley 1872k, 500) In this same discourse, an example appears that constitutes the purposeful list in reverse, similar to the one in the poem mentioned in chapter 1. Here, he spoke about the commandment of God and the demands it makes of our entire person: "The "commandment" of God "is exceeding broad;" as extending not only to all *our actions, but to every word which goeth out of our lips, yea, every thought that rises in our heart.*" (Wesley 1872k, 500 (italics added))

I close this chapter with a final example of the purposeful list proper. However, in this case, the progression comes in an entire paragraph. The example comes from discourse one focused on poverty of spirit. First, Wesley spoke of those who become aware of evil tempers. He quickly followed this with a catalog of attitudes, including evil thinking that betrays the evil tempers. Later, he mentioned and catalogued various offenses of the tongue and the innumerable evil works. This example appears to be the purposeful list expanded through an entire paragraph. The example shows how powerfully this inward outward perspective pervaded Wesley's thinking. The piece speaks for itself. Wesley wrote:

> He sees more and more of the evil tempers which spring from the evil root; the pride and haughtiness of spirit, the constant bias to think of himself more highly than he ought to think; the vanity, the thirst after the esteem or honor that cometh from men, the hatred or envy, the jealousy or revenge, the anger, malice, or bitterness; the inbred enmity both against God and man, which appears in ten thousand shapes; the love of the world, the self-will, the foolish and hurtful desires, which cleave to his inmost soul. He is conscious how deeply he has offended by his tongue; if not by profane, immodest, untrue, or unkind words, yet by discourse which was not "good to the use of edifying," not "meet to minister grace to the hearers," which, consequently, was all corrupt in God's account, and grievous to his Holy spirit. His evil works are now likewise ever in his sight: If he tells them, they are more than he is able to express. He may as well think to number the drops of rain, the sands of the sea, or the days of eternity. (Wesley 1872i, 338 (italics added))

Chapter 3

Mapping the Soul: Liberty and the Apprehending Faculties of the Soul

God's Intended Work in the Human Soul

"The soul is placed in the body like a rough diamond; and must be polished, or the lustre of it will never appear." So wrote Daniel Defoe, famed author of *Robinson Crusoe*. (Defoe) Defoe wrote these words as an argument for the education of women. But in some sense, the words could apply to God's larger purpose in the human soul. Of course, we know God intends more than some glittery outward refinement of the human soul. At the same time, being polished suggests a cleaning up. Like silver, rendered dull through years of neglect, misplaced use or abuse, the human soul stands in need of cleansing. But because of fallen nature, it also stands in need of a radical makeover. And this is exactly what God seeks to accomplish. Through his work of salvation, God intends to radically remake the human soul into His divine image. In the language of the purposeful list, God essentially remakes and *polishes* the soul, transforming humans from the inside out. He undertakes this work at a definitive point through His sanctifying grace in the soul of the redeemed. But the idea of *polishing* implies this is not a once for all experience. Rather, it implies that once begun, this holy transformation continues through life. This suggests that sanctification involves both crisis and process. God begins this revolutionary makeover in our religious affections, transforming our tempers and affections into holy affections. Moreover, He transforms our minds, creating in us the mind of Christ. Of course, to be remade and *polished* at the core of our being means that this change represents more than superficial decoration; it goes deep within persons, penetrating and pervading our entire being at its deepest level, and changing the very nature of our dispositions. What's more, it radically reshapes who we are on the inside as well as on the outside. Holy being becomes concretized in holy living. Wesley partly conveyed this intent and trajectory of the soul's transformation in his purposeful list.

In this chapter I propose to chart the soul in which God does His transforming work. In a sense, in so doing, I follow Kenneth Collins who in an early article described Wesley's topography of the soul. (Collins 1998) However, I will expand on this discussion by presenting a broader view of the soul beyond the religious affections. That is, I will broadly discuss the faculties or powers of the soul Wesley described. In this chapter I will address Wesley's presentation of liberty as a power of the soul. Furthermore, I will also devote attention to the apprehending faculties of understanding, memory, imagination and conscience. In the chapter that follows, focus will shift to the will, the motivating faculty of the soul. Through these two chapters, I hope to build a foundation that might help one better understand Wesley's view of the soul in which God does His redemptive and perfecting work. As a result, I hope to suggest ways in which God's *polishing* impacts the entire soul.

Wesley's Faculties of the Soul

To speak of the soul essentially involves a discussion of the imago dei, God's image resident in human persons. Wesley saw this image as involving three aspects. Thus, he spoke about the moral, political and natural image. By the moral image, he meant the righteousness and holy state in which humans were first created. However, through the fall, this moral image was completely destroyed. Because of its annihilation, humans stand in need of a total makeover, only accomplished by virtue of Christ's redemptive work. (Collins 1989; Wesley 1872n; Wesley 1872d; Wesley 1872p) By the political image, Wesley referred to humans' responsibility to govern creation. In his own words, this entailed being "...the governor of this lower world having "dominion over the fishes of the sea, and over all the earth;" (Wesley 1872p, 84) The third aspect of the soul of which Wesley spoke, was the natural image. For him, this last aspect of the imago dei denoted humans as spiritual beings who possessed "... understanding, freedom of will, and various affections." (Collins 1989, 23; Wesley 1872p, 84)

In other places, he named additional aspects of the natural image including memory, imagination, conscience and liberty. (Wesley 1872h; Wesley 1872i; Wesley 1872q; Wesley 1872r; Wesley 1872s; Wesley 1872ah) For example, in *The Good Steward*, he clearly referenced imagination and memory. Here, he noted: "First, God has entrusted us with our soul, an immortal spirit, made in the image of God; together with all the powers and faculties thereof, understanding, imagination, memory; will, and a train of affections, either included in it, or closely dependent upon it;" (Wesley 1872i 161) Moreover, he identified conscience as a faculty of soul in *The Witness of Our Own Spirit*. (Wesley 1872ah) It is likewise so identified in *The Doctrine of Original Sin*. In this latter place, he linked conscience to the other aspects of the soul previously mentioned. Here, he noted: "Man, in his natural state, is altogether corrupt, through all the faculties of his soul: Corrupt in his understanding, his will, his affections, his conscience, and his memory." (Wesley 1872v, 506-507) He also referred to liberty in this manner in sermons like *The General Deliverance*. Here, he referenced liberty as an aspect of the soul that empowered the other faculties. It also made service to God possible. (Wesley 1872h)

These references all indicate that he considered these aspects as *powers* or *faculties* of the soul. Ancient writers such as Thomas Aquinas predominantly used the term *power* in reference to the soul. (Aquinas 1997) However, it seems clear that along with *power*, Wesley also used the term *faculty* to speak about the soul, and to a large degree employed them in an interchangeable manner. For example, in *The Witness of Our Own Spirit*, when speaking about conscience, he referred to it as a faculty or power implanted in every soul; from the context, it seems clear that he intends these words be understood synonymously or at least closely related. (Wesley 1872i; Wesley 1872ah) Most likely, he employed these terms in a similar sense to Aquinas. In the latter, *powers* seem like capabilities exercised by the soul. Aquinas saw some of these powers exercised through one's bodily organs. In this sense, he described sight as actualized by the eyes and hearing by the ear. However, he believed that the body did not exercise intellect and will. (Aquinas 1997) Rather, it would appear that these latter aspects come directly under the operation of the soul itself.

Powers Implanted by God

In his sermons and other writings, it seems patently clear that Wesley traced the origin of these capabilities to God. These faculties came as gracious gifts implanted by God. Thus, speaking about conscience, he described it as: "...a faculty or power, implanted by God in every soul that comes into the world, of perceiving what is right or wrong in his own heart or life, *in his tempers, thoughts, words, and actions*." (Wesley 1872ah, 210, (italics added)) But he did not hold such views simply in regards to conscience. In fact, he understood this divine source as the genesis of all faculties of the soul, endowed to humans at creation. This claim appeared in places such as his sermon, *The Original, Nature, Property, and Use of the Law* written around November 1749. (Wesley Center Online 2009) In it, he offered these words in regard to the creation of humans: "It pleased the great Creator to make these, his first-born sons, intelligent beings, that they might know Him that created them. For this end he endued them with understanding, to discern truth from falsehood, good from evil; and, as a necessary result of this, with liberty, — a capacity of choosing the one and refusing the other. By this they were, likewise, enabled to offer him a free and willing service; a service rewardable in itself, as well as most acceptable to their gracious Master." (Wesley 1872u, 532)

He expressed similar thoughts in a letter to his brother Charles from June 25, 1746 where he wrote: "I believe firmly, and that in the most literal sense, that "without God we can do nothing;" that we cannot think, or speak, or move a hand or an eye, without the concurrence of the divine energy; and that all our natural faculties are God's gift, nor can the meanest be exerted without the assistance of his Spirit." (Wesley 1872o, 91) One final example comes from *Thoughts Upon Necessity* where he also included a reference to the will:

> God created man an intelligent being; and endued him with will as well as understanding. Indeed, it seems, without this, his understanding would have been given to no purpose. Neither would either his will or understanding have answered any valuable purpose, if liberty had not been added to them, a power distinct from both; It may be doubted whether God ever made an intelligent creature without all these three faculties; whether any spirit ever existed without them; yea, whether they are not implied in the very nature of a spirit. Certain it is, that no being can be accountable for its actions, which has not liberty, as well as will and understanding. (Wesley 1872ac, 552)

Besides identifying these faculties of soul as gifts of God, in this latter quotation, Wesley made several observations relative to the faculties of the soul. First, these faculties made one an intelligent being. Moreover, they serve as the essential aspects of a spiritual being. In fact, these qualities form an essential part of what it means to be a human created in the image of God; indeed, one wonders whether one would be truly and fully human in the sense God intended without them. Second, he implied that the will was critical to understanding; without it, understanding could not play its defined purpose. But will also needs understanding to function as it was designed. The same might be said about the addition of liberty to will and understanding, because without it, these latter two faculties would be rendered useless in carrying out their defined purpose. Essentially, Wesley implied that the faculties of the soul function as a system, informing each other and needing each other to reach their intended divine purpose and design in human life. Finally, all three faculties are important to exercising moral choice and responsibility. However, elsewhere, Wesley discussed liberty as most critical to the exercise of moral choice and responsibility. (Wesley 1872h; Wesley 1872s)

Because these aspects of soul come as divine gifts, they carried with them an obligation of stewardship. In relation to this matter, in *The Good Steward*, Wesley wrote: "Now, of all these it is certain, we are only stewards. God has entrusted us with these powers and faculties, not that we may employ them according to our own will, but according to the express orders which he has given us; although it is true that, in doing His will, we most effectually secure our own happiness; seeing it is herein only that we can be happy, either in time or in eternity. Thus we are to use our understanding, our imagination, our memory, wholly to the glory of Him that gave them." (Wesley 1872i, 162) Clearly, the faculties serve the purpose of accomplishing God's will. When they are thus employed, they become properly ordered. This ordered quality, involving the alignment of the human will with God's will, makes the faculties holy and good. On the other hand, they can also become disordered. This occurs when they are employed to serve the self rather than God. In this case, these God-given qualities themselves become unholy and vile.

The Work of the Holy Spirit in the Soul

In discussing these gifts, Wesley carved out a role for God's enabling through the Holy Spirit. This enabling rings true in every aspect of salvation; without the Holy Spirit's enabling no one could truly come to a knowledge of the truth, appropriately respond to God or experience justification and sanctification. Thus, speaking of his own conversion, he wrote: "My whole heart was filled with a divine power, drawing all the faculties of my soul after Christ, which continued three or four nights and days. It was as a mighty rushing wind, coming into the soul, enabling me from that moment to be more than conqueror over those corruptions which before I was always a slave to." (Wesley 1872m, 189) The Holy Spirit also played a renewing role in the human faculties of the soul. Because of the fall, human affections had become completely depraved. Humans also came to exhibit self-will standing in full opposition to the will of God. The Holy Spirit addressed both problems; He renews human affections and works to shift the will, making it responsive to God. Indeed, the Holy Spirit works to renew every part of the human soul. (Wesley 1872f) According to Wesley, this work of the Holy Spirit involves a two-fold operation whereby He both opens and enlightens the eyes of the soul. As a result of this operation: "… we see the things which the natural "eye hath not seen, neither the ear heard." We have a prospect of the invisible things of God; we see the *spiritual world*, which is all round about us, and yet no more discerned by our natural faculties than if it had no being: And we see the *eternal world*; piercing through the veil which hangs between time and eternity. Clouds and darkness then rest upon it no more, but we already see the glory which shall be revealed." (Wesley 1872y, 63)

Wesley pictured this transformation as the beginning of sanctification whereby persons become renewed by the power of God. (Wesley 1872y) This renewal largely involves the Holy Spirit shedding God's love in human hearts. By this radical change, the Spirit produces "...love to all mankind, and more especially to the children of God; expelling the love of the world, the love of pleasure, of ease, of honor, of money, together with pride, anger, self-will, and every other evil temper; in a word, changing, the earthly, sensual, devilish mind, into "the mind which was in Christ Jesus." (Wesley 1872y, 61) Moreover, the shedding of love in the believer's heart enables one to love God completely. This complete love to God constituted the very heart of being *altogether a Christian*. Of this real and complete Christian experience, he wrote:

> "What more than this is implied in the being *altogether a Christian*?" I answer, **(I.)** 1. First. The love of God. For thus saith his word, "Thou shalt love the Lord thy God, with all thy heart, and with all thy soul, and with all thy mind, and with all thy strength." *Such a love is this, as engrosses the whole heart, as takes up all the affections, as fills the entire capacity of the soul, and employs the utmost extent of all its faculties.* (Wesley 1872a, 85-86 (Italics added))

Later, in the same sermon, he added a second and third aspect which makes one altogether a Christian. Not surprisingly, the second critical aspect involves loving one's neighbor as self. The third element involves faith in Jesus Christ that makes the whole experience possible. (Wesley 1872a)

As demonstrated in this sermon, love clearly held a central and foundational place in Wesley's view of salvation and his understanding of the altogether Christian. He saw love transforming the soul through its dispersion throughout the whole heart. This love possessed objective qualities in that it derives from focus on God. (Land 1993) What's more, this focus transforms relationship with Him (and with others) while radically reshaping the entire being. As a result of this dispositional shaping, one's entire soul with all its capacities comes under the guidance of love. Love becomes the directing force in reshaping all affections. But additionally, love harnesses and guides every faculty of the soul. It employs understanding, memory, imagination, conscience, liberty and will, bending these to divine and godly purposes. One can only begin to imagine the glorious possibilities when each of these aspects of the soul becomes guided by love. Understanding and its associated properties become holy entities so that one now "thinks for the glory of God." (Sire 2000) Even imagination, sometimes seen as a frivolous and almost trivial faculty, becomes a tool for holy creativity and actualizing godly purposes. (Beecher 1995; Hurlbut and Kalanithi 2001; Tozer 1995) Furthermore, the human will, redeemed from its skewed bent towards accomplishing its own purposes, now lives for doing the will of God. Such are the transformations forged by love in the altogether Christian. Nevertheless, one ought always to remember that the energizing force producing this holy transformation is the Holy Spirit. It is this Spirit who stands as the very embodiment of all forms of grace working in the life of the Christian. (Maddox 1994; Outler 1980)

Liberty: the Enabling Faculty of the Soul

In his discussion of the faculties of the soul, Wesley clearly placed central emphasis upon the necessity of human liberty. However, he remained fully aware that his position was not necessarily a popular one. In *Thoughts Upon Necessity*, he lamented the all too common tendency for humans to locate the principle of their action outside themselves; that is, humans possessed an innate tendency to transfer responsibility for their actions onto other persons. (Wesley 1872ac) He traced this tendency back to Adam and Eve after the fall. He also discovered the tendency in human religious history among groups such as the Manichees. Their system made gods responsible for the evil and good in the world. In a somewhat related fashion, in the century before his time, he saw a similar tendency in the Westminster Divines. According to him, this group attributed human actions, even sinful ones, to God who they saw as foreordaining them. In his own time, he recognized the same mistake in persons such as Jonathan Edwards who allowed no place for liberty in human actions. Wesley even saw the error in the scientific theories of his day; they variously attributed sinful actions to vibrations of the brain, motions of the blood, flow of animal spirits and to God. (Wesley 1872ac) Any explanation would suffice as long as responsibility for behavior and its consequences was not laid at the door of humans. But in so doing, these various persons and groups stripped humans of their ability to choose and of any legitimate sense of moral responsibility.

This undermining of liberty and human responsibility carried personal relevance for Wesley. It lay at the heart of the Calvinist controversy of 1770 that he confronted. In response to and following it, he added liberty as a faculty of the soul. According to Kenneth Collins, he did so because he believed the Calvinist emphasis on irresistible grace undermined human freedom and responsibility. (Collins 1998) Essentially, such beliefs placed sin at God's door. (Wesley 1872ac) Such a thought was anathema to him. He knew that "If all the passions, the tempers, the actions of men, are wholly independent on their own choice, are governed by a principle exterior to themselves, then there can be no moral good or evil; there can be neither virtue nor vice, neither good nor bad actions, neither good nor bad passions or tempers." (Wesley 1872ac, 548) Only through an appropriate emphasis on liberty could one legitimately affirm the notion of moral responsibility. But liberty was important for another reason; through liberty one could freely respond to the prevenient grace of God made possible in Jesus Christ. However, even in this latter emphasis on liberty, Wesley included the activity of the Holy Spirit and prevenient grace. Prevenient grace embodied in the Holy Spirit acted to restore precious human liberty devastated in the fall. (Langford 1980; Leffel 2004; Maddox 1994; Myers 2006; Wesley 1872s)

But the denying of liberty and the concomitant attribution of responsibility outside humans was not the only error Wesley encountered. Specifically, those who acknowledged human liberty tended to confuse it with understanding and will. (Wesley 1872h; Wesley 1872ag) Regarding this problem, Wesley wrote: "I am conscious to myself of one more property, commonly called liberty. This is very frequently confounded with the will; but is of a very different nature. Neither is it a property of the will, but a distinct property of the soul; capable of being exerted with regard to all the faculties of the soul, as well as all the motions of the body." For him, liberty remained distinct from both understanding and will. (Wesley 1872ac) In fact, he saw liberty as fundamental to the other faculties of the soul; without it, they would be rendered useless, and make service to God impossible. This idea finds support in his sermon *The General Deliverance* where he wrote:

> He was, after the likeness of his Creator, endued with understanding; a capacity of apprehending whatever objects were brought before it, and of judging concerning them. He was endued with a will, exerting itself in various affections and passions: And, lastly, with liberty, or freedom of choice; without which all the rest would have been in vain, and he would have been no more capable of serving his Creator than a piece of earth or marble. (Wesley 1872h, 273-274)

But how did he define liberty? He described it as "a power of choosing for himself, a self-determining principle." (Wesley 1872ac, 552) It involved: "... a power of directing his own affections and actions; a capacity of determining himself, or of choosing good or evil." (Wesley 1872s, 244) Wesley also acknowledged a "liberty of contradiction," the power to act or not act. Furthermore, he ascribed to a "liberty of contrariety," that is, the power to choose one action as opposed to a contrary one. (Wesley 1872ag) Liberty indicates that God did not intend human beings to live as automatons, fundamentally moved by forces outside of themselves. Rather, He intended them to live and be moved by an internal principle grounded in personal liberty. In fact, one could affirm with Wesley that this power of self-determination lies at the heart of what it means to be a person created in God's image. (Wesley 1872ac)

Modern writers would affirm this. For example, psychologists sometimes speak about the importance and necessity of agentic action. (Richardson 2012; Tjeltveit 2006) In fact, some like Shapiro think the restoration of agency (although not in a moral sense) is fundamentally linked with the ability to experience a therapeutic cure. (Shapiro 2000) Agentic action can be defined as purposeful action especially evident when humans pursue personal goals. What's more, such actions tend to fundamentally shape the direction of one's life, determining what one becomes. (Richardson 2012; Tjeltveit 2006) Agentic action fundamentally revolves around the power to choose and to build one's life in a particular fashion. It stands in stark contrast to a life dictated and constructed by a principle outside the self. Agentic action largely involves another way of speaking about human liberty. Some would even say that human agency or liberty coupled with mind and moral awareness is that which provides a sense of personal existence. (Hurlbut and Kalanithi 2001)

Such thinking places a rather different spin on liberty or self-direction. Some segments of the Christian community seem to view self-direction with a jaundiced eye; they view it as an evil, terrible thing and one that stands completely contrary to the divine purpose. From this presentation, human self-direction should be seen in a different light. One ought to see it as divinely endowed and therefore a gift worth cherishing. Not surprisingly, even though God wills that humans serve Him, He yet restores the freedom to choose whom they will serve; He allows this knowing full well they might choose to serve others instead of Him. This thought alone ought to reinforce the value of human liberty. From this perspective, varied efforts to erode human liberty ought to be seen as demonic in nature in that they undermine what God has Himself established. No wonder despotic rulers who would become *gods* to their people, very quickly strike at the heart of human liberty! In so doing, they endeavor to reduce persons to something less than human; once dehumanized, they can more brutally mistreat them and rule from without. In demonic fashion, they seek to do that which God himself will not do; that is, rob individuals of their freedom and thus become the primary mover and determiner of their subjects' affections and actions.

However, one wonders if this all too common denigration of self-direction arises from confusing it with self-will. Interestingly, Wesley treated these two concepts rather differently. Evidenced by this discussion, he viewed liberty in a positive light. In stark contrast, he always described self-will in a negative light, associating it with pride and rebellion against the will of God. (Wesley 1872g; Wesley 1872j; Wesley 1872w; Wesley 1872x; Wesley 1872ad; Wesley 1872ae) I will speak about self-will in further detail in the next chapter when I discuss the human will. Suffice it to say that for Wesley, self-direction should always be accepted and embraced as God's good gift that truly makes us human. The same cannot be said about self-will. Rather than being embraced, it is something God designs to uproot in us.

Liberty's Enablings

One can describe liberty as the enabling faculty of the soul. I will now discuss three critical areas enabled by liberty according to Wesley. He believed grace enabled human response to God; without it, humans could not freely respond and commit themselves to the service of God. (Wesley 1872h; Wesley 1872s) Interestingly, in a quotation from *On The Fall of Man*, he produced a statement remarkably similar to that from *The General Deliverance*, quoted earlier. In the latter place, he showed liberty as vitally important in enabling service to the Creator. (Wesley 1872h) In *On The Fall of Man*, after speaking of understanding and will, he wrote: "To crown all the rest, he was endued with liberty; a power of directing his own affections and actions; a capacity of determining himself, or of choosing good or evil. Indeed, had not man been endued with this, all the rest would have been of no use: Had he not been a free as well as an intelligent being, *his understanding would have been as incapable of holiness, or any kind of virtue, as a tree or a block of marble."* (Wesley 1872s, 244 (italics added)) The italicized words likely filled out what Wesley generally meant by liberty enabling the service of God indicated in *The General Deliverance*; service to God likely meant serving God in holiness and becoming persons of virtuous character. Moreover, it would appear from this statement that he believed only free beings could truly become holy and virtuous; this idea fits with the general tenor of his thinking. As I will make clear in a later chapter, love lies at the heart of Wesley's vision of holiness and love must be freely given. Mildred Bangs Wynkoop expressed this biblical and Wesleyan truth well when she noted: *"Love can only exist in freedom.* It cannot be coerced." (Wynkoop 1972, 25) Later, in the same book, she added similar sentiments when she noted: ""Coerced" love is not love at all. At no point is the human person more responsible, therefore more "free" than the ordering of his love." (Wynkoop 1972, 157) Wesley likely would have heartily endorsed such statements. As a result, any Christian understanding of holiness must include the idea of freedom and liberty.

Second, he believed freedom of choice was necessary to the effective functioning of the other faculties of the soul. (Wesley 1872h; Wesley 1872s) Liberty, according to him was"... capable of being exerted with regard to all the faculties of the soul, as well as all the motions of the body." (Wesley 1872ag, 257) In *On The Fall of Man*, he referenced liberty's implications for understanding. He also implicated liberty relative to the will, directing as it did one's affections that are exercised by the will. (Wesley 1872s) Elsewhere, he included passions as another area directed by liberty. (Wesley 1872h) Thus, one could offer that liberty enabled the apprehending and motivating aspects of the soul. Without freedom of choice, apprehending faculties such as understanding might function to perceive and comprehend the self and the world. However, the results of such comprehension would play no meaningful role in one's life; that is, in the absence of freedom of choice, one would be powerless to exercise and apply the results of one's thinking and understanding. Likewise, one could make similar statements regarding the use of the will. Wesley saw the will exercised through one's affections and passions. But how does one engage these aspects without liberty? It would appear that in the absence of liberty, the will would play no practical role in one's life; that is, one could not engage the will and exhibit it in one's affections and passions. These aspects would be completely determined by forces outside the self. In fact, without, liberty, understanding and will, one could not meaningfully speak about accountability and responsibility for actions done and sins committed. We may consider this enabling of moral responsibility as a third thing enabled through liberty. Thus, in *Thoughts on Necessity*, after reinforcing the necessity of liberty, understanding and will, Wesley offered this statement: "Certain it is, that no being can be accountable for its actions, which has not liberty, as well as will and understanding." (Wesley 1872ac, 552)

However, although liberty exerted itself in the apprehending and motivational aspects of the soul, Wesley seemed to believe that it exerted itself more directly and more fully in one's visible behaviors, that is, in words and actions. Thus, he wrote of liberty: "*It is a power; which although it does not extend to all our thoughts and imaginations, yet extends to our words and actions in general, and not with many exceptions.* I am full as certain of this, that I am free, with respect to these, to speak or not to speak, to act or, not to act, to do this or the contrary, as I am of my own existence." (Wesley 1872ag, 257 (Italics added)) One can infer from this statement that in his view, liberty did not always extend to all of one's apprehensions, especially one's thoughts and imaginations. That is, some thoughts and imaginations lay outside of voluntary control, and were more influenced by other elements such as disease. This way of thinking helps explain his allowance for problems such as wandering thoughts and even nervous disorders in the Christian person. Although he saw some wandering thoughts springing from sinful tempers, he attributed others to the wedding of the soul with the body. In the latter instances, he highlighted how human problems such as disease and mental disorders might disrupt understanding and thought. (Wesley 1872af) Similarly, in nervous disorders, one's thoughts and imaginations might also find their source in bodily ailments. (Headley Summer, 1997; Wesley 1872ab) But with little or no exception, he saw liberty extending more fully to one's words and actions. This way of thinking fits well with psychological systems such as cognitive-behavioral theories which generally see overt behavior evident in words and actions as lying under more direct control than emotions and cognition. (Lazarus 1989)

The Apprehending Faculties of the Soul: Reason

In several places, Wesley described an aspect of the soul that served the purpose of apprehension and making judgments about the same. (Wesley 1872h) Elsewhere, he added a third way in which this faculty exerted itself; that is, by discourse. (Wesley 1872b) He provided a definition for each of these ways. He wrote: "*Simple apprehension* is barely conceiving a thing in the mind; the first and most simple act of the understanding. *Judgment* is the determining that the things before conceived either agree with or differ from each other. *Discourse*, strictly speaking, is the motion or progress of the mind from one judgment to another." (Wesley 1872b, 391-392) He linked all these functions to understanding that he equated with reason. (Wesley 1872b) This way of thinking stands in line with Jonathan Edwards who described understanding as being capable of perception and speculation. (Clapper 1985; Edwards 1997)

All these terms, whether apprehension, perception or speculation point to a facet of understanding whereby one grasps meaning. They all envision some degree of observation and contemplation facilitating meaning making.

For example, in perception, meaning derives from stimulation of the senses or through mental processes bringing sense data into awareness. (Kaplan and Sadock 1991) But Wesley did not ascribe this function to understanding alone; understanding or reason has its companions that share in the task of apprehension. These companions are imagination, memory and conscience. (Wesley 1872ah; Wesley 1872ag) In fact, it might not be unfair to conclude that even when he employed the term *understanding*, he likely envisioned these other aspects. One clue to this way of thinking derives from part 7 of his treatise on *The Doctrine of Original Sin*. In describing the fallen nature of human understanding and its natural bias toward evil, Wesley offered as part proof of it, the corruption of the human imagination:

> Consider how the carnal 'imagination' supplies the want of real objects to the corrupt heart. The unclean person is filled with speculative impurities, 'having eyes full of adultery.' The covetous man fills his heart with the world, if he cannot get his hands full of it. The malicious person acts his revenge in his own breast; the envious, within his own narrow soul, sees his neighbor laid low enough; and so every lust is fed by the imagination. These things may suffice to convince us of the natural bias of the mind to evil.(Wesley 1872v 510)

Because these apprehending aspects constitute one systemic reality, they share several features; they all stand corrupted by the fall. For example in relation to understanding, Wesley noted several effects of the fall: It was corrupted in terms of its created glory and now "covered with confusion," in regard to spiritual things. This confusion created great difficulty in understanding spiritual things, enveloped as it was in darkness relative to such things. But this difficulty in apprehending spiritual things was not simply passive; rather, because of a fallen understanding, humans exhibit an active opposition and aversion to the truth. Beyond these, the human understanding possessed a natural bias toward evil and a tendency to high-mindedness. (Wesley 1872v) Similarly, imagination also exhibited the effects of the fall. Because of its separation from God, imagination works to conjure up its own objects of worship. Thus, Wesley described imagination as a species of idolatry and associated it with the desire of the eyes. That is, it was chiefly through the eyes and the gratifying of the imagination that one sought happiness. (Wesley 1872l; Wesley 1872z) In similar fashion, all the apprehending faculties exhibit the effects of a fallen nature. As such, they can easily be marshaled in support of evil.

But because these faculties come as divine gifts with potential for serving holy purposes, they should be received and neither overvalued or undervalued. In *The Case of Reason Impartially Considered*, Wesley made this precise point relative to reason. He referred to those who elevated reason far more than they should. They did so believing that by itself, reason could provide a guide to truth and virtue. At the same time, others devalued reason. To the first group, and to place reason in proper perspective, he focused on things it could not accomplish. Although he perceived reason as consistent with faith, it could not produce scriptural faith. Neither could it produce scriptural hope by itself. Finally, no matter how cultured and enhanced, reason alone could not produce the love of God grounded as it was in faith and hope. Moreover, since reason could not produce the love of God "... so neither can it produce the love of our neighbor; a calm, generous, disinterested benevolence to every child of man." (Wesley 1872b, 398) Given this disability, reason by itself could not produce virtue since it depended on faith, hope and love. Additionally, one could not experience happiness by reason alone since it too was tied to faith, hope, love and virtue. One might experience momentary pleasures, but true happiness, if pursued through reason alone, lay beyond their grasp. (Wesley 1872b)

In spite of these limitations, Wesley believed reason yet had an important role to play. After all, God had given it to humans as a guide to life. (Wesley 1872b) Given his thinking, to those who devalued reason, he offered natural and supernatural reasons for embracing it. Among the former, he showed how reason guides individuals in the able performance of their obligations. He applied reason's scope in this regard to areas such as agriculture, apparel making, the arts, seafaring life, political life and the medical arts. Moreover, he showed how reason facilitated study in the arts and the sciences. Reason could also serve as an able guide in the discharge of social responsibilities in the public or private sphere. Basically, reason applied to all of life particularly as it pertained to relationships; that is, it enabled one to a life void of offense against God and man. Thus, he wrote:

> Many cases of conscience are not to be solved without the utmost exercise of our reason. The same is requisite in order to understand and to discharge our ordinary relative duties; — the duties of parents and children, Of husbands and wives, and (to name no more) of masters and servants. In all these respects, and in all the duties of common life, God has given us our reason for a guide. And it is only by acting up to the dictates of it, by using all the understanding which God hath given us, that we can have a conscience void of offense towards God and towards man. (Wesley 1872b, 393-394)

These areas constituted some of the natural purposes for which God gave reason as a guide. But besides these, God gave reason to help accomplish spiritual purposes; that is, reason helped one understand and explain the truths of God. In support of this precept, Wesley wrote the following:

> Is it not reason (assisted by the Holy Ghost) which enables us to understand what the Holy Scriptures declare concerning the being and attributes of God? — concerning his eternity and immensity; his power, wisdom, and holiness? It is by reason that God enables us in some measure to comprehend his method of dealing with the children of men; the nature of his various dispensations, of the old and new covenant, of the law and the gospel. It is by this we understand (his Spirit opening and enlightening the eyes of our

understanding) what that repentance is, not to be repented of; what is that faith whereby we are saved; what is the nature and the condition of justification; what are the immediate and what the subsequent fruits of it. By reason we learn what is that new birth, without which we cannot enter into the kingdom of heaven; and what that holiness is without which no man shall see the Lord. By the due use of reason we come to know what are the tempers implied in inward holiness; and what it is to be outwardly holy, — holy in all manner of conversation: In other words, what is the mind that was in Christ; and what it is to walk as Christ walked. (Wesley 1872b, 393)

This particular passage sheds light on how reason serves spiritual purposes when opened and enlightened by the Spirit. When enlightened, it helps one understand the intricacies of salvation including the nature of the new birth and justification and its requirements. What's more, it promotes understanding of the holiness God required. Interestingly, as Wesley affirmed reason's contribution to holiness, he resurrected the language and sequence encountered in the compacted form of the purposeful list; namely, reason facilitates understanding of inward and outward holiness. In relation to the former, it helps one grasp the nature of the religious affections and the tempers constituting inward holiness. In so doing, one could better apprehend the holy transformation required to conform to God's requirements. But in addition, reason informs outward holiness; it helps one better discern how to harmonize one's outward and inward life and to bring both into conformity with Christ. (Wesley 1872b) As such, reason and the other apprehending faculties demand stewardship of the highest kind. In support, Wesley struck this emphasis in *The Good Steward*, especially in reference to the apprehending faculties. He wrote: "*Thus we are to use our understanding, our imagination, our memory, wholly to the glory of Him that gave them.* Thus our will is to be wholly given up to him, and all our affections to be regulated as He directs. We are to love and hate, to rejoice and grieve, to desire and shun, to hope and fear, according to the rule which He prescribes whose we are, and whom we are to serve in all things. *Even our thoughts are not our own, in this sense; they are not at our own disposal; but for every deliberate motion of our mind we are accountable to our great Master.*" (Wesley 1872i, 162 (italics added))

Imagination

Besides reason, imagination, memory and conscience merit discussion. In regard to imagination, I found it interesting how Wesley set it in opposition to reason when discussing the appropriate discharge of one's responsibilities. Though these two normally complement each other, they can work in opposition to each other. According to Wesley, those who despised and repudiated reason invariably turned to imagination to supply their visions of the revelation of God. Wesley called such persons enthusiasts. (Wesley 1872b) Even the venerable William Law developed an unhealthy relationship between reason and imagination. Thus, in an extract of a letter written to Law, Wesley laid this problem at his door. He accused Law of blending philosophy and religion in an unscriptural manner as well as advancing views derived from this unholy alliance. In this spirit and in critique of Law, he wrote: "And I fear they who stop the workings of their reason, lie the more open to the workings of their imagination." (Wesley 1872e, 581) But though imagination can be misused in this manner, one should not leave it off. It too can serve godly purposes, creating good and profitable things. One could easily argue that the many great and valuable inventions the world has seen came as the product of imagination. As such, like reason, imagination should neither be devalued nor over-valued. Rather one ought to strike a balance regarding it.

But what exactly is the nature of the imagination of which Wesley spoke? He described imagination as a source of delight as one contemplates and apprehends the created world. Such delight proceeded from a contemplation of the grand, the uncommon (the novel) and the beauty of God's created world. (Wesley 1872z; Wesley 1872k) But imagination does more than apprehend; it demonstrates anticipative and creative properties reflective of a creative God. In Wesley's language, imagination acted as a framer creating its own internal objects. (Wesley 1872v) In *Original Sin*, he provided a rather succinct description of the facets of the imaginative element of the soul. Thus, he wrote: "It includes whatever is formed, made, fabricated within; all that is or passes in the soul; every inclination, affection, passion, appetite; every temper, design, thought. It must of consequence include every word and action, as naturally flowing from these fountains, and being either good or evil according to the fountain from which they severally flow." (Wesley 1872t, 73) In this description one sees his use of affectional language, normally associated with the will. Additionally, it incorporated the varied aspects one finds in Wesley's purposeful list, including its internal and external dimensions. As a result, one can detect the very close relationship between imagination and the will of the soul.

Modern writers largely agree with this assessment of the creative powers of imagination. Thus, the authors of one article wrote the following about imagination: "The capacity for imagination, however, goes far beyond adapted anticipation. Imagination is not mere memory or imitation, but envisioned creation. Forming mental images, maintaining them in the mind and achieving their realization, signifies intention, planning, and implementation of ideals." (Hurlbut and Kalanithi 2001, 336) As such, imagination itself involves an aspect of mind that envisions, strategizes and seeks to actualize its internal creations. One can even engage in envisioned creation even if it was not possible to implement the product of those ideas; that is, imagination possesses the power to create its own internal world, unrelated to the external world. In keeping with this idea, though in a negative light, Wesley spoke about imagination's ability to supply the lack of real objects to the corrupt heart; the covetous man can create in his heart the riches and possessions of the world which he does not possess in reality. Likewise, the person seeking revenge can act it out internally if this option does not avail itself in actuality. (Wesley 1872v)

These statements from Wesley fit well with Scripture's precepts. For example, in Psalm 73, while speaking about arrogant and evil persons, the author indicated: "From their callous hearts comes iniquity; their evil imaginations have no limits." (Psalm 73:7, NIV) From the context, it appears evident that acts of malice, oppression and violence proceed from the hearts of such persons. Furthermore, through imaginations, they conjure up limitless possibilities for doing evil. But Jesus himself provides several examples of the evil possibilities created within the internal world of humans. In several places, he envisioned this imaginative quality of mind relative to sin. For example, in Matthew chapter 5:28, he noted that anyone who looks at a woman lustfully had already committed adultery; though the deed was not done outwardly, it had already been accomplished in the imagination of the heart. In similar fashion, Jesus observed that the heart served as the source for all kinds of evil. Thus, in Matthew 15:19 he said: "For out of the heart come evil thoughts, murder, adultery, sexual immorality, theft, false testimony, slander." (NIV). Verses such as these would suggest that it is within one's internal world, including the imagination that one first conjures up evil. Furthermore, these internal acts constitute some degree of reality even if they do not get acted out in the external world. This reality necessitates the radical renewal of the human soul in its imaginations as well as tempers and affections. And God does exactly this task through His perfecting work in the human heart.

In keeping with this idea of internal creation, some have referred to imagination as *symbolic mind*. The term points to imagination's ability to create with or without implementation. Imagination as symbolic mind possesses the capability to detach images from the actual objects. In this way, the imagination experiences a freedom to innovate; through detaching images from objects, these same images can be internally recombined in a variety of configurations. This results in an infinite number of scenarios and sequences. But imagination does more; it can also detach envisioned scenarios and sequences from time and space. Additionally, it can anticipate the implications and outcomes of one's imaginative thinking. (Hurlbut and Kalanithi 2001) One can only begin to imagine the creative potential when one is able to frame internal images and recast them in an exponential range of possibilities outside of space and time, and sometimes, give them life.

My son Aaron, who is an artist, helps me in this regard. Sometimes I stand in awe of his fertile imagination and the real images that spring from it. Perhaps it's because I possess minute ability in this area, not being gifted in drawing, painting, sculpting, animation or other accomplished art forms. However, I make my backyard my canvas. Sometime ago, I discovered that

Aaron and I engage in a very similar process as we create our respect art; he with his varied art and animation and I with my backyard canvas. One day we stood on the deck of my home and peered over the backyard. He commented on how nice it looked and expressed appreciation for my creation even though a work in progress. I told him that I actually create pictures in my head of my envisioned plan for the backyard. He immediately said to me "That's exactly how I create my art. I see it in my head long before I produce it." Given my respect for his creative ability, I felt strangely complimented by his comment. That's the nature of imagination; it images independently of what presently exists, it recasts, remakes and reshuffles objects and in the process creates an infinite number of possibilities. Sometimes it even gets to the point of implementation. But even before that period in time, the internal created object is very real. For me, this ability constitutes a much less expensive process. In my mind, I can contemplate the placement of the envisioned objects I desire; but I can also manipulate them, move them from place to place until I find the desired effect, all without spending a dime until I actually make them real in time and space. I can only imagine the creative possibilities which exist for much more fertile minds who possess artistic and scientific capabilities to make their imagined creations live.

I suppose this quality of imagination gets somewhat objectified in computers and other gadgets that can simulate possibilities without implementation. Sometime ago, I saw the movie, *Iron Man 2*. In it, his alter ego, Tony Stark faced the daunting task of finding an alternate power source for the energy that kept him alive and which powered Iron Man's gadgetry. To create such a possibility, Stark turned to his computer, Jarvis. Jarvis explored various possibilities and made them visible to Stark through holographic type images. Stark could then view, move and otherwise manipulate these images, creating various configurations and possibilities. Through this process, he was able to discover the new and more powerful power source he desired. In many ways this sequence of events from the movie reminds me of the power of imagination; imagination does all the work Jarvis and Tony Stark accomplished. Imagination detaches images from objects, even suspending them outside of space and time. As a result, it remains free from the constraints of such elements. Freed from such limitations, the imagination is free to plan, create and innovate. In the process, infinite possibilities arise, sometimes to be implement and sometimes waiting more opportune moments.

In other words, imagination possesses the power to bring to virtual or real life, the imagined ideal. In the mind of some authors, this ability constitutes the "fullest manifestation of human freedom." By this ability to imagine the ideal, "... humans have the freedom to draw the past into the present from learning stored as memory and the freedom to draw the future into the present through the creative imagination." (Hurlbut and Kalanithi 2001, 336) Furthermore, these authors indicated that the capacity for imagination coupled with the drive to pursue it, actually brings about the aspiration towards a moral ideal. Henry Ward Beecher pointed to this same connection of imagination to morality; he indicated that imagination functions as "the true germ of faith." That is, imagination has a faith-like quality in that it is able to conceive "... as definite the things which are invisible to the senses, - of giving them distinct shape." (Beecher 1995, 216) As such, imagination stands as a critical element in perceiving spiritual things. A.W. Tozer echoed a similar thought relative to imagination. According to him, the cleansed imagination possesses the power to look beyond that which is natural and perceive spiritual things. It represented for him *the sacred gift of seeing*; that is, the ability to look at the beauty and mystery of created things and gaze more intently at that which is holy and eternal. (Tozer 1995)

Memory

But imagination sometimes uses another apprehending faculty; that is, it draws upon memory. Beyond using the raw material around it, or conjuring up its own images, it can also draw from information resident in memory. It then uses this material as the basis for its creative imagination. (Hurlbut and Kalanithi 2001) The apprehending faculty of memory thus serves as an ally to imagination. In regard to memory, Wesley believed it exerted itself in at least three ways that seemed to exist in a kind of hierarchy. He named the functions of remembering, reminiscence and recollection. He considered simple remembering as a passive function of the mind in that persons exhibit little ability to determine what they will or will not remember. Furthermore, as he rightly pointed out, this ability to remember is sometimes determined by whether the remembered event produced pleasure or pain. However, he considered reminiscence and recollection as examples where the mind functioned more actively to deliberately pull up past events. What's more, he considered recollection as a more deliberate aspect of memory whereby one studiously pulled together memories and events, even those that might have long escaped memory. By this statement, he likely meant to imply that this activity of mind proceeded from deliberate purpose as well as systematic effort. (Wesley 1872aa) Additionally, he suggested that there existed a facet of memory beyond these three. One might refer to this as memory's ability to accurately replicate events the individual had experienced. He used examples such as the ability to recall discourse, verses or a tune heard in one's mind and to reproduce these accurately with little if any variation. Furthermore, one can replicate that event without opening one's lips or without any verbal expression. He referred to this as a sort of *inward voice*. (Wesley 1872aa) Here too, one might surmise the association of memory and imagination, in that one remembers, reminisces, recollects or replicates in imagination.

However one understands memory, it seems clear that it exists to apprehend events. This might occur even when one did not consciously focus on the event. Whether consciously or unconsciously, the human mind can apprehend objects and events of all sorts, storing them for a more opportune moment when they become resurrected in consciousness. This quality of memory can be harnessed to achieve spiritual purposes. In proof, one can point to the countless number of times in Scripture where God sought to remind his people of his mighty acts on their behalf. For example, in Deuteronomy 5: 15, as part of the giving of the Ten Commandments, God spoke the following words: "Remember that you were slaves in Egypt and that the Lord your God brought you out of there with a mighty hand and an outstretched arm. Therefore the Lord your God has commanded you to observe the Sabbath day." (NIV) As seen here, the reminder of God's faithful acts on their behalf placed on them the obligation to remain faithful to Him through keeping His commandments. Sometimes, in Scripture, the individual deliberately engaged such acts of recollection to call forth hope. One discovers good examples of this in places like Psalms 42 -43 and 77, where memory inspired faith and hope. Psalm 77 serves as a particularly good example; here, many of the apprehending faculties of the soul work in tandem to restore hope in the psalmist. In support, I provide a large portion of the psalm below, italicizing the apprehending words.

> 1 I cried out to God for help;
> I cried out to God to hear me.
> 2 When I was in distress, I sought the Lord;
> at night I stretched out untiring hands,
> and I would not be comforted.
>
> 3 *I remembered you*, God, and I groaned;
> *I meditated*, and my spirit grew faint.
> 4 You kept my eyes from closing;
> I was too troubled to speak.
> 5 *I thought about the former days,*
> *the years of long ago;*
> 6 *I remembered my songs in the night.*
> *My heart meditated* and my spirit asked:
>
> 7 "Will the Lord reject forever?
> Will he never show his favor again?
> 8 Has his unfailing love vanished forever?
> Has his promise failed for all time?
> 9 Has God forgotten to be merciful?
> Has he in anger withheld his compassion? "
>
> 10 *Then I thought*, "To this I will appeal:
> *the years when the Most High stretched out his right hand.*
> 11 *I will remember the deeds of the* LORD;
> *yes, I will remember your miracles of long ago.*

> ^{12} *I will consider all your works*
> *and meditate on all your mighty deeds."* (NIV)

Clearly, in this psalm, the author stood in a precarious place. Later in the psalm, it appears that the precarious problem involved the community. Nevertheless, as is often the case, national and communal events all have personal repercussions, even if this involves despairing for the nation. Whatever the nature, the problem carried deep personal consequences. Thus, he described himself as standing in great distress, direly in need of comfort and help. In this trouble, he reached out in desperation to the Lord. But his trouble seemed so deep he despaired of help. To bolster hope of relief, he turned to memory of God's action. In verses 3-6, we find apprehending language, prominently focused around memory. Even verse 5 which uses the word *thought* is really memory at work, pulling up God's acts in the past and his joyful appreciation in song. But questions still remained. Thus, verses 7-9 poured forth his many questions about God in relation to his predicament. The verses all revolve around his despairing of God's help. He wondered aloud about rejection, loss of favor, failed promises, forgotten mercies and withheld compassion; all possible evidences of God's failure. Taking verses 3-6 and 7-9 together reminds one of psalms 42-43 where the psalmist alternately wavered between despair and hope. But in verses 10-12, remembrance rises to the rescue, and brings to mind God's mighty acts. This final plunge into the depths of memory brings hope triumphantly to the surface. As a result, verses 13-20, rises like a crescendo of praise of God's mighty acts on Israel's behalf: God is the God of miracles who displays His greatness and power on behalf of Israel and who constantly leads them like a flock. This spirit finds expression in all of these verses, but 13-15, it reverberates:

> ^{13} Your ways, God, are holy.
>   What god is as great as our God?
> ^{14} You are the God who performs miracles;
>   you display your power among the peoples.
> ^{15} With your mighty arm you redeemed your people,
>   the descendants of Jacob and Joseph. (NIV)

No wonder Jesus often made an appeal to memory, often calling His disciples to remember His acts. In Mark 8: 15, following the feeding of the four thousand, He warned His disciples to be on guard against the leaven of the Pharisees and Herod. Misunderstanding Him, they wondered if He was referring to their lack of bread. Jesus then asked them: "Why are you talking about having no bread? Do you still not see or understand? Are your hearts hardened? Do you have eyes but fail to see, and ears but fail to hear? And don't you remember? When I broke the five loaves for the five thousand, how many basketfuls of pieces did you pick up? ... And when I broke the seven loaves for the four thousand, how many basketfuls of pieces did you pick up?" (Mark 8:17-20, NIV) In this way Jesus called them to believe in

Him. He also sought to rouse their spiritual understanding. It's interesting how in this passage He connected understanding, the hardened heart, sense data and memory. The message seems to indicate that in order to apprehend spiritual realities, one should include all the senses and understanding, including the power of memory.

But memory can also provoke spiritual repentance. Perhaps the most obvious example of this comes in the aftermath of Peter's denial of Jesus. Jesus had predicted this denial and Peter had vehemently denied the possibility. However, he took it to heart following his disavowal of his Lord. Following the crowing of the rooster, Matthew 26:75 recorded: "Then Peter remembered the words Jesus had spoken: "Before the rooster crows, you will disown me three times." And he went out and wept bitterly." (NIV). Evidently, this weeping represented mourning for his sins, befitting of a godly repentance and through it, Peter found redemption. Memory can also serve to confirm belief. This evidences itself following the death and resurrection of Jesus. Prior to His death, he had constantly reminded His disciples that He would die and rise the third day. Following these events, the disciples firmly placed their trust in Him. John's gospel records: "After he was raised from the dead, his disciples recalled what he had said. Then they believed the Scripture and the words Jesus had spoken." (John 2:22, NIV) No wonder the church practices rituals that invoke memory. The sacrament of Holy Communion constitutes one such example. Through visible acts, memory and imagination vividly recalls God's acts on our behalf and they become for us, means of grace. Thus, in I Corinthians 11, in regards to the bread, Paul reminds us of this reality in the communion ritual: "This is my body which is for you; do this in remembrance of me." (I Corinthians 11:24, NIV) Similarly, regarding the cup, He gave the same refrain: "This cup is the new covenant in my blood; do this, whenever you drink it, in remembrance of me." (I Corinthians 11: 25, NIV)

Conscience

Before concluding this chapter, another apprehending aspect of the soul deserves attention. This aspect is conscience. I have already established that Wesley saw conscience as a faculty of the soul. (Wesley 1872i) Furthermore, in his description he saw it serving a perceptive or deciphering role. Thus he described it as "...a faculty or power, implanted by God in every soul that comes into the world, of perceiving what is right or wrong in his own heart or life, in his tempers, thoughts, words, and actions." (Wesley 1872ah, 210) Conscience enables moral sensibilities whereby one is able to perceive right and wrong. But, in this description, Wesley invoked the purposeful list in its concise and expanded forms. Thus, conscience helps one to discern right and wrong in heart and life (concise form). But it also helps one assess the rightness or wrongness of one's "... tempers, thoughts, words and actions" (expanded form). Given Wesley's employment of the purposeful list in discussing Christian perfection, he likely intended it consideration in relationship to conscience

But by what rule does one determine right or wrong? Such an important matter should not be left to personal whim, unguided by nothing else but one's own imagination, thoughts or beliefs. It required a surer standard of moral behavior and this requirement was met in the word of God. This word of God served as the final arbiter and the Christian rule determining right and wrong. Wesley believed four things were absolutely required if one should maintain a conscience void of offense. Significantly, these four all revolved around the word of God. These four included the following:

1. A right understanding of the word of God.
2. Self-knowledge that facilitated measuring life against God's word.
3. Bringing one's known life into conformity with God's word.
4. An internal perception that inward and outward holiness accorded with the rule of God's word. (Wesley 1872ah, 209-219)

Wesley's first requirement of a right understanding of the word of God included its application to life. After all, one could only walk by a rule if one understood its meaning. Conscience also required self-knowledge. Here, he did not mean some superficial knowledge; rather he referred to a deep knowing of one's inward and outward life. Without this in-depth knowledge, one could not truly measure one's life against God's word as the rule for life. But in this requirement, one intuits another truth: Intimacy with self becomes a necessary ingredient to intimacy with God demonstrated through a life void of offense. At first blush, this conclusion might appear a leap of logic but it is not. After all, God's word to us is fundamentally meant to help us become like Him and intimate Him. But such intimacy is profoundly bound up with having experienced intimacy with the self. In their book, *Spiritual Wholeness for Clergy*, Hands and Fehr made this very point highlighting that intimacy with God required intimacy with self and vice-versa. As we know ourselves better, it creates space to become more intimate with God. On the other hand, intimacy with God facilitates a fuller understanding and appreciation for the self. Without intimacy with God, we miss the ultimate basis for love and self-acceptance. (Hands and Fehr 1994) This way of thinking lends support and legitimacy to giving time and space to knowing and promoting intimacy with the self. This is no quick or easy task; it requires effort and introspection. Here, I do not mean a morbid introspection that becomes an exercise in navel-gazing and which drowns one in depression and despair. Rather, I think about intentional efforts to know the self with a view to bringing life into greater conformity to God's rule. In this sense, introspection becomes a spiritual discipline and a path to transformation. It forms a part of the discipline of solitude whereby we create space for God to reach us. (Foster 1993)

But the journey to greater self-knowledge requires one's own efforts as well as the help of others. Self-knowledge might come through spiritual friends who mutually nurture the development of each other's souls and thereby promote wholeness and holiness. But structured forms of contact such as spiritual direction also facilitated self-knowledge. (Benner 2002) Additionally, so-called secular processes can also aid the journey. Here I refer to interpersonal processes such as psychotherapy. Viewed from my perspective, therapy might become a means of grace, helping to plumb the depths of personality. It might help one become more self-aware and thereby lead to greater self-integration. Concomitantly, this might awaken a deeper spirituality and relationship with God. In this sense, psychotherapy becomes a handmaid of spiritual formation. (Benner 1998; Leffel 2004; Strawn and Leffel 2001; Strawn 2004) Psychotherapy and other therapeutic arts can serve spiritual purposes largely because humans constitute wholes. In humans, the spiritual and the psychological do not exist separate from each other. Rather, they exist as mutually influencing aspects of personhood. David Benner has described this reality as a psycho-spiritual union. Given this reality, that which helps us psychologically has the distinct potential to aid our spiritual growth and vice versa. (Benner 1988)

To speak of the help of others in knowing the self suggests a social dimension to conscience. And why not! After all, the root of the word *conscience* points to a social dimension. Conscience derives from two words highlighting the reality of joint or mutual knowledge. That is, conscience partly comes about through the sharing of knowledge with another, especially in relation to moral matters. Thus, Hurlbut and Kalanithi while discussing the moral nature of humans suggested that conscience is deeply oriented towards people. In fact, this also holds true for a related word, *consciousness*, since both words derive from the same root. Moreover, according to them, consciousness was originally included in the term conscience. From this perspective, consciousness primarily meant consciousness about moral matters. (Hurlbut and Kalanithi 2001) But of course, consciousness also involves apperception, a full awareness of oneself, especially as modified by one's emotions and thoughts. (Kaplan and Sadock 1991) Thus, one can conclude that conscience and consciousness as related to moral and other forms of self-awareness also require social contact. Such thinking affirms the necessity of varied forms of social contact such as spiritual friends, accountability relationships, varied forms of mentoring and even psychotherapeutic relationships when necessary. Each of these can promote self-awareness in the sense of consciousness. But they also enhance conscience in the sense in which Wesley employed the term.

The third requirement relative to the word required bringing one's known life into harmony with God's word. Here Wesley again invoked the language of the compacted and expanded purposeful list: "Thirdly, an agreement of our hearts and lives, of our tempers and conversation, of our thoughts, and words, and works, with that rule, with the written word of God. For, without this, if we have any conscience at all, it can be only in evil conscience." (Wesley 1872ah, 211-212) In the last requirement, he proposed that there ought to exist an internal perception of the alignment of inward and outward holiness with the rule of God's word. What's more, he believed that this inward perception ought to continually exist. It would appear that this internal perception constituted a form of assurance, likely aided by the presence and confirmation of the Holy Spirit. For Wesley, having this continual internal perception constituted possessing a good conscience, void of offense toward God and others. (Wesley 1872ah)

Faculties of the Soul and Christian Perfection

Earlier in this discussion of conscience, I cited two occasions from *The Witness of our Own Spirit* where Wesley associated it with the purposeful list. According to him, conscience helped one perceive the moral rightness of one's inward and outward life. It also helped assess the congruence between one's heart and life and internal and external righteousness with the word of God. (Wesley 1872ah) As demonstrated at the beginning of this book, the purposeful list primarily relates to inward and outward holiness. Thus, the connection of the purposeful list in Wesley's discussion of conscience suggests that it is principally designed by God to facilitate holiness; that is, it exists to help us perceive and ultimately conform our inward and outward lives to God's vision of holiness. But this role does not simply apply to conscience; it applies to every apprehending aspect of the soul. Wesley made a similar connection between inward and outward holiness and reason as he had for conscience. (Wesley 1872b) Reason served the holy purpose of creating in us a true understanding of the nature of inward and outward holiness required by God. In fact, all the apprehending faculties of the soul work together to promote understanding and a living into God's vision of holiness. Of course, these faculties might work together in a variety of ways and might begin with any of these elements. But if one looked at understanding and imagination, in a rudimentary way, it might look thus: After having more fully comprehended God's requirement of holiness through reason or understanding, imagination might help us picture what life could be if it incorporated this vision. That is, one might picture in imagination the kind of saint God wants us to become. Then, in tandem with His Spirit, God works in us cooperantly to make this imagined vision a reality in space and time.

Is this not the way change sometimes occurs? Sometimes individuals change their lives by first picturing what they would like to become. Then, through focus on the vision and deliberate effort, the imagined self becomes reality. Arnold Lazarus, the founder of Multimodal Therapy believed this relative to the change process. He believed that before anything became reality, it first had to be rehearsed in imagery. Related to this, he believed that unless persons could picture themselves doing an act, they probably would not be able to perform it. (Lazarus 1989) Along a similar line, I once had a colleague say to me that the image on which one focused dictated what one became. For example, if a man had an abusive father and fixed his mind on the father's image as a reminder of what he did not want to become, he eventually conformed to that image. The abusive father image fed imagination, eventually producing a product of the same kind. On the other hand, if he created an image of what he actually wanted to be, that image would lead to a different kind of person. This way of thinking finds support in another concept indicated in this book; that is, the object of one's focus, dictates what one becomes. Might this or a similar process be at work in the lives of those who seek to conform their lives to the holy image of Christ? Might we image Christ as God's ideal of the holy human person and thereby facilitate Christlikeness? Might imaging and concentration on Christ constitute part of the process whereby we find our tempers and affections transformed? Might such concentration help to transform carnal, worldly minds into the mind of Christ? It certainly seems plausible. Of course, such holy transformation does not simply involve these cooperant actions by the individual; it fundamentally involves the work of God's Spirit in the human soul.

But though the apprehending faculties of the soul help move us toward inward and outward holiness, they also help set the limits of Christian perfection. Faculties of the soul such as reason can point us toward Christian perfection. However, these very areas provide proof that we never become absolutely perfect. Each involved some degree of infirmity and Wesley allowed space for such in his teachings on Christian perfection. Of course, some infirmities largely derive from living in a corruptible body. But besides these, he spoke of inward and outward infirmities not of a bodily or moral nature. These he related to the apprehending faculties of the soul as demonstrated in the following excerpt from *Christian Perfection*:

> But I mean hereby, not only those which are properly termed bodily infirmities, but all those inward or outward imperfections which are not of a moral nature. Such are the weakness or slowness of understanding, dullness or confusedness of apprehension, incoherency of thought, irregular quickness or heaviness of imagination. Such (to mention no more of this kind) is the want of a ready or retentive memory. Such, in another kind, are those which are commonly, in some measure, consequent upon these; namely, slowness of speech, impropriety of language, ungracefulness of pronunciation; to which one might add a thousand nameless defects, either in conversation or behavior. These are the infirmities which are found in the best of men, in a larger or smaller proportion. And from these none can hope to he perfectly freed, till the spirit returns to God that gave it. (Wesley 1872c, 17)

Of course, just as the apprehending faculties play in role in salvation, including Christian perfection, so too does liberty. As an enabling faculty of soul, it also works to make us holy creatures. To reiterate previous statements in succinct form, liberty relates to several aspects of salvation. It is liberty, enabled by God's Spirit that permits response to God and service to God. And as previously noted, service to God equates with the virtuous and holy life. Moreover, it is this faculty of soul that permits moral responsibility and accountability. Without this capability, virtue or even vice would not even be possible. But because of this power to choose, one can exercise it to move towards the good or the evil. This capacity relates both to one's inward nature and outward action; that is, through liberty, one can direct one's tempers as well as actions in ways that make for inward and outward holiness. But supremely, to come to Christian perfection, means that one has learned how to love as God intends. But even here, liberty plays a pivotal role. Although God Himself gives us the ability to love through shedding his love in our hearts, it yet requires liberty if we will live into love. Love must spring from a free act of the human will rather than being wrenched and coerced from unwilling humans. (Wynkoop 1972) Thus enabled, we are free to exercise liberty to live a holy life. Paul placed it rather succinctly and poignantly in his letter to the Galatians: "You, my brothers and sisters, were called to be free. But do not use your freedom to indulge the flesh; rather, serve one another humbly in love. For the entire law is fulfilled in keeping this one command: "Love your neighbor as yourself." If you bite and devour each other, watch out or you will be destroyed by each other." (Galatians 5: 13-15, NIV)

Chapter 4

Mapping the Soul: The Will and the Religious Affections

The Consecrated Will

Frances Ridley Havergal's memorable hymn, *Take My Life and Let it Be*, speaks a great deal about the consecrated life. Havergal wrote the hymn during a five-day visit to a family. During the last night of her trip, she found it difficult to sleep. Joy and happiness over the family's successful transactions with God and receipt of His blessings kept sleep safely at bay. Unable to sleep, she spent most of the night renewing her consecration to God. During this period she penned the words to the famous hymn. According to her, the many couplets of the hymn "... formed themselves and chimed in my heart one after another till they finished with "Ever, only, ALL for thee." (Bailey 1950, 404) The final words of the hymn capture its essence; Havergal pictured an exclusive consecration to God lasting forever. What's more, it meant the surrender of her entire being and possessions to God, for all time. As a result, the entire hymn detailed significant areas of surrender; the essential aspects her life, represented by hands, feet, voice and lips, she offered up to God. But besides surrendering these bodily instruments, she also willingly offered the outward accouterments of her life such as silver and gold. This proffered, tangible sacrifice represented more than written verse; she actually gave up her treasures. In proof, she wrote in one of her letters: "Take my silver and my gold' now means shipping off all of my ornaments, - including a jewel cabinet which is really fit for a countess – to the Church Missionary Society where they will be accepted and disposed of for me." (Bailey 1950,405) Her written words of sacrifice became concretized in the outward expressions of a surrendered life.

These surrendered areas of her life found their culmination in a surrendered will and consecrated heart. Thus, as they appear in many hymnals, Havergal wrote verses four and five:

Take my will and make it Thine; It shall be no longer mine.
Take my heart; it is Thine own! It shall be Thy royal throne.
It shall be Thy royal throne.

Take my love; my God, I pour at Thy feet its treasure store
Take my self and I will be Ever only, all for Thee;
Ever, only, all for Thee. (Lillenas 1972, 281)

Havergal knew a surrendered will and heart laid at the core of the consecrated life. Without such dedication, life could easily degenerate and become mired in self-will. Such a stance involved placing self on the throne and worshipping at one's own shrine. In this sense, Jesus' prayer in the Garden of Gethsemane "... not as I will, but as you will," represents the ultimate surrender and the needed cry of the human heart. All of us, if we will truly dedicate our lives completely to God, must understand that the crux of that surrender lies in the yielded will. Thus, in verse four, Havergal offered the surrender of her will in a radical manner, aligning it fully with God's will. Moreover, the second part of verse four spoke to God's rightful ascension to the throne of her heart, a place reserved for Him alone. Of course, all of this finds its source in complete love towards God. Havergal highlighted this in verse 5 where she offered all of her life as a living sacrifice. This giving over of one's will, heart and love truly make for a complete surrender.

The Will in Wesley's Writings

John Wesley would likely have agreed with Havergal and her ideas about the will and the need to surrender it to God. For him, the will played a significant role in the holy life when surrendered to and aligned with God. As a result, he spoke often of the will which he considered a faculty of the soul. (Wesley 1872t) But unfortunately, it can also rebel against God seeking to make self-will the governing basis of one's life. This stance opens one up to living life solely for the self and pursuing the love of the world, the flesh and the devil rather than love for God. This latter stance derives from the fallen nature of the will. Just as Wesley viewed other aspects of the soul as fallen, he held similar views relative to the will. He depicted its fallen nature in several places but I mention two instances. First, in his sermon, *The Way to the Kingdom*, he painted a picture of the utter corruption of the will and its affections, along with the other faculties of the soul.

> Know that thou art corrupted in every power, in every faculty of thy soul; that thou art totally corrupted in every one of these, all the foundations

being out of course. The eyes of thine understanding are darkened, so that they cannot discern God, or the things of God. The clouds of ignorance and error rest upon thee, and cover thee with the shadow of death. Thou knowest nothing yet as thou oughtest to know, neither God, nor the world, nor thyself. *Thy will is no longer the will of God, but is utterly perverse and distorted, averse from all good, from all which God loves, and prone to all evil, to every abomination which God hateth. Thy affections are alienated from God, and scattered abroad over all the earth. All thy passions, both thy desires and aversions, thy joys and sorrows, thy hopes and fears, are out of frame, are either undue in their degree, or placed on undue objects.* So that there is no soundness in thy soul; but "from the crown of the head, to the sole of the foot," (to use the strong expression of the Prophet,) there are only "wounds, and bruises, and putrefying sores." (Wesley 1872z, 151-152 (Italics added))

To put it mildly, he painted a rather dismal picture. Like the rest of the soul, the will became thoroughly corrupted, perverse and distorted away from its original purpose. Prior to the fall, God intended the human will to fully align itself to His will and act out of that motivation. But the fall destroyed this design. Now instead of allegiance to the will of God, the human will prostrated itself in service to the self. As such, it disavowed all the good and all that God loved while enthusiastically embracing and devoting itself to everything God hated. Having made this declaration regarding the will, Wesley turned his attention to the religious affections, specifically the affections and passions (Wesley 1872k; Wesley 1872n; Wesley 1872b; Wesley 1872d). The simple logic for this shift arose from seeing the affections and passions as elements exercised by the will. These too had become perverse and distorted. Relative to the affections, he described them as totally alienated from God. This suggests that they were no longer centered on God. Not surprisingly, once detached from God, they appeared like wandering spirits, destitute of a home, vainly seeking a place of rest; accordingly, they vigorously attached themselves to whatever evil they encountered in the world. But the passions also became disordered. Wesley described them as out of frame and judging from the statements that followed, this suggests several possibilities: They often appeared unwarranted, excessive and unjustified. Sometimes they exhibited themselves even though unnecessary. Moreover, these undue passions displayed this quality either by disproportionate excess or by attaching themselves to unworthy and evil objects. One should understand undue objects as anything that is not God. One might render the passions thus displayed as inordinate or disordered.

Wesley provided a similar depiction of the fallen human will and affections in *Part 7 of The Doctrine of Original Sin*. Here, he wrote: "Man, in his natural state, is altogether corrupt, through all the faculties of his soul: Corrupt in his understanding, his will, his affections, his conscience, and his memory." (Wesley 1872p, 506-507) Elsewhere in the same document, he added: "Nor is the will less corrupted than the understanding. It was at first faithful, and ruled with God; but now it is turned traitor against God, and rules with and for the devil." (Wesley 1872p, 512) In this last quotation, he gave additional emphasis to the perverse nature of the human will. Once again he emphasized how far the human will had fallen away from its original design and full alignment with the will of God. In their un-fallen state, Adam and Eve possessed a will fully aligned with the will of God. According to him: "His will lay straight with the will of God. There was no corruption in his will, no bent or inclination to evil; for that is sin properly so called; and, therefore, inconsistent with that uprightness with which it is expressly said he was ended at his creation. The will of man was then naturally inclined to God and goodness, though mutably. It was disposed by its original make to follow the Creator's will, as the shadow does the body. It was not left in an equal balance to good and evil; for then he had not been upright, or conform to the law; which no more can allow the creature not to be inclined to God as his end, than it can allow man to be a God to himself." (Wesley 1872p, 497) Moreover, given the will's alignment with the will of God, the religious affections that flow from it, functioned as God intended; that is, they functioned in an ordered rather than disordered fashion. In support of this reality, Wesley added the following statement: "His affections were regular, pure, and holy. All his passions, yea, all his sensitive motions and inclinations, were subordinate to his reason and will, which lay straight with the will of God. They were all, therefore, pure from all defilement, free from all disorder or distemper; because in all their motions they were duly subjected to his clear reason and his holy will." (Wesley 1872p 497) However, following the fall, the human will transferred its allegiance; it rebelled against God and cast its lot fully on the side of the devil. In speaking about this treacherous shift in allegiances, Wesley used the term *rule*. Being aligned with God, the will moved humans to do God's will in the world. Humans ruled and governed creation on His behalf. Now in a fallen state, humans aligned their wills to fulfilling the devil's will in the world; that is, instead of God's, they aimed to make the devil's will and purposes victorious in the world.

Following his statement of the will's treachery, Wesley discussed the numerous ways in which the will acts perversely and rebelliously against God. First, he saw the un-renewed will totally lacking in any ability to do good in the sight of God. Given his views on the enabling faculty of liberty, he believed that the unconverted possessed the capacity to choose and do what was materially good. However, though such persons could will, such persons could do nothing spiritually good apart from God. As proof, he pointed to some of the ways in which this manifests itself. For example, though one might know the good to be chosen and the evil to refuse, yet one's heart finds it impossible to choose the good. Moreover, though conscience itself might instruct in the right way, here too one finds it impossible to follow this path. Second, he believed there existed in the will of fallen humanity an awareness of God coupled with a firm and contrasting commitment to sin. Because of this commitment, such persons spurn Christ, refusing His healing. But in addition, they actually actively rebel against the light which God gives, preferring to live in darkness. Third, and related to the previous point, there existed in fallen humanity a natural proneness to evil that instinctively chooses sin and rejects holiness. Fourth, they also exhibit a natural contrariety, that is, a direct opposition to God himself. Finally, the will became completely perverse. This perverseness exhibits itself in humans' obstinate efforts to turn to themselves rather than to the God who made them. Though created as dependent beings that find their truest existence and goodness in Him, they willfully seek to find these essentials in themselves. In a sense, they perversely run after a kind of self-idolatry where they become their own gods. Thus, Wesley noted:

> And thus man was created looking directly to God, and his last end; but, falling into sin, he fell off from God, and turned into himself. Now, this infers a total apostasy and universal corruption in man; for where the last end is changed, there can be no real goodness. And this is the case of all men in their natural state: They seek not God, but themselves. Hence though many fair shreds of morality are among them, yet 'there is none that doeth, good, no, not one.' For though some of them 'run well,' they are still off the way; they never aim at the right mark. Whithersoever they move, they cannot move beyond the circle of self. They seek themselves, they act for themselves; their natural, civil, and religious actions, from whatever spring they come, do all run into, and meet in, this dead sea. (Wesley 1872p , 523)

Self-Will and Rebellion against God

One can consider the commitment to rebellion against God a manifestation of self-will. This should not be identified with true liberty or self-direction. Wesley always discussed self-will in a negative light! In contrast, he often described liberty or self-direction in a positive light. Self-will represented for him the rebellious and perverse turning of the human will towards itself rather than to a commitment to God and his will. But as implied in our previous discussion, a commitment to self-will really represents a commitment to the rule of the devil in one's life. This holds true for at least two reasons. First, being governed by self-will indicates a rejection of God's image and instead allowing Satan to engrave his image within us. By rejecting God's image, we mimic Satan's stance when he rebelled against God. Second, in mimicking this stance we fully align ourselves with Satan, choosing to pursue our own path independent of and in opposition to God's. (Wesley 1872o) But those who follow this path often fail to see its devilish connection. They believe living by self-will means they only live for themselves! Some even see this way of living as an appropriate expression of self-direction or liberty. In reality, such notions represent an exercise in self-deception. Living by self-will represents a commitment to the dark side and everything devilish while casting one's lot firmly with the devil. Perhaps this truth finds some support in the temptations of Jesus. In the temptations, Jesus came face to face with the ultimate choice humans face: To live by God's rule or capitulate to the devil. The devil's temptations came as an invitation for Jesus to live by his rule. They invited Jesus to live his life governed by his own will. This meant fulfilling all His desires and needs in ways contrary to what God intended. But such choices always come at a price; in order to live in such a manner, Jesus would have to fall down and worship the devil. So too, in worshipping at our own altars of self-will, in reality we bow in service to the devil. This thought relative to self-will naturally leads us to a further consideration of this term that I briefly introduced in chapter one.

The actual term self-will occurred in several places in Wesley's sermons. It appears in such places as *First Fruits of the Spirit, Repentance of Believers, The Righteousness of Faith, Upon Our Lord's Sermon on the Mount, Discourse 9 and Heaviness through Manifold Temptation.* In these places, he consistently identified self-will as an expression of sin. It also involved an inordinate love of self, contrasted with a love for God. What's more in his view, self-will, constituted a type of idolatry because it placed the self on the throne, devolving into self-worship. (Wesley 1872q; Wesley 1872x) The sainted Bernard of Clairvaux held a similar perspective relative to the will, particularly as it exemplified self-rule in opposition to the will of God. In his classic, *On Loving God*, Bernard wrote of self-will: "Furthermore, the slave and the hireling have a law, not from the Lord, but of their own contriving; the one does not love God, the other loves something else more than God. They have a law of their own, not of God, I say; yet it is subject to the law of the Lord. For though they can make laws for themselves, they cannot supplant the changeless order of the eternal law. Each man is a law unto himself, when he sets up his will against the universal law, perversely striving to rival his Creator, to be wholly independent, making his will his only law." (Clairvaux 1997, 41) Cardinal Špidlík added another dimension to self-will when he equated it with the "… tendency to justify with holy pretexts the inclination towards evil." (Špidlík 2010, 20)

But self-will does not exist alone. Rather, it exists along with evil attitudes such as pride. Not surprisingly, pride also comes stained with idolatry because it ascribes to the self the honor that belongs to God alone. Through pride, according to Wesley, "… we rob God of his unalienable right, and idolatrously usurp his glory." (Wesley 1872o, 77) Thus, in *The Repentance of Believers*, he noted: "Now self-will, as well as pride, is a species of idolatry, and both are directly contrary to the love of God. The same observation may be made concerning the love of the world." (Wesley 1872q, 236) Later, in the same sermon, he wrote: "There does still remain, even in them that are justified, a mind which is in some measure carnal; (so the Apostle tells even the believers at Corinth, "Ye are carnal;") an heart bent to backsliding, still ever ready to "depart from the living God;" a propensity to pride, self-will, anger, revenge, love of the world, yea, and all evil; a root of bitterness, which, if the restraint were taken off for a moment, would instantly spring up;" (Wesley 1872q, 238) Similarly, in *The*

Righteousness of Faith, he connected self-will with pride and inordinate affections, including love of the world and pleasure and pictured these as standing in opposition to the love of God: "For, what is it more, than to acknowledge, with our heart as well as lips, the true state wherein we are? to acknowledge that we bring with us into the world a corrupt, sinful nature; more corrupt, indeed, than we can easily conceive, or find words to express? *that hereby we are prone to all that is evil, and averse from all that is good; that we are full of pride, self-will, unruly passions, foolish desires, vile and inordinate affections; lovers of the world, lovers of pleasure more than lovers of God?*" (Wesley 1872r, 141 (italics added)) Finally, in the ninth discourse on the Sermon on the Mount, he struck the same emphasis. The notable difference here is that instead of identifying self-will with love of the world and pleasure, he connected it to an inordinate love of self, among other things:

> To resemble, to be conformed to, the world, is a Third thing we are to understand by serving mammon; to have not only designs, but desires, tempers, affections, suitable to those of the world; to be of an earthly, sensual mind, chained down to the things of earth; to be self-willed, inordinate lovers of ourselves; to think highly of our own attainments; to desire and delight in the praise of men; to fear, shun, and abhor reproach; to be in patient of reproof, easy to be provoked, and swift to return evil for evil (Wesley 1872x, 476)

Several observations appear here that also were reflected in previously quoted passages. First, self-will clearly connected with many of the internal dispositions associated with Wesley's purposeful list. As a result, this statement included words expressive of internal dimensions such as desires, tempers and affections, albeit, proceeding from a worldly soul. Second, he associated self-will with having a "sensual mind," and one would think this ought to be contrasted with having the mind of Christ. Third, self-will connected to inordinate love, in this case, a love of self which stands in direct opposition to the love of God and likely to love of others. One should note that Wesley qualified this love of self by the adjective *inordinate*. That is, it depicts a love excessively or disproportionately showered on the self and thus left little if any space for God or others. However, if love of self can be disproportionately lavished on the self, there must also exist a love for self that is quite appropriate, balanced and ordered. But I reserve this discussion for the next chapter. Suffice it to say that self-will expressed as an inordinate love of self truly constitutes a "species of idolatry;" it displaces love for God, reserving it entirely for the self. Yet there exists another sense in which self-will undercuts love for God and others. This derives from its relationship to pride: Hurlbut and Kalanithi suggested that self-will manifests itself psychologically through pride. In turn, pride undercuts love for others since it preempt the ability to empathically respond to others. (Hurlbut and Kalanithi 2001)

No Wonder Wesley saw God's true religion as specifically intended to address issues like pride and self will! According to him, God's salvation constituted a therapy of the soul. God designed it to heal humans' corrupted souls. Thus he wrote:

> We may learn from hence, in the Third place, what is the proper nature of religion, of the religion of Jesus Christ. It is θεραπεια ψυχης, God's method of healing a soul which is thus diseased. Hereby the great Physician of souls applies medicines to heal this sickness, to restore human nature, totally corrupted in all its faculties. God heals all our Atheism by the knowledge of Himself, and of Jesus Christ whom he hath sent; by giving us faith, a divine evidence and conviction of God, and of the things of God. — in particular, of this important truth, "Christ loved me, and gave himself for me." By repentance and lowliness of heart, the deadly disease of pride is healed; that of self-will by resignation, a meek and thankful submission to the will of God; and for the love of the world in all its branches, the love of God is the sovereign remedy. Now, this is properly religion, "faith" thus "working by love;" working the genuine meek humility, entire deadness to the world, with a loving, thankful acquiescence in, and conformity to, the whole will and word of God.(Wesley 1872o, 80-81)

Christian religion served as the ultimate cure of souls. It addressed the deepest needs of human life and restored it to its intended state and purpose. This healing involved all the faculties of the soul, including the will. God heals a distorted and corrupted understanding that prompts atheism, through a true knowledge of God through Jesus Christ. But more pertinent to our focus, God heals the diseases of the will: God cures pride by bringing true repentance and poverty of spirit; he heals rebellion demonstrated by self-will, through bringing Christians to submit their wills to the will of God. But self-will and pride do not only produce rebellion and self-worship; they also produce a disordered love which undermines love for God and inevitably undercuts love for others. Concomitantly, an inordinate love for self and love of the world, the flesh and the devil reigns supreme. God heals these disordered expressions by producing love for Him within Christian persons. This reality provides the fundamental building block for ordered love; in loving God with all our hearts, souls and minds, love in all its aspects becomes ordered. Ultimately, this ordered love of God then orders love for self and others in the way God intended. For Wesley, such lay at the heart of God's cure of soul. What's more, this therapy of the soul fundamentally involved the will and its psychological partner, pride. No wonder Oswald Chambers quite aptly wrote: "Surrender is not the surrender of the external life, but of the will; when that is done, all is done. There are very few crises in life; the great crisis is the surrender of the will. God never crushes a man's (sic) will into surrender. He never beseeches him, he waits until the man yields up his will to Him. That battle never needs to be refought." (Chambers 1963, September 13)

Some readers might recall the 2011 movie, *The Adjustment Bureau* starring Matt Damon and Emily Blunt. The movie actually carried a powerful message relative to human freedom, determinism and free will. In one part of the movie, the Matt Damon character, David Norris was locked in an empty studio. Thompson, a member of the adjustment bureau walked into the scene. He questioningly said to Norris: " Frustrating, isn't it? My name is Thompson." Norris asked him: "Whatever happened to free will?" Thompson responded: "We actually tried free will before." Thompson then took Norris on a brief verbal journey through human history that demonstrated the failure of the human free will project. As a result of this failure, the chairman and the adjustment bureau made the decision to step back in and revoke human free will. Thompson then added poignantly: "You don't have free will, David. You have the appearance of free will." (Nolfi 2011) Many might be tempted to see God in this light. We might see him as The Chairman and organizer of some heavenly Adjustment Bureau, who constantly seeks to bring human life into conformity with a fixed plan already laid out. Along with Thompson, we might think that God merely gives us the illusion of free will when in reality no such thing exists. However, the opposite is true. Honoring His divinely granted gift of free will, God aims to have us freely choose to bring our lives into conformity with his will. That's why the will plays such a central role in spiritual healing. Indeed, the will lies at the heart of becoming a holy person; to live holy in this sense means that we have fully surrendered ourselves to all the will of God.

The Will and the Religious Affections

The human will serves as a major source for human choice and action; it dictates where we cast our allegiances and in turn, how these commitments inform our choices and behaviors. Such realities apply to the will because of its motivating role. Wesley described it as the spring of action for humans in his sermon *What is Man*:

> This inward principle, wherever it is lodged, is capable, not only of thinking, but likewise of love, hatred, joy, sorrow, desire, fear, hope, etc., and a whole train of other inward emotions, which are commonly called passions or affections. They are styled, by a general appellation, the will; and are mixed and diversified a thousand ways. And they seem to be the only spring of action in that inward principle I call the soul. (Wesley 1872aa, 256)

Clapper affirmed this motivational aspect when he noted that the will "...either is pleased or displeased, approving or rejecting the thing perceived." (Clapper 1984, 82) However, beyond this emphasis, Wesley connected the motivational actions of the soul to the affections and passions and equated these with emotions. Specifically, he affirmed what one might term primary emotions such as love and hatred, joy and sorrow, desire, fear and hope. But, the emotional life of the human soul was not limited to these named emotions. Indeed, he saw them as building blocks for an innumerable variety of emotions.

Wesley associated these emotions with the affections and passions, and these he inextricably linked to the will. Indeed, Wesley, in line with Jonathan Edwards viewed the religious affections as the manifested exercises of the will. (Clapper 1987; Clapper 1985b; Clapper 1985a; Edwards 1997; Wesley 1872b) They believed the religious affections constituted the essence of the Christian faith. (Clapper 1984; Clapper 1985a) Moreover, according to Clapper, "Edwards' affectional "sense of the heart" was at the center of his psychology, epistemology, ethics and, indeed, his whole theology." (Clapper 1984, 78) One might ascribe a similar statement to Wesley for at least two reasons: First, Wesley, like Edwards, placed significant emphasis on the religious affections, especially as they pertained to his understanding of Christian perfection. In many of his sermons such as *Salvation by Faith* and *The Circumcision of the Heart*, one finds continual emphasis on the affective life. One encounters a similar emphasis in his Explanatory Notes on the New Testament. (Clapper 1984; Clapper 1985b) Second, Wesley drew heavily from Edwards on the topic of religious affections, publishing an abridged copy of the latter's treatise. This would suggest that he shared much of what Edwards wrote about this topic. However, as indicated elsewhere, because he rejected Edwards' determinism, he purged from the publication those elements portraying this emphasis. Moreover, though he shared a good deal in common on the topic with Edwards, it seems useful to highlight another point; namely, his thoughts on this subject, visibly reflected in some of his sermons, predated his publication of the abridgment of Edwards' treatise. (Clapper 1984; Clapper 1985b; Collins 1998) Notwithstanding this latter evidence, it seems fair to say that the religious affections also stood at the heart of Wesley's theology and psychology particularly as it pertained to Christian perfection.

Transformed Affections: from Disordered to Ordered

But, though the religious affections played a central in Christian faith, Wesley saw them as corrupted by the fall just like the various faculties of the soul. As a result, he considered them completely disordered and distempered when cut off from God. (Wesley 1872p) Given their disordered nature, affections can be employed for evil. Indeed, without the transforming grace of God, they remain unholy, and almost completely given over to evil purposes. In other words, affections can serve holy or unholy purposes depending on their source. For this reason, in addition to the term, *holy,* Wesley often attached adjectives such as *unholy, vile and unclean* to the religious affections when cut off from relationship with God. For example, in his seventh discourse on the Sermon on the Mount, he showed the affections as corrupted and vile or holy and transformed. In speaking about fasting, he indicated how having fullness of bread could help to increase "... carelessness and levity of spirit, but also foolish and unholy desires, yea, unclean and vile affections." (Wesley 1872w, 441) Later in the same sermon, speaking about how fasting could become a means for exercising holy affections, he noted the following: "But let us take care to afflict our souls as well as our bodies. Let every season, either of public or private fasting, be a season of exercising all those holy affections which are implied in a broken and contrite heart." (Wesley 1872w, 451)

Similar depictions of the affections appear in several other places. (Wesley 1872f; Wesley 1872r; Wesley 1872s; Wesley 1872z; Wesley 1872w) For example, one good instance appeared in a section of the sermon, *The Righteousness of Faith*, previously referenced. Among other things, Wesley wrote:

> "...that hereby we are prone to all that is evil, and averse from all that is good; that we are full of pride, self-will, unruly passions, foolish desires, vile and inordinate affections; lovers of the world, lovers of pleasure more than lovers of God? (Wesley 1872r, 141)

Here, he identified the vileness and inordinate nature of the affections with all that's gone wrong in the human soul; the passage contained a veritable plethora of the ills of the human heart, described from the perspective of both the evil and the good. Thus, he described corrupted humanity as prone to evil but also antagonistic to the good. Next, he highlighted the various ills of the will through placing emphasis on pride and self-will. In addition, he addressed the corrupted internal life demonstrated in corrupted passions, desires and affections. What's more, he related these unholy attributes of the heart to loving the world and pleasures more than loving God. Implicit in this statement one discovers a truth that often appears in Wesley; namely, love is objective and that on which one focuses attention transforms one's inward and outward lives, for evil or good. Elsewhere, Wesley described other attributes that relate to corrupted affections. For example, affections can also be alienated from God, undue in degree or placed on the wrong objects. (Wesley 1872z) Apart from God, affections can go astray resulting in affections and passions run amok. Said another way, to be locked into the world corrupts affections. Moreover, affections can become disordered when they are expressed excessively, or due to a lack of appropriate regulation. In a similar vein, affections appear disordered when expressed to a lesser degree than they should be. But supremely, affections become holy and gracious or unholy and ungracious depending on the object of focus.

But that which became disordered by separation from and rebellion against God can also become ordered when focused on God; just as affections come "disordered and distempered" apart from God, they can become ordered, tempered and regulated in God. That's because the affections derive their holy character from God's divine work in the human heart. (Clapper 1984) When God transforms the heart, rather than being employed for evil and unholy purposes, the religious affections become the motivation for good purposes and holy expressions of the will. For this reason, the religious affections are often termed gracious or holy affections;

they take on the nature of the holiness and the gracious character of the God who makes them possible. (Clapper 1984; Clapper 1985b; Clapper 1985a) This transformation centrally revolves around love; it is the very love of God imbibed in the human soul that has the power to transform human affections, bringing them under holy regulation, balancing and ordering them. This indeed is God's purpose in transforming affections: not to extinguish them but rather to balance them and place them in the servitude of holy purposes. (Wesley 1872u) Thus, for Wesley, "... even the harsher and more unpleasing passions are applicable to the noblest purposes; even hatred, and anger, and fear, when engaged against sin, and regulated by faith and love, are as walls and bulwarks to the soul, so that the wicked one cannot approach to hurt it." (Wesley 1872u, 348)

Other Marks of Transformed Affections

In addition to describing affections as holy or gracious, Clapper suggested other characteristics of gracious affections. First, they come accompanied by "... a conviction of the reality and certainty of divine things." (Clapper 1984, 83) I take this to mean that the affections involve a conviction of the truth and that this dynamic connects them to assuring faith as well as aspects of mind and understanding. Second, Clapper indicated that affections usually come attended by "evangelical humiliation;" meaning that affections can only be transformed through humbly coming to God and seeking His transformation. To remain proud dooms one to continual corruption in the affections; in fact, the proud individual likely sees no need for transformed affections. Instead, such a person tends to rest satisfied. In contrast, the gracious affections create in a transformed individual a hungering and thirsting after greater spiritual attainment. (Clapper 1984) Finally, Clapper indicated that the gracious affections promote a Christ-like spirit; they promote the mind of Christ accompanied by the fruit of the Spirit evident in Galatians 5:22 such as love, joy, peace, patience, goodness and self-control among others. Jonathan Edwards gave special attention to affections such as meekness, quietness, forgiveness, mercy and love, and placed the heightened emphasis on the latter. (Clapper 1984) Following in this train, Wesley placed significant emphasis on love and possessing the mind of Christ. He closely related love to meekness as well as other attributes such as kindness, benevolence, compassion and tender-heartedness. (Clapper 1984; Clapper 1985b; Wesley 1872u; Wesley 1872x)

The Affective and Cognitive Nature of the Religious Affections

In an earlier quotation from Wesley's *What is Man*, he described an emotional principle. Furthermore, he identified the emotional principle with the religious affections, commonly termed passions or affections and indicated that they were exercised by the will. This emotional language of affections and passions might lead one to think that the religious affections simply relate to emotions. Nevertheless, in the same sermon, he also described a thinking principle, very much related to the emotional principle. Given this dual emphasis on emotions and thinking relative to the aspects of soul, and especially the will, a further discussion of these issues seems merited.

Several authors have related the religious affections to emotions. (Clapper 1987; Collins 1998; Leffel 2007; Kilian and Parker 2001; Maddox 1994) However, they generally indicate that the affections involve more than emotions. For example, Leffel indicated that though the terms affections and tempers partly capture what we call emotions, they involve more than feeling states. Given this distinction, it is possible for one to possess the temper of love, but not always feel loving. As a result, Leffel distinguished between having the dispositional temper of love, described as an action tendency and the phenomenological experience of feeling loving. (Leffel 2007) Additionally, he saw the affections as "...wholistic response tendencies, patterned tendencies to perceive, experience and move towards others and events in a particular way." (Leffel 2007, 301) Given these elements, he described them as more akin to "character virtues" than feelings. (Leffel 2007) It is these tempers and affections that serve as the motivators in human personality; they incline individuals towards various attitudes, choices and actions; that is, they serve as the motivators of moral choice and action in the individual. (Leffel 2007; Maddox 1994) Taken together, these assertions demonstrate various realities of Christian perfection evident in the holy Christian. It asserts that one might not always feel loving toward another all the time, but can maintain the holy temper of love with regard to the same individual. Furthermore, and related to the first point, given love's action tendency, the holy person might yet act lovingly though not feeling the emotion of love; that is, the phenomenological absence of loving feelings does not short-circuit the possibility of acting in loving ways. Rather, love can become a temper so deeply embedded in the person that one acts out of it in virtuous ways regardless of how one feels in the moment.

Wesley identified the tempers and affections and their motivational element with the pure or right heart. That is, it is the pure heart, filled with the love of God, that leads persons to right relationships with others as well as right words and actions in the world. To invoke the central concept inherent in Wesley's purposeful list, inward holiness marked by a loving heart sparks outward holiness. But the right heart also makes possible the virtuous life and the dispositional character consistent with Christian perfection. Given its critical importance, Wesley saw the pursuit of the right heart as foundational to Christian perfection. He also saw the right heart as that which one ought to pursue supremely. Accordingly, Leffel described

Wesley's vision of Christian spirituality as a quest story focused on the transformation of the affective and motivational aspects of heart. (Leffel 2007) Leffel also provided further insights into Wesley's vision of the pure heart. Drawing from moral character theory, he described the heart as "an associative network of moral capacities which "... function as innate activators of moral behavior." (Leffel 2007, 301) One can also regard these elements of the network as affective capacities. But this does not mean that the affections themselves are moral; rather they tend to result from and stimulate moral behavior. Additionally, moral affects though related to both affective traits and emotional states, are not identical with either. Rather, Leffel saw them as "nonconscious knowledge systems" which operate relationally; they dictate to those who possess them the appropriate way to be with and relate to others. He further connected these moral affective capacities to virtues, indicating that they can be considered "affective virtues." Earlier, he had described the affections as more like "character virtues." Fundamentally, however conceptualized, the affections precipitate a movement towards the acquisition of virtue. At the same time, they serve to move one away from vice or what Leffel described as "neurtue," the opposite of virtue. (Leffel 2007)

But though one can relate the affections to emotions and moral affect, this does not mean they lack cognitive linkages. Various authors have reinforced the connection between the affections and understanding. For example, Clapper, following Saliers, linked the affections to categories such as judgment and religious or non-religious belief. (Clapper 1987) Additionally, in line with the discussion of Wesley's purposeful list, the relationship between the affections and the mind (thinking) seems reciprocal in nature. Accordingly, Clapper noted that in some cases, the heart has to be right in order for the mind to function appropriately. (Clapper 1985a) This connection of the emotional and rational elements in the affections also appears in Wesley. In *Part 7 of The Doctrine of Original Sin*, Wesley noted that the passions and the affections functioned subservient to both the reason and the will. This suggests that the operation of these affections involved both rational and affective dimensions. (Wesley 1872p) Similarly, in *On Perfection*, he connected the affections and the understanding. Having previously noted the human inability to always "... think right, to apprehend things distinctly, and to judge truly of them," he drew the following conclusion: "In consequence hereof, his affections, depending on his understanding, are variously disordered. And his words and actions are influenced, more or less, by the disorder both of his understanding and affections." (Wesley 1872l, 456) Similar connections between the emotional and rational aspects of the soul appear in *What is Man* and *A Caution Against Bigotry*. (Wesley 1872ab; Wesley 1872a) In the latter work, he described the varied transformations that God performs in the human soul. He described these as taking place in the understanding and affections, seemingly together: "The understanding of the sinner is now enlightened, and his heart sweetly drawn to God. His desires are refined, his affections purified; and being filled with the Holy Ghost, he grows in grace till he is not only holy in heart, but in all manner of conversation." (Wesley 1872a, 584) Thus, Clapper affirmed that Wesley espoused a rational element in the gracious affections; these renewed and holy affections arise from the mind being enlightened so that it might be able to apprehend divine things. For Clapper, this combination of mind and will connotes the heart. (Clapper 1984; Clapper 1985b) Furthermore, the religious affections serve to integrate the rational and emotional dimensions of life. In this sense, one can consider them wholistic in nature in that they prompt certain attitudes, choices and actions. (Leffel 2007) This integration of the rational and affective dimensions of life appears a necessary recipe for religious devotion and the life of holiness. In fact, William Law considered devotion as the amalgamation of both elements. Accordingly, he offered: "Devotion is nothing else but right apprehensions and right affections towards God. All practices, therefore, that heighten and improve our true apprehensions of God, all ways of life that tend to nourish, raise, and fix our affections upon Him, are to be reckoned so many helps and means to fill us with devotion." (Law 1997, 154) From Law's perspective, affections such as devotion combine the apprehending aspects of soul as well as affectional aspects of will. One would think that this applies to all the religious affections.

Wesley's Affectional Language: Affections, Tempers and Passions

Having provided some background to understanding the will and the religious affections, I turn to a discussion of these motivational aspects of the will. Specifically, I will address the tempers, the affections and the passions. I do so because each of these relate to the will, though they can be distinguished from the will. In addition, the tempers relate to the will in that they indicate the direction of the will. (Collins 1998) However, at the outset, it seems wise to highlight the debate that exists regarding the nature of the tempers, affections and to some extent, the passions. For example, Clapper indicated that tempers and affections connote the same reality and that Wesley largely used the terms in an interchangeable manner. (Clapper 1987; Clapper 1985a; Clapper 1984; Clapper 1985b) On the other hand, Collins distinguished between tempers and affections. He reserved the former term for the fixed posture of the soul that is not easily shaken; in other words, tempers represented stable dispositions that show up in one's orientation towards various behaviors. (Collins 1998; Collins 2003; Collins 2004) Despite these differences, Clapper and Collins seem to hold similar views regarding the passions, seeing them as more sudden expressions where the mind has less control. (Clapper 1984; Clapper 1985b; Collins 2003; Collins 1998) In considering this matter, I wonder if there are not two separate but related issues wrapped up in the debate. Furthermore, I wonder if treating these issues together can serve to confound the distinction between the tempers and affections and even the passions. The first issue revolves around the question as to whether Wesley at times used the terms as interchangeable or near parallels. The second issue involves whether tempers and affections actually connote the same reality for Wesley. Do they both indicate a fixed posture of the soul? Or do they point to different realities with tempers indicating a fixed posture of the soul and affections (and passions) indicating more transient expressions?

The Similarities among Tempers, Affections and Passions

In addressing the first question, I affirm that Wesley often discussed the tempers, affections and passions in somewhat close association with each other. This makes sense given the commonalities they share. For instance, the nature and character of each largely depends upon the object of focus and the source from which they spring. Love and/or meekness also regulate each of them, seeking to balance and make them appropriate in their use. (Wesley 1872g; Wesley 1872u) Additionally, just like the tempers, the affections and even the passions, can be holy, just and good or given over to unholy purposes. (Wesley 1872m; Wesley 1872f; Wesley 1872y) But the tempers, affections and passions connect in another way; each relate in some fashion to growth in grace and holiness. Moreover, each believing person holds responsibility for the state of the tempers, affections and passions. Given this reality, one must be careful to aim to cultivate holy and godly tempers, affections and passions. (Collins 1998)

But besides these common threads, one also finds instances where Wesley seemed to use the terms in an interchangeable way. For example, in his journal entry for Thursday, September 13, 1739, he associated the two while speaking of holiness and the new birth:

> I believe it to be an inward thing; a change from inward wickedness to inward goodness; an entire change of our inmost nature from the image of the devil (wherein we are born) to the image of God; a change from the love of the creature to the love of the Creator; from earthly and sensual, to heavenly and holy affections; — in a word, a change from the tempers of the spirits of darkness, to those of the angels of God in heaven. (Wesley 1872ac, 253-254)

From the context, it appears one should understand the last two clauses pertaining to the new birth as coordinate in nature. This coordination associates affections and the tempers. Specifically, one could logically associate or even equate the transformation from earthly to heavenly and holy affections with a similar transformation in the tempers. The latter transformation moved the tempers from those that inhabit spirits of darkness to those befitting the angels of God. In other words, these two clauses represent alternate ways of speaking of the real change that takes place in transformed persons in the new birth.

But other examples of this association or near equation exist. For example, in his sixth discourse on the Sermon on the Mount, Wesley wrote: "IN the preceding chapter our Lord has described inward religion in its various branches. He has laid before us those dispositions of soul which constitute real Christianity; the inward tempers contained in that "holiness, without which no man shall see the Lord;" the affections which, when flowing from their proper fountain, from a living faith in God through Christ Jesus, are intrinsically and essentially good, and acceptable to God." (Wesley 1872v, 418) Here it appears that he saw both the tempers and affections as dispositions of the soul. I infer this from the fact that Wesley used the plural *dispositions*. This means that more than one disposition followed. In fact, the last two clauses that followed fleshed out what Wesley meant by *dispositions*. In these clauses, he specifically mentioned the inward tempers and the affections. It may be the case that the term *disposition* is most often used in association with tempers. However, judging from this example, this might not be done so exclusively.

Furthermore, in *On Perfection*, Wesley associated the tempers and the affections with having the mind of Christ. Here, he noted: ""Let this mind be in you which was also in Christ Jesus." For although this immediately and directly refers to the humility of our Lord, yet it may be taken in a far more extensive sense, so as to include the whole disposition of his mind, *all his affections, all his tempers*, both toward God and man. Now, it is certain that as there was no evil affection in him, *so no good affection or temper was wanting*. So that "whatsoever things are holy, whatsoever things are lovely," are all included in "the mind that was in Christ Jesus." (Wesley 1872l, 457-458 (italics added)) Here one observes two instances italicized in the quotation where affections and tempers appear equated. Additionally, it also seems clear that Wesley saw transformations of the tempers and affections as constituting real Christianity. In fact, transformation in the tempers and affections and even the passions stand as hallmarks of the holy life. In *The New Birth*, Wesley made this very point. After arguing for the necessity of the new birth, he clearly linked it to holiness; the new birth served as a necessary precursor to holiness. Wesley proceeded to define holiness as the image of God stamped on the human heart: "Gospel holiness is no less than the image of God stamped upon the heart; it is no other than the whole mind which was in Christ Jesus; it consists of all heavenly affections and tempers mingled together in one." (Wesley 1872i, 89) According to this statement, Wesley equated both the tempers and the affection with holiness and possessing the mind of Christ. Furthermore, it seems clear that the mingling of these two religious affections partly constitute holiness. One even finds evidence for a close association between the words tempers and passions. In *The General Spread of the Gospel*, speaking of Christians, Wesley spoke of a time when: "All their desires, meantime, and passions, and tempers, will he cast in one mold; while all are doing the will of God on earth, as it is done in heaven." (Wesley 1872e, 318) Similarly, in *Of Evil Angels*, he spoke of how the devil seeks to "... awaken evil passions or tempers in our souls." (Wesley 1872j, 418) These examples would seem to provide evidence of the close linkage Wesley made between the tempers and affections and the passions.

The Differences in Tempers and Affections.

But does the close association, or even what sometimes seems like an interchangeable use mean that Wesley conceptualized these terms as exactly the same? Contrary to Clapper's perspective, this does not appear to be the case. In fact, one might even argue that the phrase "mingled together in one," from *The New Birth*, made in reference to the tempers and affections, could also be used to substantiate their distinctness. That is, one could argue that the phrase suggests two distinctive elements coming together to form a new reality. In this sense, it might be akin to a statement by Wesley regarding the mingling of self-love and social love. Speaking about the Christian's love Wesley noted: "His love, as to these, so to all mankind, is in itself generous and disinterested; springing from no view of advantage to himself, from no regard to profit or praise; no, nor even the pleasure of loving. This is the daughter, not the parent, of his affection. *By experience he knows that social love, if it mean the love of our neighbor, is absolutely different from self-love, even of the most allowable kind; just as different as the objects at which they point. And yet it is sure, that, if they are under due regulations, each will give additional force to the other, till they mix together never to be divided.* (Wesley 1872h, 85, Italics added) Here, Wesley clearly differentiated between love of self and love of neighbor as separate entities. However, from his perspective, one can grow in holy love to the point that the love expressed to oneself looks no different than that given to others. Something similar might exist between the tempers, and affections (as well as the passions). Each constitutes different ways in which the holy life manifests itself. But because of their systemic link to the holy life, they can be conceived together, almost as one reality. That is, in order to be holy, one needs to possess the dispositional character of the tempers as well as the more transient, day-to-day holy expressions of the affections and passions.

At any rate, one can admit to an imprecise use of the words *tempers*, *affections* and *passions* in some of Wesley's writings. This does not mean that he saw them as the same reality. But if he did not conceptualize tempers and affections as constituting the same reality, why then use them in a seeming interchangeable manner? A clue to this dilemma might be found in a letter from Wesley written to William Law. In this letter, Wesley seemingly allowed interchangeable use of terms for related passions and dispositions. At the same time, he insisted on the differences between them.

In the letter, Wesley offered the following: *"I must premise, that I have no objection to the using the words wrath (or anger) and justice as nearly synonymous; seeing anger stands in the same relation to justice, as love does to mercy; love and anger being the passions (speaking after the manner of men) which correspond with the dispositions of mercy and justice.* Whoever therefore denies God to be capable of wrath or anger, acts consistently in denying his justice also." (Wesley 1872c, 554, italics added) This quotation offers a few interesting insights into Wesley's use of affectional language. It presents a good example of his imprecision or permissive use of affectional language. In this instance, he referred to love as a passion, whereas it many other places, he designated it a temper or disposition. Moreover, he gave the title of disposition to mercy which one would generally think flows from love. However, this shift might have been made because he was referencing God's mercy that spurs love towards humanity. But more pertinent to our point, he allowed the use of dispositional terms, in this case mercy and justice, as near equivalent terms for the manifested passions (love and anger). Nevertheless, he made it clear that they were not exact replicas of each other. Rather, they appeared "nearly synonymous." His comments in this quotation might shed light on the interchangeable use of the language of tempers, affections and passions; namely, Wesley sometimes allowed the passion (or affection) to denote the related disposition or temper.

In fact, the distinction between the dispositional nature of the tempers and the more transient nature of the affections and passions appear several places in Wesley. I have chosen to cite two examples. A good example comes from his commentary on I Thessalonians 2:17. In chapter 2, Paul described his ministry in Thessalonica. In keeping with this, Verse 17 described his intense longing that drove a desire to see them again. Commenting on this passage, Wesley wrote:

> In this verse we have a remarkable instance, not so much of *the transient affections of holy grief, desire, or joy, as of that abiding tenderness, that loving temper,* which is so apparent in all St. Paul's writings, towards those he styles his children in the faith. This is the more carefully to be observed, because *the passions occasionally exercising themselves, and flowing like a torrent, in the apostle, are observable to every reader; whereas it requires a nicer attention to discern those calm standing tempers, that fixed posture of his soul, from whence the others only flow out, and which more peculiarly distinguish his character.* (Wesley 1997, 689 (italics added))

Several elements in this commentary merit comment. First, all three terms commonly used in in describing the religious affections appear here. Second, it's worth noting that Wesley even saw the transient affections such as grief, desire and joy as possessing a holy quality. Third, he described the affections as transient and contrasted them with the enduring nature of the temper. In reference to the latter he employed adjectives such as *abiding*, and *calm standing*. These terms support the sense of permanency he envisioned in the tempers. Later, he made an implicit contrast between the tempers and the passions. In this instance, he described the passions as *occasionally* being exercised. This would suggest that like the affections, they too possess a less than permanent nature. Additionally, the phrase *flowing like a torrent* suggests that the passions may be less under one's control, though clearly visible. In contrast, he described the tempers as calm, standing and less discernible though very real. In fact, adding to his earlier description of the temper of love as abiding and calm standing, he now described the tempers as entailing a "fixed posture of his soul."

In this instance Wesley likely had in mind the love Paul exhibited towards all his spiritual children. Thus, he referred to *abiding tenderness* equated with *that loving temper*. Specifically, we have here a notion encountered elsewhere where love was described as a master temper out of which all other tempers flow. Additionally, he linked the language of character to the tempers; it was through the tempers, representing the fixed posture of one's soul, that one's character was most markedly discernible. This likely does not mean that the display of affections and passions reveal nothing of character. The affections and passions may *indirectly* reveal character, whereas in the tempers, character is more *directly* revealed. It might also be that in the affections and passions, character may not be as fully and clearly visible as it is in the tempers. Wesley might also have been suggesting that the true bedrock of character derives from one's standing disposition.

A similar description of tempers versus passions appears in Wesley's sermon *Heaviness Through Manifold Temptations*. Speaking about heaviness, he wrote:

> It is probable our translators rendered it heaviness, (though a less common word,) to denote two things: First, the degree, and next the continuance, of it. It does indeed seem, that it is not a slight or inconsiderable degree of grief which is here spoken of; but such as makes a strong impression upon, and sinks deep into the soul. Neither does this appear to be a transient sorrow, such as passes away in an hour; but rather, such as, having taken fast hold of the heart, is not presently shaken off; but continues for some time, as a settled temper, rather than a passion, even in them that have living faith in Christ, and the genuine love of God in their hearts. (Wesley 1872g, 114)

Here too Wesley distinguished between the tempers and the passions, this time in reference to the Apostle Peter's grief. He declared that Peter's grief was likely not of the passionate sort. According to his reasoning, if it was, Peter's grief would have been more transient, the kind that passes away in an hour. Additionally, a sorrow of the passionate sort would constitute a surface emotion rather than one that became deeply embedded in the soul. In contrast, he described Peter's grief as a temper for two reasons: First, in terms of its degree; that is, it was a grief rooted deeply in the soul. Second, he saw Peter's grief as continuing as a settled temper rather than a sorrow which quickly passed away as would a passion. These examples confirm that though Wesley sometimes used the terms in an interchangeable way, he firmly distinguished between them; for him, the term temper denoted enduring aspects of the religious affections, whereas the affections involved passing states, considerably less habituated than the tempers. As evident in our previous discussion, the passions share the ephemeral characteristic of the affections. In fact, according to Collins, one can describe the passions as intensified affections. (Collins 2003; Collins 1998; Kilian and Parker 2001)

Despite the differences within the tempers, affections and passions there exists a clear relationship between them. For one, the dispositional nature of the tempers seems to give rise to the more transient expression of the affections and passions in everyday situations. Persons such as Collins appear to draw this conclusion. (Collins 1998) This conclusion also finds support in Wesley's commentary on 1 Thessalonians 2:17. The phrase "... that fixed posture of his soul from whence the others only flow out..." would seem to suggest this assertion. (Wesley 1997, 689) Interestingly, in this statement Wesley used the plural "others," suggesting the elements that flow from the tempers involve more than just the affections. Ultimately, he might have intended to connect the passions to the tempers, even if the former are construed as vitally related to the affections. But their relationship is not one directional; it is not simply the case that the tempers produce the affections and passions. The affections and passions also have a reciprocal effect on the standing tempers. In fact, several authors suggest that affections can be transformed into tempers. (Kilian and Parker 2001; Maddox 1998) They believe that growth in grace via sanctification transforms the affections, solidifying them as tempers. That is, through this work of grace, the affections become "strengthened and focused" so as to render them into tempers or dispositional aspects of the soul. (Collins 1998; Kilian and Parker 2001; Maddox 1998) This kind of transformation likely provides a gauge of how one has progressed in the life of faith. This consideration also suggests that the relationship between the tempers, affections and passions is systemic in nature.

The Tempers and Moral Responsibility

But the very idea of standing tempers raises questions regarding responsibility. If habituated tempers give rise to predetermined behaviors, whether holy or unholy, does this make one less free? Could one legitimately avoid responsibility by saying "my temper made me do it?" Collins raised this pertinent question and the inherent risk of "a practical determinism" in Wesley's conceptualization. He wrote: "... if the tempers and the dispositions of the heart are habituated, as seems to be the case, if they represent orientations towards behavior, whether good or evil, then their predisposing tendency renders one less free to do otherwise." (Collins 1998, 173) Put another way, having a habituated disposition might make its expression determined to the point that one is not free to act otherwise.

Given this way of thinking, the person who had cultivated a standing evil disposition could not be held responsible for the resulting behavior.

An example from the clinical world might provide a useful example of the dilemma. In the clinical field we speak of persons who have dispositional or personality disorders. These are described as "an enduring pattern of inner experience and behavior." (American Psychiatric Association 2000, 685) In this sense, they can be considered reflections of the psychological equivalent of tempers. A noxious example of these disorders would be antisocial personality disorder. The person with antisocial personality disorder is described as one who exhibits "... a pervasive pattern of disregard for and violation of the rights of others occurring since age 15 years. This disregard demonstrates itself in ways such:

1. Failure to conform to social norms with respect to lawful behaviors.
2. Deceitfulness as indicated by repeated lying, use of aliases or conning others for
3. personal profit or pleasure.
4. Impulsivity or failure to plan ahead.
5. Irritability and aggressiveness, as indicated by repeated physical fights or assaults.
6. Reckless disregard for safety of self or others.
7. Consistent irresponsibility, as indicated by repeated failure to sustain consistent work behavior or honor financial obligations.
8. Lack of remorse, as indicated by being indifferent to or rationalizing having hurt, mistreated or stolen from another. (American Psychiatric Association 2000, 706)

Such a description clearly defines one who is unholy, with a clear disposition towards evil. Could such a person claim a lack of moral responsibility for crimes committed? Many often do, but is this a legitimate claim? If standing tempers predetermined one to evil behaviors, then one could make this argument. On the hand, if one believed this, neither could one receive moral credit for having a holy disposition eventuating in holy behavior since this too would be predetermined. What is the way out of this "practical determinism?" Collin offered a solution to this dilemma. He proposed that the predisposing power of the tempers should be understood within the context of grace and freedom. Specifically, he offered: "... Wesley's understanding of the grace of God not simply as divine favor and approval but also as divine empowerment indicates that though the tempers predispose, one can always do otherwise." (Collins 1998, 173; See also Maddox 1994) In other words, the temper does not eliminate freedom of choice. Thus, even one steeped in evil behaviors may by the grace of God be transformed so that she or he might move in the direction of holy behavior. But on the other hand, one who has been characterized by holy tempers may fall away from grace and choose evil again. (Collins 1998) But choice connects to the tempers in another sense; that is, having habituated dispositions in the first place, implies choice. For one who possesses the temper of love, habitual personal choice helped established that temper. Over a period of time, the individual made choices that served to help establish that habit of the heart. This perspective does not neglect the work of God in the human heart. However, it does say that humans play a vital role in the construction of their own heart and this too makes them morally responsible for it.

For this reason, God has all right to hold us responsible for the state of our hearts; by our choices and actions, we help cultivate our hearts. Truly, the heart is partly our own construction. It partly depends on our choices and the ways in which we school our emotional life, thereby forming right character. (Goleman 1995) But God also holds us responsible for the holy cultivation of the tempers, affections and passions because this supremely captures the holy life he envisions for us. God envisions a holiness of heart that entails a "...renewal of the soul in all its desires, tempers and affections." (Wesley 1872x, 482) What's more, by grace, God has made ample provision for such a renewal of the soul. Lying at the heart of this renewal is a transformation in the temper of love. This means that holiness in the sense God intends, involves more than a transformation of our standing dispositions and our inner being; rather, along with this characterological transformation, God also intends a transformation of our affections and passions as they lovingly evidence themselves in everyday life. It is transformation in this total sense that gives the fullest meaning to what it means to live holy. No wonder God's purpose regarding the tempers, affections and passions is not to extinguish them; rather He intends to bring them under the due regulation of love, to order them appropriately and reorient them to their original divine design. (Wesley 1872u) When this happens, love can become the master tempers of the heart creating within us a right disposition that gives rise to right thinking, right words and actions. Furthermore, when love becomes the guiding temper of the heart, it strives for outward expression; it shows itself in right loving relationships with God, self and others. That's truly getting it right!

Chapter 5
Relational Love and Christian Perfection

A wonderful habit exists among faculty at Asbury Theological Seminary. Several times per week, many of us meet for lunch. The group varies widely in several ways; it often represents a nice cross section of the disciplines represented in the faculty. It also tends to vary by the number of people present at any given time. Sometimes the group becomes so large, we join a couple of tables together to accommodate everyone. It also varies in the topics we discuss; sometimes we talk about funny stuff. We have heard students usually expect raucous laughter to erupt from our table when we meet. Sometimes we discuss the latest exploits of the Kentucky Wildcat basketball team. At other times, we participate in serious discussions about theological subjects. Actually, on any given day, we might cover all the above. Not too long ago, I arrived at lunch and surprisingly only two persons were present and I joined them. When I joined, my two colleagues were already deeply engrossed in a discussion of Christian perfection. Having entered a conversation already begun, I mostly listened to catch the general tenor of the conversation. As I listened, I was struck by the many themes and emphases they raised. These emphases largely paralleled those discussed to this point in the book. For instance, even though each of us grew up in the Wesleyan holiness tradition, we noted an emphasis on purity that sometimes bordered on the legalistic. Likewise, we noted the lack of any emphasis on the means of grace in our experience, at least using this terminology. I was mostly taken by the conclusion made: Namely, Christian perfection fundamentally revolves around the notion and practice of love. That's the focus of this chapter.

Wesley's Relational Emphasis on Love

In the initial discussion of *the purposeful list* earlier in this book, I noted that Wesley began his vision of Christian perfection with a focus on the right heart. Very closely connected to this, he emphasized right thinking and the outward expression of these in right words and works. (Wesley 1872h; Wesley 1872l; Wesley 1872p; Wesley 1872x; Wesley 1872ab; Wesley 1872ad) In fact, he considered the Christian faith "a religion of the heart." For him, the true root of religion laid in the heart, that is, in the inmost soul of humans. (Wesley 1872ad) He emphasized this to such a degree that any religion devoid of this inward emphasis, he considered worthless. (Wesley 1872ad) Thus, he wrote: "It is also true, that bare outside religion, which has no root in the heart, is nothing worth; that God delighteth not in *such* outward services, no more than in Jewish burnt-offerings; and that a pure and holy heart is a sacrifice with which he is always well pleased. But he is also well pleased with all that outward service which arises from the heart...." (Wesley 1872ad, 392) He highlighted the heart because in this most sacred place God placed his love and his life. For Wesley, the right heart placed the focus on the inward being of persons, transformed by the power of love. In the real Christian, love sets up its seat in the inmost recesses of the soul. This possession of the heart/soul by love produced genuine religion and lay at the very heart of Christian perfection. (Wesley 1872y; Wesley 1872ac; Wesley 1872ad)

In keeping with this emphasis, Wesley consistently described love in a way that placed it at the center of Christian perfection. From my perspective, this heightened focus on love faithfully reflected the biblical message. In chapter two, I described the Sermon on the Mount as the primary source from which Wesley defined his understanding of Christian perfection. Given this thought, it should not be surprising that the Sermon on the Mount placed major emphasis on the primacy and pivotal role of love. Significantly, at the end of chapter 5, starting at verse 43, the passage mandated love for one's enemies patterned after God's love for humanity. As pictured here, God loved impartially, extending His care to the righteous and the unrighteous, the evil and the good. This passage concluded with the admonition: "Be perfect, therefore, as your heavenly Father is perfect." From the context, it appears quite clear that perfection envisioned by Matthew centered on love; to be perfect means to be perfected in love.

Wesley took seriously Matthew's message endorsing love as the center of Christian perfection. As a result, his thirteen sermons on the Sermon on the Mount teemed with the centrality of love. The recurrence of love in these sermons parallels a similar emphasis on holiness in its inward and outward forms. This concurrent emphasis makes sense given love's role in Wesley's understanding of holiness. Given this understanding, it seems reasonable to expect that any emphasis on holiness would come hand in hand with an equal accent on love. Thus, as with holiness, love consistently appeared in these sermons regardless the focus of the passage. For example, in Discourse 7 while speaking about fasting as an aid to prayer, he noted that the virtuous life was the goal of prayer and other works of piety (and works of mercy). However, the virtuous life found its culmination in the love of God and transformations in one's affectional life. (Wesley

1872af) Similarly, in Discourse 4, focused around letting one's light shine, Wesley equated light with various internal attitudes of the heart, including love to neighbor and to God. (Wesley 1872ad) Not surprisingly, given the connection between love and holiness, he also equated light with holiness. (Wesley 1872ag) For him, through these inward tempers and their outward reflection in the world, one shone one's light. As a result, he wrote: "Ye Christians are "the light of the world," with regard both to your tempers and actions." (Wesley 1872ad, 389) By tempers, he likely meant to imply that love serves as the master temper that transforms other tempers of the heart as well as inward and outward holiness. (Wesley 1872g; Wesley 1872ab; Wesley 1872ah) This reality becomes clear later in the sermon where he noted:

> "Let your light so shine:" — Your lowliness of heart; your gentleness, and meekness of wisdom; your serious, weighty concern for the things of eternity, and sorrow for the sins and miseries of men; your earnest desire of universal holiness, and full happiness in God; your tender good will to all mankind, and fervent love to your supreme Benefactor. Endeavor not to conceal this light, wherewith God hath enlightened your soul; but let it shine before men, before all with whom you are, in the whole tenor of your conversation. Let it shine still more eminently in your actions, in your doing all possible good to all men; and in your suffering for righteousness' sake, while you "rejoice and are exceeding glad, knowing that great is your reward in heaven." (Wesley 1872ad, 397)

Truly, For Wesley, love constituted the essence and end of religion. Thus, he noted elsewhere: "In the same manner have the end and the means of religion been set at variance with each other. Some well-meaning men have seemed to place all religion in attending the Prayers of the Church, in receiving the Lord's supper, in hearing sermons, and reading books of piety; neglecting, mean time, the end of all these, the love of God and their neighbor." (Wesley 1872af, 436) Elsewhere, he described love to God and men as the grand principle that provided evidence of the change God works in human hearts. (Wesley 1872v) For him, love was more central than works of piety. In fact, for him, ordinances such as works of piety ought to lead one to love. (Wesley 1872ab) He also ascribed to love a heavenly quality when he described heaven as the "region of love." (Wesley 1872ab) From this perspective, to love on earth was to participate in the very nature of heaven and of God. Along the same line, he described a religion of love as the only kind worthy of God. As a result, he offered: "We are grieved at the sight; and should greatly rejoice, if by any means we might convince some that there is a better religion to be attained, — a religion worthy of God that gave it. And this we conceive to be no other than love; the love of God and of all mankind; the loving God with all our heart, and soul, and strength, as having first loved *us*, as the fountain of all the good we have received, and of all we ever hope to enjoy; and the loving every soul which God hath made, every man on earth, as our own soul." (Wesley 1872e, 8) However, he always believed love should become visible in the world by its fruits; it should avoid doing ill to one's neighbor, and instead engage in beneficent action, as well as "spreading virtue and happiness all around it." (Wesley 1872e, 9)

Wesley also frequently described love as the fulfilling of the Law and as its intended goal. (Wesley 1872ac; Wesley 1872ad; Wesley 1872af) In Discourse 4, he discussed the sense in which love was the fulfilling of the law. However, he was careful to note that this did not mean overriding faith or good works. Rather, "It is "the fulfilling of the law," not by releasing us from, but by constraining us to obey it. It is "the end of the commandment," as every commandment leads to and centers in it." (Wesley 1872ad, 392) Given this thinking, Wesley wrote to Miss Furly admonishing her: "I want you to be all love. This is the perfection I believe and teach. And this perfection is consistent with a thousand nervous disorders, which that highstrained perfection is not. Indeed, my judgment is, that (in this case particularly) to overdo, is to undo; and that to set perfection too high, (so high as no man that we ever heard or read of attained,) is the most effectual (because unsuspected) way of driving it out of the world." (Wesley 1872j, 240) By highstrained perfection, he referred to an absolute perfection that made no allowance for sometimes thinking or speaking amiss. Such perfection was inconsistent with living in a corruptible body. Rather, though characterized by love, the perfection he invited allowed for various errors of thought and was open to mistakes. (Wesley 1872j, 240)

One can describe Wesley's emphasis on love from three perspectives: the relational, dispositional and objective. (Kilian and Parker 2001; Land 1993) The relational element means that religious affections like love express themselves in relationship "with God, the church and the world." The dispositional refers to the fact that the affections become like virtues, transforming persons at the core of their being. Finally, the objective highlights that the religious affections, including love, always require an object. (Kilian and Parker 2001; Land 1993) The rest of this chapter highlights the relational aspect of love. In the process of this discussion, I will also touch on love's metaphysical, ethical and agentic aspects. In the next chapter, the focus will shift to the dispositional emphasis. However, because love requires an object, it would be difficult to speak about its relational or dispositional aspects without incorporating some reference to the objective. Thus, in both chapters, the objective aspect comes into play. However, this focus will be more concentrated in the next chapter.

Relational Love to God

In his description of love, Wesley focused on the great commandment and its mandate to love God and neighbor as self. Contrary to those who focus only on love for God and neighbor, he kept all three loves objects together. Wesley likely knew that God intended these loves to complement each other rather than oppose and contradict each other. (Olthuis 2006) However, he always began with an emphasis on the love of God. We can understand this emphasis in at least two ways. First, in the sense of a love initiated by God and which comes *from* God. Second, the term also connotes human's loving response *toward* God. In this sense, God serves as the object of human affections. This is love in the objective sense. Wesley spoke of the love of God in both senses. However, everything began with God's initiating love towards humans. This reality makes all forms of love truly possible; love springs from God and because we have experienced it, we love for His sake. (Wesley 1872x; Wesley 1872ab; Wesley 1872ac) Without God pouring His love in our hearts, human love as He required becomes impossible. But having experienced the love of God, our response is to love God with all of our heart, soul and mind. Thus, in discourse 10, Wesley wrote: "Thou wilt love the Lord thy God, because he hath loved thee." (Wesley 1872y, 498) For him, loving God formed a large part of what it meant to worship God. This thought appeared in his fourth discourse on the Sermon on the Mount. In response to his own question of what it meant to worship God, he focused a large part of his answer around loving God and the implications of such affection. Thus he wrote:

> It is, to love him, to delight in him, to desire him, with all our heart, and mind, and soul, and strength; to imitate him we love, by purifying ourselves even as He is pure; and to obey him whom we love, and in whom we believe, both in thought, and word, and work. Consequently, one branch of the worshipping God in spirit and in truth is, the keeping his outward commandments. To glorify him, therefore, with our bodies, as well as with our spirits; to go through outward work with hearts lifted up to him; to make our daily employment a sacrifice to God; to buy and sell, to eat and drink, to his glory; — this is worshipping God in spirit and in truth, as much as the praying to him in a wilderness. (Wesley 1872ad, 394)

As evidenced here, love toward God possessed an all encompassing quality, permeating all of life. But love also vitally connected to joy, happiness and longing. Thus, he associated it with *delight* and *desire*. This association appears elsewhere in his sermons. For example, we find it in discourse 9 on the Sermon on the Mount. Here, speaking of the meaning of loving God, he wrote: "— it is to *desire God alone for his own sake*; and nothing else, but with reference to him; — to rejoice in God; — *to delight in the Lord*; not only to seek, but find, happiness in him; to enjoy God as the chiefest among ten thousand; to rest in him, as our God and our all; — in a word, to have such a possession of God as makes us always happy." (Wesley 1872ah, 474 (italics added)) In the initial chapter in this book, I indicated that *desire* and *delight* as well as *design* constituted affectional language. Along with *tempers* and *affections* they reflect internal attitudes of the heart. His use of them in these contexts seems to confirm this assessment. But besides these terms, he heightened the comprehensiveness of love to God by adding the phrase "heart, and mind, and soul, and strength." This phraseology, mimicking Scripture's emphasis, occurs in many places in his writings including his discourses on the Sermon on the Mount. (Wesley 1872aa; Wesley 1872ac; Wesley 1872ag; Wesley 1872ah;) He also linked this complete love to God with having the single eye or a single intention. Accordingly, he wrote: "This eye of the soul is then said to be single, when it looks at one thing only; when we have no other design, but to "know God, and Jesus Christ whom he hath sent," — to know him with suitable affections, loving him as he hath loved us; to please God in all things; to serve God (as we love him) with all our heart, and mind, and soul, and strength; and to enjoy God in all, and above all things, in time and in eternity." (Wesley 1872ag, 454)

But a complete love for God always carried moral implications; it meant imitating Him and becoming pure like Him. Moreover, it demanded obedience that harmonized all thoughts, words and deeds with the love professed. That is, for Wesley, love involved more than sentiment; it conformed the inward and outward life to the law of love. This fundamentally meant exhibiting inward and outward holiness. Furthermore, it meant glorifying God in spirit and body, making them holy places for the Spirit to inhabit. But outward holiness did not simply involve what we do with our bodies and its parts. It also involves the way we live in the world. We ought to live outwardly holy lives in the world. But besides this, we ought to make all our employment in the world a sacred expression of devotion to God. (Wesley 1872ad) For Wesley, God intended that those who profess to know Him should live out this all-consuming love. This notion finds expression in places such as his collection of prayers. He began the collection with the many reasons that call forth human love for God. He called these reasons *titles* and named several: God's command, God's holiness, His creation of humans and His providential blessings, God as the end for which humanity was created and the source of happiness, God sending Christ to bring about redemption, God providing all necessary aids to bring us to glory and working in humans to work out these purposes. (Wesley 1872c) These reasons centered on the God's love and the prevenient grace displayed in making salvation possible. These many reasons showed that salvation only became possible because of the initiating work of God. Because of these *titles*, Wesley made the following prayer:

> Upon these, and many other titles, I confess it is my duty to love thee, my God, with all my heart. Give thy strength unto thy servant, that thy love may fill my heart, and be the motive of all the use I make of my understanding, my affections, my senses, my health, my time, and whatever other talents I have received from thee. Let this, O God, rule my heart without a rival; let it dispose all my thoughts, words, and works; and thus only can I fulfill my duty and thy command, of loving thee "with all my heart, and mind, and soul, and strength." (Wesley 1872c, 233-234)

Love to Self and Others: Metaphysical, Ethical and Agentic Aspects

When one speaks of relational love, especially in respect to self and others, one ought to also consider its metaphysical, ethical and agentic aspects. (Tjeltveit 2006a) The metaphysical sense refers to the loving nature of God; that is, God is love. Because of His loving nature, He seeks to make us loving by shedding His love abroad in our hearts. It is this reality that makes possible an appropriate love of self and others. (Tjeltveit 2006b) Without God's love, human love remains disordered, distorted and inordinate; either perversely focused on the self, on others or on the world. (Wesley 1872x; Wesley 1872y; Wesley 1872z) But one can also point to love's ethical dimensions. This element points to its focus on that which is "good, right, obligatory, and virtuous." (Tjeltveit 2006b, 9) Among these obligations comes the responsibility to love God and one another. Wesley highlighted this obligation in the tenth discourse on the Sermon on the Mount when he noted:

> Believe in the Lord Jesus Christ, and thou shalt be saved:" Thou shalt be saved now, that thou mayest be saved forever; saved on earth, that thou mayest be saved in heaven. Believe in him, and thy faith will work by love. Thou wilt love the Lord thy God, because he hath loved thee: Thou wilt love thy neighbor as thyself: And then it will be thy glory and joy, to exert and increase this love; not barely by abstaining from what is contrary thereto, from every unkind thought, word, and action, but by showing all that kindness to every man, which thou wouldest he should show unto thee.(Wesley 1872y, 498)

Earlier, I highlighted a small part of this quotation to demonstrate that God's love to us required us to love Him. But this longer version demonstrates that God's love requires us to love our neighbors and ourselves. For Wesley, this envisioned love was not static but dynamic and changing. He envisioned it as a love to be practiced and one that could increase. Furthermore, he described it both negatively and positively; that is, love avoids unkind thoughts, words and actions while embracing kindness in these same areas.

Before speaking about the implications of love to self and neighbor, a brief word about the agentic aspect of love seems appropriate. Agency means one can exert choice and this constitutes a critical in the morally responsible life. (Headley 2006; Maddox 1994; Tjeltveit 2006b) Borrowing from earlier authors, Richardson noted that agentic action includes aspects of human intention and action. It involves purposeful human actions made visible when individuals pursue their goals. Furthermore, such actions play a fundamental role in shaping individual lives. (Richardson 2012) When one relates this concept of agency to Christian love, it suggests that though God requires us to love, it cannot be forced; it must be freely chosen. Wynkoop spoke directly to this point when she noted: "*Love can only exist in freedom*. It cannot be coerced. Freedom is the most fundamental ingredient of love." (Wynkoop 1972, 25) In a later part of the book, she added: ""Coerced" love is not love at all. At no point is the human person more responsible, therefore more "free" than the ordering of his love." (Wynkoop 1972, 157) She was absolutely right! Thus, along with affirming the metaphysical and ethical dimensions of love, one ought also to leave space for agency. This inclusion is fundamental to understanding the love that lies at the heart of Christian perfection.

As demonstrated in chapter 3, this emphasis on choice and liberty permeates Wesley's writings. His idea of liberty mirrored the elements seen in the definition of agentic action. For him, liberty in humans involved: "... a power of directing his own affections and actions; a capacity of determining himself, or of choosing good or evil." (Wesley 1872s, 244) This emphasis appears in places such as his sermon *The End of Christ's Coming*. Here, he devoted a section to describing the nature of the human person. After speaking of God endowing humans with will and affections, he noted: "... He was likewise endued with liberty; a power of choosing what was good, and refusing what was not so. Without this, both the will and the understanding would have been utterly useless." (Wesley 1872f, 303) One finds similar statements in his sermons that attest to the necessity of freedom of choice. (Wesley 1872i; Wesley 1872m; Wesley 1872n; Wesley 1872o; Wesley 1872s;) This emphasis also appears in later writers on Wesley where it is often discussed in relation to the concept of prevenient grace. (Collins 1989; Leffel 2004; Maddox 1994; Myers 2006)

Love to Self

From an ethical perspective, the love of God calls us to love our neighbor as ourselves. However, some Christians often miss or ignore the latter part of this equation and thereby nullify an appropriate love for self. As one author noted, such thinking magnifies love's sacrificial elements, making love to others the only real possibility. (Tjeltveit 2006b) Others sometimes affirm a watered down love for self, limiting it to simply giving oneself due self-respect. (Wynkoop 1972) Each of these perspectives share the implicit notion that self-love is in some ways evil. Furthermore, these perspectives seem to imply that only love of self can be disordered. In fact, all forms of love that do not spring from God stand disordered. This would include some expressions of love to God and others and not just expressions of love to self. In contrast to these perspectives, Tomas Špidlík wrote that self-love should not be considered evil; after all, the great commandment never called us away from loving ourselves. Rather, it called us to love our neighbor as ourselves. In support, he noted that the scholastics often repeated the maxim: "Whoever is not good toward himself, will not be good even to others." (Špidlík 2010, 65) It is gratifying to see that in some quarters of Christendom the negation of love to self is changing. In fact, in a

2006 volume in the Journal of Psychology and Theology, the horizontal dimension of love was described as loving *neighbor-as-self*. (Tjeltveit 2006a) Apparently, the hyphenation was deliberately done to highlight the validity of self-love. In one article, Tjeltveit described it rather succinctly: "Jesus said "love your neighbor *as* yourself,"' ... not "love your neighbor *instead* of yourself."'" (Tjeltveit 2006b, 15) Furthermore, the various authors used the hyphenation to indicate how inextricably linked are love of self and love of others; the former provides the model by which one loves another.

John Wesley took this same stance; he kept love of God, self and neighbor together. Though he often referenced love of God and neighbor, he assumed a love of self. (Lindstrom 1980) In this regard, he followed in the train of biblical writers like Paul where a love of self seemed assumed (Ephesian 5: 28-29). But in other places, the emphasis on an ordered self-love rings clear and explicit. For example, in *The Way to the Kingdom*, he devoted attention to describing the great commandment. After speaking about loving God and equating this with righteousness, he devoted attention to the horizontal expression of love. From the sermon, it appears clear that he aimed to treat each part separately. First, he treated the command to love, associating it with goodwill, affection, and seeking all possible good. Next, he described the meaning of neighbor equating it with every human creature God made, whether know or unknown. Lastly, he defined the phrase *as yourself*. Here, he noted that loving others as self meant doing it "... with the same invariable thirsts after his happiness in every kind; the same unwearied care to screen him from whatever might grieve or hurt either his soul or body." (Wesley 1872aj, 149) From the context, it seemed clear that he believed these constituted actions one did to oneself and which ought to extend to one's neighbor.

Similarly, in other places, he carefully maintained the distinction and connection between love of neighbor and love of self. In relation to the former, he distinguished social love (the love of neighbor) from self-love. Speaking of the Christian, he wrote: "By experience he knows that social love, if it mean the love of our neighbor, is absolutely different from self-love, even of the most allowable kind; just as different as the objects at which they point. And yet it is sure, that, if they are under due regulations, each will give additional force to the other, till they mix together never to be divided." (Wesley 1872k, 85) This portion of his letter to Rev. Conyers Middleton affirmed at least a couple of realities about these two expressions of love: First, he recognized and affirmed these two kinds of love. Second, he believed both expressions of love required regulation. Unregulated, both can become inordinate forms of affection; however, duly regulated, they become appropriate and necessary, mutually empowering the other.

Following the biblical mandate to love one's neighbor as self, Wesley conceived self-love as the model for neighbor love. For example, in the second discourse on the Sermon on the Mount, he noted the command to love one's neighbor as self and then proceeded to pray that God would fill the heart with such love. (Wesley 1872ab) From the context, it seems apparent that the "such love" harks back to the love one displays toward oneself; one ought to give to one's neighbor the same love one displayed toward oneself. Similarly, in discourse 10, he admonished: "Love thy neighbor as thyself! Love friends and enemies as thy own soul! And let thy love be long-suffering and patient towards all men. Let it be kind, soft, benign; inspiring thee with the most amiable sweetness, and the most fervent and tender affection." (Wesley 1872y, 529) Here too one finds the implicit thought that self-love serves as the pattern for loving others. This affirmation of self-love also occurred in places such as Wesley's commentary on Ephesians 5:28. Speaking about loving one's wife as one's own body, he described it as an "indisputable duty," rather than sin. Clearly, the indisputable duty applies to loving one's own body that then becomes a pattern for loving one's wife. (Lindstrom 1980; Wesley 1997) Furthermore, in his commentary on 11 Timothy 1:7, he kept love of God, self and others together. This section of scripture pertained to God's gift of a spirit of power, love and sobriety instead of fear. In commenting on the latter two, he wrote: "These animate us in our duties to God, our brethren, and ourselves. Power and sobriety are two good extremes. Love is between, the tie and temperament of both; preventing the two bad extremes of fearfulness and rashness." (Wesley 1997 722) A least three major thoughts relative to love appear here. First, it seems clear that he saw love as a motivator in exercising our responsibilities and obligations. Second, he perceived our obligations as legitimately expressed towards God, others and self. Third, he saw love (along with sobriety) serving a kind of balancing mechanism keeping one from extremes. One such balance point that avoids extremes involves holding love to God, self and others in dynamic tension.

But Wesley also attached these relational obligations to other tempers besides love. Meekness constitutes a good example of this phenomenon. In speaking about the ways in which meekness expresses itself, he related it to God, self and others. In fact, he indicated that meekness most properly related to the self. When related to the self, he described it as patience or contentedness. (Wesley 1872ab) However, he also saw meekness applying to God and our neighbor. In reference to God, he described it as resignation to the will of God; applied to one's neighbor, he described it as "... mildness to the good, and gentleness to the evil." (Wesley 1872ab, 348) These ways in which meekness expresses itself closely parallels the various obligations to love in the great commandment. The similarity of expression might also lend support to the need to express love in these three forms.

At first blush, it might appear a stretch to imply that the threefold expression of meekness lends support for a similar expression of love. However, in reading Wesley, one quickly realizes the vital relationship that exists between meekness and love. In several places, he described meekness in a similar fashion to love. For one, like love, meekness served a kind of homeostatic and regulatory purpose. This idea appeared in his explanatory notes on Matthew 5:5. Here, he described the meek as: "They that hold all their passions and affections evenly balanced." (Wesley 1997, 27) Furthermore, in discourse 2 on the Sermon on the Mount, he described meekness as steering clear of extremes; he saw it serving the purpose of balancing and regulating the affections, rather than seeking to destroy them. Wesley saw this creation of balance in relation to the affections as God's ultimate design and purpose. Thus, he wrote: "Nor does Christian meekness imply, the being without zeal for God, any more than it does ignorance or insensibility. No; it keeps clear of every extreme, whether in excess or defect. It does not destroy but balance the affections, which the God of nature never designed should be rooted out by grace, but only brought and kept under due regulations. It poises the mind aright. It holds an even scale, with regard to anger, and sorrow, and fear; preserving the mean in every circumstance of life, and not declining either to the right hand or the left." (Wesley 1872ab, 348) However, in the same discourse, he also attributed this regulatory mechanism to love. Having described the meek as not attempting to extinguish passions but balance and use them appropriately, he offered the following statement in relation to love, namely: "... And thus even the harsher and more unpleasing passions are applicable to the noblest purposes; *even hatred, and anger, and fear, when engaged against sin, and regulated by faith and love*, are as walls and bulwarks to the soul, so that the wicked one cannot approach to hurt it." (Wesley 1872ab, 348 (Italics added)) Moreover, he described meekness in a manner similar to love. For example, he described it as the essence of Christianity. (Clapper 1984) But such language also applies to love; it stands at the apex of the gracious affections, being the more excellent way. (Wesley 1872ac; Wesley 1872ad; Wesley 1872ah) As a result, the argument from meekness to love might not be so far-fetched as it first appears.

Love to Neighbor-as-Self

From my perspective, the love of God calls forth love of self and love of neighbor. This more excellent way only becomes possible because God Himself floods our heart with His love. (Romans 5:5) Without this divine reality, loving as God requires remains impossible. However, loving others also requires a model and without this, loving becomes difficult. But what provides the model? Scripture serves as a prominent model; one can follow the dictates of scripture and thereby avoid those things inconsistent with love. It also provides a template for doing those things consistent with love. In these ways, one can be said to love others. But loving others appears most authentic when in addition to springing from the love of God it also arises from a genuine love for self. Bernard of Clairvaux referred to this as loving self for God's sake. (Clairvaux 1997) Without this concomitant love of self, loving others can tie one up in emotional knots. One must deal with the contradiction of not being able to love oneself while endeavoring to love others. (Headley 2006) Given this perspective, Harald Lindstrom described self-love as an "obvious pre-requisite" for loving others. Moreover, he though love for others ought to be balanced with love for self. (Lindstrom 1980) Tomas Špidlík came to the same conclusion in regards to the need to balance love of self and neighbor. Thus he wrote: "Christianity wants to unite both loves, of self and others, in one love. Whoever rejects this union possesses self-love, but on its own it is self-centered, perverse. Loving self, the egoist also destroys himself because he breaks the relationship with others and thereby diminishes his being "person."" (Špidlík 2010, 65) However, Špidlík did not speak to the aberration that occurs when one focuses on loving others exclusively without appropriate love to oneself. But from the tenor of this statement he might have said something similar to his statement about self-love. He might have continued by saying that loving others in this inordinate way also becomes perverse. Similarly, he might have said that in so doing, such persons destroy themselves because they break relationship with themselves and diminish their own persons.

Špidlík's words regarding Christianity's aim to unite love of self and love of neighbor recalls an earlier quoted statement from Wesley. Wesley admitted that self-love and neighbor love existed as different realities. However, he acknowledged that when duly regulated, they mutually reinforced each other, and eventually became one love. (Wesley 1872k) Because Wesley believed they needed to be balanced, he considered the command to love neighbor as self as a most "equitable rule." (Wesley 1872e; Lindstrom 1980) But he also believed that rightly understood, both love of self and neighbor needed regulation. One would assume that he meant that they should be regulated, by the love of God shed abroad in the human heart. This is the stance Lindstrom took. He noted that in Wesley's sermon, *The Use of Money*, love of self and neighbor both constituted ordered love originating in the love of God. (Lindstrom 1980) Without such regulation, love of self or of others can become distorted and perverted. In regards to the self, unregulated love might make self a false center. (Wynkoop 1972) This unregulated love then becomes a way in which sin manifests itself. (Lindstrom 1980; Wynkoop 1972) But unregulated love of others can also become inordinate; it involves loving the creature more than the creator. In short, self-love and love of neighbor can be unregulated or regulated. When regulated, they become legitimate expressions of the horizontal dimension of the command to love.

The Disinterested Nature of Neighborly Love

Wesley sometimes attached the adjective *disinterested* to love. In those instances, the adjective mostly connected to love of one's neighbor or as he described it "to every child of man." (Wesley 1872a; Wesley 1872r)

Sometimes he employed alternate terms for love to convey the same idea. For example, he sometimes employed the phrases *disinterested benevolence* or *disinterested goodwill.* (Wesley 1872a; Wesley 1872q; Wesley 1872w) However, from the context, these alternate terms clearly referred to love. This concept of disinterested love appeared several places in his writings. It appeared in diverse places such as his sermons *The New Birth, The Duty of Reproving our Neighbor,* and even in his sermon on the death of George Whitefield. (Wesley 1872d; Wesley 1872l; Wesley 1872r) It also appeared coupled with love in a letter to Rev. Conyers Middleton, *A Farther Appeal to Men of Reason and Religion, Part 2* and *A Case of Reason Impartially Considered.* (Wesley 1872a; Wesley 1872g; Wesley 1872k) Moreover, given the many references to love in his discourses on the Sermon on the Mount, it is not surprising to also find it there. One example comes from his fourth discourse on the Sermon on the Mount. Here he wrote:

> Be this your one ultimate end in all things. With this view, be plain, open, undisguised. Let your love be without dissimulation: Why should you hide fair, disinterested love? Let there be no guile found in your mouth: Let your words be the genuine picture of your heart. Let there be no darkness or reservedness in your conversation, no disguise in your behavior. Leave this to those who have other designs in view; designs which will not bear the light. Be ye artless and simple to all mankind; that all may see the grace of God which is in you. And although some will harden their hearts, yet others will take knowledge that ye have been with Jesus, and, by returning themselves to the great Bishop of their souls, "glorify your Father which is in heaven." (Wesley 1872ad, 397)

This quotation proves particularly useful in that it provides aspects of and concomitants of disinterested love of neighbor. From the context, it is a love that demonstrates itself without guile or any ulterior motive other than to love; it accurately reflects in words and works the actual state of the heart. Wesley also connected it with the work of sanctification began in the new birth. According to him, in the new birth "...the love of the world is changed into the love of God; pride into humility; passion into meekness; hatred, envy, malice, into a sincere, tender, disinterested love for all mankind." (Wesley 1872l, 88-89) Disinterested love also served as a master temper; it produced all other holy and divine tempers, implanting in persons the very image of God. Thus he wrote: "... What benevolence also, what tender love to the whole of human kind, will you drink in, together with the love of God, from the unexhausted source of love! And how easy is it to conceive that more and more of his image will be then transfused into your soul; that from disinterested love, all other divine tempers will, as it were naturally, spring: Mildness, gentleness, patience, temperance, justice, sincerity, contempt of the world; yea, whatsoever things are venerable and lovely, whatsoever are justly of good report!" (Wesley 1872g, 224)

But Wesley's letter to Rev. Conyers Middleton provided further glimpses into the nature of disinterested love. There, he described it as "... springing from no view of advantage to himself, from no regard to profit or praise; no, nor even the pleasure of loving." (Wesley 1872k, 85) This statement conveys the sense in which Wesley meant *disinterested*. Disinterested love does not infer a lack of concern or interest in others. Rather, it should be understood from the perspective of the one who loves; that is, the lover desires nothing for self. This love does not seek reciprocity and is not moved by the desire to gain something from the one loved; it is not self-seeking. Such love harbors no designs, airs or subterfuge. (Wesley 1872u) Given this nature, in his fourth discourse on the Sermon on the Mount, he described it as "plain, open, undisguised." (Wesley 1872ad, 397) In these statements, the nature of disinterested love appears patently clear; it revolves around loving the other simply as other. (Watson 2000)

A Love which Corrects and Sets Priorities

However, the love Wesley envisioned, although generally marked by benevolence, kindness and goodwill, also possessed corrective qualities. This tough aspect of disinterested love appeared in his sermon *The Duty of Reproving our Neighbor*. He based the sermon on Leviticus 19:17 which denounced hating one's brother from the heart. The latter part of the verse indicated the manner in which this is done, namely, by refusing to rebuke one's neighbor regarding sin. To Wesley, the other side of this verse required a love strong enough to correct those who fell into sin or were on the verge of doing so. As a result, he wrote: "Love indeed requires us to warn him, not only of sin, (although of this chiefly,) but likewise of any error which, if it were persisted in, would naturally lead to sin. If we do not "hate him in our heart," if we love our neighbor as ourselves, this will be our constant endeavor; to warn him of every evil way, and of every mistake which tends to evil." (Wesley 1872d, 332) He then described the acts needing reproof, those to whom this duty is owed, as well as how to do it.

In relation to the acts needing reproof, he clearly meant undeniably sinful and evil actions. One ought not to correct one's neighbor over disputable matters. Neither should one reprove others for actions the reprover's conscience disallowed. Instead, the actions needing reproof included profane cursing, drunkenness and profaning the Lord's Day. He also described the manner in which one ought to reprove. Briefly stated, reproof should be exercised with the spirit of love, humility, meekness, prayer and seriousness while paying attention to scripture. Reproof ought also to vary with the situation. However, it did not always require words but could sometimes be conveyed even through a gesture or a look. (Wesley 1872d) Wesley also described the persons Christians ought to reprove. This duty applied to one's neighbor in the broadest possible sense, namely, every child of man. However, this loving duty should be carried out with clear priorities. That is, such loving reproof was first owed to one's nearest neighbor. In keeping with this idea, he believed the first priority for correction extended to one's parents. Following them, in order of priority, one owed loving reproof to biological brothers and sisters, relatives by blood or marriage, one's servants and fellow citizens and members of one's society. Following these, this responsibility applied to every human creature. (Wesley 1872d) This description of the way in which all-embracing, disinterested love operates, suggests that it acknowledges different levels of priority and responsibility.

One can discern these different priorities and responsibilities in expressing love elsewhere in Wesley's writings. For example, in *The Use of Money*, these differences clearly appeared. In it, he also made explicit connections between love and money. Money when loved and valued above God constituted inordinate affection. In such cases, the love of money became the root of all evil. But as he made clear, "The fault does not lie in the money, but in them that use it." (Wesley 1872ai, 149) Money connects to love in other ways; through inordinate love of it, one pursued gain at the expense of loving one's neighbor. For Wesley, true love of neighbor did not permit such things. On the other hand, one could use money to benefit one's neighbor thereby making it a legitimate means of expressing love. (Wesley 1872ai) But even in the latter case, Wesley saw clear priorities in the loving use of money. The loving use of money ought to begin with providing adequate care for oneself. Following this, one respectively provided for one's spouse and children, one's servants and others in one's household. If money yet remained after the exercise of these duties, one provided for those in the household of faith, followed by other persons outside the faith. (Wesley 1872ai)

Lindstrom apparently held similar views to Wesley relative to the priorities of love. (Lindstrom 1980) Furthermore, he provided a model supporting the idea of priorities in love. In it he differentiated between the all-embracing love of neighbor and brotherly love. According to him, in later life, Wesley increasingly spoke of a brotherly love considered different than the all-embracing love. The latter love embraced all humankind whereas the former only applied to the Christian brotherhood. However, Lindstrom admitted that both loves were of the same kind though different in degree. (Lindstrom 1980) In his model, he posited three circles each representing different levels of priority. All-embracing, disinterested love formed an outer circle reserved for all of humanity, including enemies of God and strangers is the truest sense of the word. Within this outer circle, he posited two inners circles both comprising brotherly love. The first inner circle applied to "... friends, brothers in Christ, citizens of the New Jerusalem, comrades in the same war and under the same leader." (Lindstrom 1980, 192) The second and innermost circle more peculiarly applied to "... those to whom the Christian is joined not only in the Spirit but also by all the outward bonds of Christian fellowship; those who belong to the same congregation and in whose company he received the means of grace." (Lindstrom 1980, 192) Lindstrom suggested that these three circles represented three kinds of love: all-embracing love and two forms of brotherly love.

Although I commend Lindstrom for recognizing different priorities in love, I differ with his statement about brotherly love in Wesley. As indicated, he noted that the idea of a brotherly love different from all-embracing love came later in Wesley's life. (Lindstrom 1980) What he did not say is that even in Wesley's later life, he continued to speak of the all-embracing love that extended to all human kind. This appeared in the earlier referenced sermon *The Duty of Reproving our Neighbor*. Timothy L. Smith dated this sermon to the latter years of Wesley's life, specifically to July 28, 1787. (Smith 1982) This sermon established priorities in love's expression. Moreover, it very closely identified neighborly and brotherly love in ways suggesting no difference between the two. As a result, I disagree with Lindstrom in differentiating all-embracing love and brotherly love in the fashion he proposed. Perhaps Lindstrom saw a need to differentiate these loves because he was taken aback by Wesley requiring a love to brothers that seemed higher in degree than that required for the bulk of humankind. (Lindstrom 1980; See Wesley 1872b) Yet as he rightly noted, all-embracing, disinterested love as well as brotherly love shared the same characteristics described I Corinthians 13.

In contrast to Lindstrom's position, Wesley's sermon *The Use of Money* seems to equate neighborly love and brotherly love; they describe the same love but differ depending on the human object and likely, the context. This means that one should not think about the three different circles Lindstrom espoused as constituting three different kinds of love. Rather, one should think of these as constituting one love expressed differently. When applied to humanity in general, it is love to neighbor or all-encompassing love. When described in the context of the community of faith, it is brotherly love. But even within brotherly love, it expresses itself differently depending on the proximity of the fellow believer; love expressed to brothers and sisters who are a part of one's fellowship might look different, be more intimate and more varied in expression than love expressed to believers far away. Yet these varied expressions all pertain to the one all-embracing disinterested love to which God calls us. But this sermon makes the same point when Wesley discussed the obligation to gain all we can. Related to this point, he noted we should do this without hurting our neighbor since this was inconsistent with loving our neighbor as ourselves. Here it seems patently clear that Wesley was speaking about all-embracing, disinterested love. He then detailed actions contrary to this love, such as devouring the increase of one's neighbors' lands through gaming, allowing them to accrue large bills, and charging exorbitant interest. (Wesley 1872ai) But in the very same paragraph, he made similar statements about brotherly love. He wrote: "...We cannot, consistent with brotherly love, sell our goods below the market-price; we cannot study to ruin our neighbor's trade, in order to advance our own; much less can we entice away, or receive, any of his servants or workmen whom he has need of. None can gain by swallowing up his neighbor's substance, without gaining the damnation of hell!" (Wesley 1872ai, 151)

But what do we do with Wesley's call in *Catholic Spirit* to a brotherly love higher in degree from love of neighbor? From my perspective, the higher degree of love he required for brothers was not a different love. Rather, it involved a love expressed *prior* to those outside the community and perhaps expressed in *different, more intimate* ways and *with greater frequency* depending on proximity. In support of this perspective, in *Catholic Spirit,* he explicated the meaning of a higher kind. (Wesley 1872b) He described this love in terms of I Corinthians 13. But he added other obligations such as commending to God in prayer; wrestling on a fellow Christian's behalf, provoking to love and good works, speaking to fellow Christians in love, quickening them in the work to which they were called as well as in love expressed in word and deed. (Wesley 1872b) Although Christians can pray for persons outside the faith community, the other obligations more specifically apply to those within the community. Additionally, these expressions of love differ depending on whether the fellow believer is near or far away; one can more likely provoke to love and good works persons who inhabit the same local community. At least one can do this on a much more regular and personal basis; one can also quicken fellow believers in the work to which they were called but this is better done when that person is part of the same community. These expressions do not apply to persons outside the faith in the same sense. These aspects, *unique* to the household of faith, likely fill out Wesley's phrase "in a higher degree." Thus, one can conclude that the love to which God calls is one love. It is this love which constitutes the fulfilling of the Law. Of this love, Wesley wrote: "How excellent things are spoken of the love of our neighbor! It is "the fulfilling of the law," "the end of the commandment." Without this, all we have, all we do, all we suffer, is of no value in the sight of God. But it is that love of our neighbor which springs from the love of God: Otherwise itself is nothing worth." (Wesley 1872ac, 364)

Perspectives on Wesley's Emphasis on Love: A Theology of Love

Wesleyan scholars generally support Wesley's emphasis on relational love as the heart of Christian perfection. For instance, Mildred Bangs Wynkoop identified it as the dynamic of Wesleyan theology. Furthermore, she argued that Wesley's hermeneutic centered on love to God and one's neighbor and ran through all his works. (Wynkoop 1972 16; Bang Wynkoop 1975) As a result, she stressed: "The principle by which to understand Wesley's doctrine is love to God and man, in the biblical sense of love. Love is the dynamic of theology and experience. Love, structured by holiness, links all that we know of man. Love is the end of the law. It is the goal of every step in grace and the norm of the Christian life in this world." (Wynkoop 1972, 269) In another place, she described love as the ultimate hermeneutic in Wesley. Then she added: "Every strand of his thought, the warm heart of every doctrine, the passion of every sermon, the test of every claim to Christian grace, was love. So central is love that to be "Wesleyan" is to be committed to a theology of love." (Wynkoop 1972, 101) I couldn't agree more with this thesis.

Wynkoop clearly highlighted this perspective to argue for a relational understanding as opposed to a substantive view of holiness and sin. From this perspective, holiness revolves around a right relationship to God; on the other hand, sin involves a wrong relationship to God marked by rebellion. Additionally, sin and rebellion largely involves centering one's love on that which is not God. In pursuing this line of thought, Wynkoop chose to center the fundamental distortion on the self; for her, sin is love misdirected toward the self. In fact, she described sin as "... love locked into a false center, the self." (Wynkoop 1972, 158) In contrast, "Holiness is love locked into the True Center, Jesus Christ our Lord." (Wynkoop 1972, 158) Elsewhere, she also described love centered on the self as a "distorting self-orientation, which flaws all other relationships because it uses them to personal advantage..." (Wynkoop 1972, 33-34)

Although I find much to commend in her views, I struggle with at least two emphases in her work. First, she gave significant arguments against a substantive understanding of sin and holiness. According to her, the substantive view identified something in humans with the image of God in persons. That *something* was seen as a "...corporeal substance or some function of the human person (such as reason, a divine spark, creative ability) or being in possession of a spirit as well as a soul and a body, distinguishes man (sic) from nonhuman beings." (Wynkoop 1972, 105) Logically related to this was the notion that the soul is some corporeal thing shaped by sin (or by holiness). From her perspective, this leads some to expect "a substance alteration of the soul which occurs below the level of rational life and which, apart from personal involvement, changes the impulsive reactions of the self." (Wynkoop 1972, 49-50) In her opinion, persons holding to this perspective interpret sin genetically seeing it as involving some kind of evil adhering in the flesh, similarly transmitted as the physical body is propagated. Given this perspective, the removal of sin involved some kind of divine operation to eliminate the offending substance. (Wynkoop 1972) But Wynkoop appeared to take this stance as a way of arguing against "crisis experiences" in holiness theology. According to her, many in the Wesleyan community placed too much confidence in such experiences, confusing these with the goal of perfection. (Wynkoop 1972)

I do not doubt that in some Wesleyan circles, some hold such views, expecting a change in substance that she envisioned. However, Wynkoop argued for her position to such a degree that it appeared she would throw out biblical language that *sounded* substantive. Here, I think about concepts such as crucifixion of the flesh, the old man, and circumcision of the heart. These terms though sounding substantive, represent metaphorical language. But even so, they point to a reality that occurs in Christian experience. Given this way of thinking, I don't believe one should discount this language as she seemed to do. Moreover, although I endorse a gradual perspective on Christian perfection, I also hold to a crisis point in the experience. Wynkoop seems to favor the gradual in contrast to Wesley's thinking on the matter. (Wesley 1872t)

Second, though agreeing with her relational definition of love, centering the perversion of love exclusively in terms of the self seems problematic. (Wynkoop 1972) Sometimes she appeared to described false love in broader terms, but most often she perceived the dominant distortion as involved centering love upon the self. No doubt this distorted focus on the self is partly true. One can focus one's love *exclusively* on the self in a disordered fashion. But is this the only way in which one can distort love? Might it not be more correct to say that the true distortion of love comes in inordinately centering one's affection on *anything* that is not God? As such, it can involve an inordinate love of others or things. In both cases, love becomes destructive. No wonder St. John admonished us against a love of the world: "Do not love the world or the things in the world. The love of the Father is not in those who love the world; for all that is in the world – the desire of the flesh, the desire of the eyes, the pride in riches come not from the Father but from the world." (1 John 2:15-16, NRSV)

Interestingly, Wynkoop herself quoted this last passage to indicate that one can substitute something else for God. Elsewhere, she apparently left space for a love directed toward the self that is not distorted. For example, in speaking about agape, she noted: "It is not first of all an emotion but a deliberate policy whereby the relations sustained with other persons are kept in balance by one's deliberate orientation to God and his own self-respect – in the right sense, self-love." (Wynkoop 1972, 33) However, this statement connected self-love with self-respect. Indeed, she apparently meant to communicate self-respect as the only legitimate form of self-love. I wonder if in this definition of sin and distorted love, Wynkoop reflected a period when it was difficult to conceive or endorse a proper, biblical love exhibited to the self. In this sense, she might have been unintentionally or unconsciously reflecting a common fallacy seen in some Wesleyan circles. This fallacy revolves around considering a healthy and appropriate love of self an unholy thing. As such, this love is sometimes denigrated in favor of love of neighbor that virtually excludes love of self. This perspective often seems to border on making self-hatred a virtue. By defining distorted love as being locking into the false center of the self, while leaving off other ways in which love might be distorted, Wynkoop seemed to support the denigration of an appropriate love of self.

Like Wynkoop, Lindstrom and Smith agreed with the central place of love in Wesley's views on Christian perfection. According to them, Wesley believed that salvation's ultimate goal involved the restoration in humans of the love of God. (Lindstrom 1980) This love delivered persons from the power as well as the guilt of sin. Moreover, faith helped one achieve both goals; it supplied the power to live holy as well as love and serve God. (Wesley 1872ae, 399-416) However, Lindstrom was careful to point out that the love Wesley emphasized was threefold in nature extending to God, neighbor and himself. As a result, Lindstrom wrote: "The law prescribes man's relation to God, his neighbor, and himself, and Wesley adopts the same pattern in speaking of love. He is not concerned only with love to God and one's neighbor; self-love also has a place." (Lindstrom 1980, 184) Speaking about this emphasis, Timothy Smith struck a similar chord when he wrote: "Christian perfection consisted, he must have written a hundred times, in loving God with all one's heart, mind, soul, and strength, and other human beings as oneself. And he understood love in Hebrew terms, of course: loyalty, or faithfulness, ground in thankful affection for the God who made and kept his promise." (Lindstrom 1980) As such Smith applauded Lindstrom's stress on love in Wesley's views of Christian perfection. [1] These latter perspectives on self-love stand in stark contrast to Wynkoop's position. Lindstrom's and Smith's discussions support a healthy appreciation for the value of relational love in its threefold expression. This seems much more in keeping with the biblical mandate to love God and love one's neighbor as oneself. I find this a refreshing emphasis that moves beyond the twofold emphasis on love to God and neighbor commonly encountered. Several years ago I was part of a dissertation hearing in which a student mentioned an inventory on love developed by Barna. However, we soon discovered that the instrument measured two dimensions - love to God and to neighbor. I quickly noted that in leaving out an appropriate love to self, the author had gotten it wrong. One often encounters this way of thinking in many Christian circles. But if we are to understand the perfection of love in Wesley's writings, we have to conceive of it in its threefold nature - love to God, self and one's neighbor. When we hold together these three, it truly becomes relational in a biblical sense. To strip away any of these emphases leaves us with a distorted view of Christian love. Unfortunately, if any emphasis is stripped away, it is typically love of self. In contrast, Wesley kept the emphasis on loving God, self and others explicit and together. According to Smith, Wesley believed part of the restoration of grace was to bring one to "... a scriptural love of self." This

---

[1] Harald Lindstrom, *Wesley and Sanctification* (Wilmore, KY: Francis Asbury Publishing Company, 1980). This line of thinking appears on the second page of Smith's foreword to Lindstrom's book.

restored regard for oneself became the standard by which one expressed love for others. (Lindstrom 1980, in Smith's Foreword)

Perspectives on Wesley's Emphasis on Love: Love as Core Notion

In *Relation Holiness,* Oord and Lodahl also described relational love as the essence of holiness. They proposed the idea of a core notion that offers insight into the love to which God calls. For them, a core notion integrates other holiness terms. Additionally, it incorporates rather than negates truths expressed in these concepts. Furthermore, it serves as an ultimate explanation. (Oord and Lodahl 2005) In contrast to it, they described other terms used for holiness (such as purity and being perfect) as contributing notions. According to them, contributing notions express something true, but are inadequate in capturing other truths. (Oord and Lodahl 2005) I tend to agree with this understanding of love as a core notion as it seems to accord with the central place Wesley gave to love. In fact, Wesley described love in a way that fits this concept well. He described it as the end of the commandment in that "... every commandment leads to and centers in it." (Wesley 1872ad, 392) For him, love integrated the other meanings of holiness. But love did more than integrate; it gave them their very meaning and nature. Given this reality, one best interprets holiness terms through the lens of love. In keeping with this centrality, I picture love as the hub of a wheel from which everything else emanates. The other holiness terms serve as spokes which show the various expressions of love. Love becomes the bottom line explanation for these terms and the basis on which one understands them. (Oord and Lodahl 2005) Wynkoop also captured this idea in understanding the other holiness terms when she wrote: "No matter which door one enters into this thinking – holiness, sanctification, perfections, cleansing, faith, man, God, salvation, or any other – not only does each of these begin to flow together and intertwine with the others, but the whole is channeled inevitably into love." (Wynkoop 1972, 21)

A few, brief examples might serve to illustrate the centrality of love and how this facilitates understanding and interpretation of other holiness terms. For example, consider the term purity! What is it? It is moral cleanliness but it involves more. In fact, purity is vitally related to love. It is nothing more than the heart completely filled with the love of God. A heart so filled by love eminently qualifies as a pure heart. In this sense, the purity which Oord and Lodahl initially described as a static and non-relational concept, is in fact eminently relational. (Oord and Lodahl 2005) Without a vital relationship with God that fills the heart with His love, no one can be truly pure. One also sees the centrality of love when one considers the term *circumcision of the heart.* Considered in the light of love, circumcision of the heart metaphorically refers to correcting the distorted curvature of the heart away from God. Without God and His perfecting love, one is oriented to loving the creature more than the creator. Circumcision of the heart restores the human heart to its expected state – a reorientation of the heart back towards God and away from all that is not God. Thus, in *The Scripture Way of Salvation*, Wesley wrote: "Then will I circumcise thy heart, and the heart of thy seed, to love the Lord thy God with all thy heart, and with all thy soul, and with all thy mind." How clearly does this express the being perfected in love! — how strongly imply the being saved from all sin! For as long as love takes up the whole heart, what room is there for sin therein?" (Wesley 1872al, 68) Similar thoughts appear in *The Circumcision of the Heart*. Here, Wesley equated the experience with a right state of the soul and a mind and spirit renewed in God's image. Later, he also associated it with holiness, being cleansed from sin of the flesh and thereby possessing the mind of Christ and exemplifying Christ's virtues. (Wesley 1872ak) More specifically, he added: "If thou wilt be perfect, add to all these, charity; add love, and thou hast the circumcision of the heart "Love is the fulfilling of the law, the end of the commandment." (Wesley 1872ak, 287)

Finally, one can consider the term *perfection*. In the Sermon on the Mount, it clearly referred to the perfection of love. But in speaking about it, Oord and Lodahl initially cited some of the problems stemming from its various meanings. Among these, they mentioned its absolute meaning and the idea of not sinning. (Oord and Lodahl 2005) But one can only view perfection in this light if it is cut off from its vital connection to love. Cut off from this connection, perfection lacks relational quality and is not the perfection God demands. Wesley knew this. In regard to perfection, he wrote: "Here it means perfect love. It is love excluding sin; love filling the heart, taking up the whole capacity of the soul. It is love "rejoicing evermore, praying without ceasing, in every thing giving thanks." (Wesley 1872al, 62) Fortunately, in their final chapter, Oord and Lodahl related perfection and the other terms for holiness to the core notion of love. Indeed, they demonstrated how the contributing notions enrich one's understanding of holiness as love. (Oord and Lodahl 2005) But love also corrects and enriches understanding of these varied holiness terms. They find their truest meaning when viewed in the light of love. Using Oord and Lodahl's language, they may not serve as core notions like love does. However, not having this status does not render them secondary or unimportant. Each term presents fundamental truths about the nature of holiness. But they all find their distinctive place when seen in the light of Christian love. To understand this integrative function of love in relation to other holiness terms makes it truly a core notion.

Chapter 6

Objective, Dispositional Love and Christian Perfection

Christian Love and Religious Affections

Christian love, according to many authors, constitutes a religious affection. (Clapper 1987; Clapper 1985a; Clapper 1985b; Collins 2003; Collins 1998; Leffel 2007; Mann 2006) Religious affections, also called *holy* or *gracious affections,* pertain to the inward attitudes of the heart. For John Wesley and others like Jonathan Edwards, they constituted the essence of true Christian religion. (Edwards 1997; Wesley 1872v; Wesley 1872w) As indicated in chapter 4, Wesley and Edwards believed they stemmed from the will of the soul; in fact, according to them, they reflected the exercises of the will. (Clapper 1987; Clapper 1985a; Clapper 1985b; Edwards 1997; Wesley 1872v; Wesley 1872w) In that chapter, I discussed the affections as appearing like emotions. However, they also possess cognitive linkages, being associated with elements such as judgments, beliefs, understanding and perception. (Clapper 1987; Edwards 1997) In addition, many commonly associate the affections with the terms *tempers* and *affections*. Such persons typically understand the tempers as enduring and stable. In contrast, affections are generally understood as transitory. (Clapper 1985a; Collins 2003; Collins 1998; Edwards 1997)

But given the addition of the adjective *religious,* the affections clearly possess spiritual linkages. One can also intuit their inherent spiritual nature in the source from which they arise. Wesley and Edwards believed the creator Himself bestowed these gracious gifts on humans and that they serve as the springboard for human action. (Clapper 1985a; Edwards 1997) One can also infer their spiritual nature since they arise from God's work in the human heart. (Clapper 1987; Clapper 1985b) Furthermore, they likewise display their essential spiritual nature in the characteristics ascribed to them: First, they come with the certitude of divine things. Second, spiritual attitudes bound up with humility also accompany them. Third, one detects their spiritual quality in that they promote a Christ-like spirit. (Clapper 1987; Clapper 1985a; Clapper 1984; Clapper 1985b; Clapper 1985b) Finally, within the affections, one locates additional spiritual qualities such as meekness, mercy and forgiveness. But reigning supreme among these is love that shapes all other tempers. (Clapper 1987; Clapper 1985b; Clapper 1985a; Edwards 1997)

Love's Transforming Object

As I previously indicated, affections possess relational, objective and dispositional aspects. (Kilian and Parker 2001; Land 1993)) Of course, since love stands as the chief affection, these aspects all apply to it. (Land 1993) But a caution seems in order when describing love in this way; this approach might make love appear a fragmented concept. However, this is not my intent. Rather, my approach largely derives from a concern for convenience while seeking to do justice to the topic. After all, God's all-encompassing, disinterested love stands as such a complex and multi-dimensional subject, speaking about it demands a multi-faceted approach. Nevertheless, these three aspects of love remain inextricably linked and constitute one reality; these are not three forms of love but three aspects that help us to better understand love in all its complexity.

In the previous chapter, I primarily focused on the relational aspects of love, although I occasionally mentioned its objective linkages. However, in this chapter, the principal focus is on dispositional love. But first, I give some attention to the objective nature of love. To reiterate, to say that the affections are objective means they always require an object on which to focus. This reality also applies to love. (Land 1993) However, when speaking of God in relation to love and the affections, it's important to remember that He is both object and subject. As subject, He stands as the very fountain from which love springs. It is this divine source that gives Christian love its distinctive character. Furthermore, this love where God stands as both subject and object lies at the center of Christian perfection.

But love's object can be God or some lesser person or thing. When principally focused on God, love truly becomes what it was meant to be; it becomes ordered, holy, produces gracious Christian character and creates a desire for greater growth in one's life. (Clapper 1987; Clapper 1985b; Wesley 1872v) However, love can also become exclusively fixated on false objects; it can become solely focused on the self or other object such as people or things. (Wynkoop 1972) When this happens, love becomes warped and destructive. (Wesley 1872c) In fact, when focused on false objects, individuals experience a deformation process that slowly erodes moral fiber; indeed, this focus tends to erode one's entire life. One could illustrate this deformation process from the world of addictions.

An Example from the World of Addictions

In addictions, an individual becomes focused on an object that serves as the source of the compulsion. The addicting element does not have to involve a tangible substance. In fact, the addicting element does not have to be a substance at all; besides alcohol and drugs, one can become addicted to stealing, gambling, setting fires, pornography or to a sexual deviancy. (American Psychiatric Association 2000) Once in place, the addiction negatively affects the individual's life in a number of deleterious ways. One can illustrate this phenomenon through a brief look at the *paraphilias*. The paraphilias section of the current Diagnostic and Statistical Manual of Mental Disorders (DSM) capture various sexual addictions such as pedophilia, exhibitionism, voyeurism and similar sexual deviancies. (American Psychiatric Association 2000) I have chosen to focus on this term because it captures the idea of a necessary object. It does so in that the term itself includes the idea of being attracted (*philia*) to an object, which in turn becomes the source of the sexual deviation (*para*). (American Psychiatric Association 2000) Once an individual becomes attracted and addicted, the addiction begins to control the person's life in several ways. The individual can become exclusively focused on the object to the neglect of other important facets of life such as significant relationships and work. In addition, one typically and persistently seeks out the object with dogged compulsivity. The addicting object also begins to pervade the person's entire life in all its aspects. (American Psychiatric Association 2000) In other words, the thing to which one had become attracted, now controls one's entire life; it dictates the individual's characteristic way of being, hopelessly tying one to depravity while continuing to erode one's moral fiber. But in contrast to such a process, making God the object of our affections sets an individual on a path of virtue acquisition and concomitantly, the diminishment of vice. (Leffel 2007)

The Nature of Dispositions: Varied Perspectives

I now turn attention to the dispositional aspect of the Christian affections. This merits attention because the affections involve more than "passing feelings or sensate episodes." Rather, they represent *standing ways of being* expressed through relationship with God and others. (Land 1993) This language signals dispositional transformation. It highlights love as it transforms human nature and character. Fundamentally, love affects individuals intrapersonally from the inside out. But when true transformation takes place in any real Christian, it does not remain there; such transformation holds the potential to precipitate dispositional change in others with whom the Christian relates interpersonally. Such transformation acts like salt and light bringing potential transformation to those with whom one interacts. (Wesley 1872u; Wesley 1872x) In this sense, love in its dispositional aspects is relational; it facilitates change in others through interpersonal relationships. One can go further; transformed persons tend to transform societies and culture one bit at a time. It is this transforming dispositional love that serves as the focus of this chapter.

Before proceeding further, it appears wise to pause and describe what is meant when characterizing God's all-encompassing love as dispositional. I do so by first defining the word *disposition*. A disposition refers to the dominant predisposition of an individual; it denotes his or her characteristic attitude reflecting the inward nature of that person. But character also becomes visible through one's thinking, emotions and outward behavior. From this perspective, one can think about dispositions as a characteristic ways of being including emotions, perceptions and action. (Brown 1996) Inherent in this understanding there exists the idea of constancy and endurance; that is, a disposition stands as a remarkably stable mark of personality and provide a window for understanding an individual's true nature. (Brown 1996) Because of these aspects and the way a disposition reveals one's typical way of being, one can also describe it as *characterological*. This last statement suggests that dispositional language comes bound up with the word *character*. As such, this latter term also provide clues to the nature of a disposition.

According to William Brown, the word *character* originally referred to an engraving tool that sends its mark deep into the material on which it is used. This mark went so deep as to make the mark virtually indelible. Given this derivation, *character* conjures up the image of the abiding and enduring aspects of a personality. The inherent and deep-seated nature of these aspects renders the personality almost impervious to modification and erosion; persons do not typically or easily shift from these ways of being. (Brown 1996) Apparently, *character* also derives some of its meaning from literary and ethical discourse. From the literary world came the idea of a *paradigm*. This term referred to the cluster of an individual's traits, also understood as stable and enduring. These distinctive traits made it possible to distinguish one character from another. In this sense, one can consider character as clearly demarcating one individual from another based on the person's distinctive way of being and acting. Moreover, from the world of ethical discourse came the notion that character referred to moral traits resident in an individual. Together, these traditions suggest that character involves somewhat fixed ways of being which are stable across time. What's more, character reveals itself in one's emotional, cognitive and behavioral life and possesses distinctive moral implications (Brown 1996)

The world of mental health diagnosis can augment an understanding of character as it relates to dispositions. Within the world of diagnostic nosology, mental health clinicians use the word *characterological* to refer to individual traits that remain enduring and stable in nature, and somewhat resistant to change. Most often they apply the term to personality disorders. The Diagnostic and Statistical Manual of Mental Disorders describes personality disorders in the following language: "... an enduring pattern of inner experience and behavior which deviates markedly from the expectations of an individual's culture, is pervasive, and inflexible, has an onset in adolescence or early adulthood, is stable over time, and leads to distress or impairment." (American Psychiatric Association 2000 685) Elsewhere, other equate character with personality indicating that these traits "... are ingrained, enduring patterns of behaving, feeling, perceiving, and thinking, which are prominent in a wide range of personal and social contexts. Personality is the psychological equivalent of physical appearance." (Maxmen and Ward 1995, 389) Because of their inherent nature, these traits express themselves in various ways, both adjusted and maladjusted. In the latter area and viewed from the perspective of mental health diagnosis, one can even speak of *characterological depression*; that is, a depression fundamentally tied to the person's basic character. (Kaplan and Sadock 1991) In line with this thinking, David Shapiro even suggested that psychopathology should be understood from the perspective of character. (Shapiro 2000) These perspectives from the mental health field integrally connect with the contributions from the literary and ethicist fields. They all offer the same picture of character as it relates to dispositions; namely, dispositions stand as enduring aspects of one's total personality exhibited in every aspect of life. Additionally, because of its characterological nature, dispositions tend to pervade one's whole life and outlook as well as one's inner and outer world.

But depending on the object of focus, dispositions can move persons in negative and destructive directions or in positive, enhancing ways; in other words, dispositions closely relate to the objective element discussed earlier. In a manner of speaking, the object of focus becomes the spring for dispositional personality. This is true not only for external objects on which one concentrates but even for internal whims and impulses. In a sense, one can makes one's whims and impulses the focused objects and thereby become slave to them. Concomitantly, one exhibits an inability to effectively manage or appropriately delay such impulses. Without learning how to appropriately channel or control one's impulses, one tends to become an impulsive character. This line of thinking relative to the impulses calls to mind Daniel Goleman's writings on emotional intelligence. In his best-selling book of the same title, he asserted that one's ethical stances in life derive from basic emotional capacities. According to him, one way in which these emotional capacities reveal themselves is through impulse management; those who allow themselves to be mastered by their impulses and who surrender to every passion tend to exhibit moral deficiency. Furthermore, the capitulation to one's passions and allowing them unrestrained flow can produce an unhealthy and diminished character. On the other hand, those who restrain and master their passions make possible the realization of a healthy and life-enhancing disposition. In fact, based on

Goleman, one can sum up the idea of emotional intelligence by the word *character*; it embodies the skills he intended when he used the phrase *emotional intelligence*. (Goleman 1995)

Interestingly, Goleman connected the ability to control and channel one's impulses to the will. (Goleman 1995) As we have previously seen, Wesley and Edwards also connected the religious affections to the will. (Clapper 1985b; Edwards 1997; Wesley 1872v; Wesley 1872w) Although not completely synonymous, Goleman's use of the term *emotional intelligence* largely seems to capture many of the aspects of the religious affections and dispositional character. One of the ways Goleman's discussion differs from Wesley and Edwards is in the source from which character springs. They discussed dispositions as springing from divine action and emphasized the moral implications of the religious affections. Although Goleman seemed well aware of the moral implications, he focused more on how individuals and institutions frame and develop healthy dispositions. For him, instruction from home and other environments can school individuals to exert control of their impulses and thereby learn how to use them appropriately. But the individual also plays an active role in this process; through exerting self-discipline, a person can form a disposition that makes for a more healthy way of being. (Goleman 1995)

Of course, the idea that one can school impulses is not foreign to the Bible. One might reasonably argue that this schooling constitutes the chief purpose of some parts of the Bible such as the Wisdom Literature. Indeed, in *Character in Crisis*, William Brown offered this perspective. He demonstrated how the various books of the Wisdom Literature illuminate the formation, deformation and reformation of character. (Brown 1996) One can also argue that the biblical narrative of the fall illuminates the deformation of character and its concomitants. In some measure, it also implies the path that returns one to healthy character. (Headley 2006) From these latter perspectives, the schooling that makes for holy character fundamentally derives from God's initiative made real through prevenient grace. This constitutes the starting point for all meaningful changes in character; God's work and obedience to His precepts laid out in Scripture makes possible radical transformation at the core of one's being. However, because grace is cooperant, perspectives such as Goleman's carry some merit; through institutional impact and one's own disciplined action, one can help work out what God has worked in.

Dispositional Language and the Virtues

Running through the previously discussed authors is an idea I have not yet discussed. This common thread revolves around the concept of virtues. For example, though morality was not necessarily Goleman's chief concern, he connected the language of emotional intelligence to the idea of virtues. From his perspective, self-discipline and self-control, hallmarks of emotional intelligence, provided the basic building blocks for the virtuous life. (Goleman 1995) William Brown made a similar linkage of dispositional language to the virtues. In fact, he equated the virtues with dispositions. He noted: "Virtue is a disposition which denotes the pattern of choices an individual makes. Dispositions comprise persistent attitudes or "habits" of the heart and mind that dispose one to a consistency of action and expression." (Brown 1996, 9) In addition, drawing on insights from Aristotle and St. Thomas Aquinas, Brown made the following conclusions relative to virtues: First, a virtue exists both as a disposition and a standard to which one ought to measure up. Second, dispositions are founded on reason and serve as the springboard for ethical conduct. Furthermore, although dispositions embody enduring tendencies and can be equated with virtue, the latter do not remain static but exist as dynamic realities. (Brown 1996)

From these ideas one can conclude that holy dispositions are not simply related to virtues; in fact, they embody one aspect of what it means to be virtuous. In this sense they are more than feelings although containing some element of emotionality (Goleman 1995; Kilian and Parker 2001). But of course, standing dispositions do not automatically produce a virtuous life. They could just as easily produce a life characterized by vice and evil. As noted earlier, the virtuous nature of the life associated with the standing dispositions derives from the object of focus. If the heart is rightly oriented towards God and the individual forms a vital relationship with God, that relationship transforms one's being and character into a virtuous life. (Collins 2003; Collins 1998; Kilian and Parker 2001) Of course, the opposite is also true; when one focuses on that which is not God, one's being and character undergoes a process of deformation, producing a life marked by evil and vice.

Dispositional Love in Wesley's View of Christian Perfection

Having provided several bases for understanding the dispositions and linking it to the virtues, I now turn to a discussion of dispositional love in Wesley's view of Christian perfection. To begin, his idea of dispositional love shares many of the characteristics already discussed. For instance, one sees in him the three aspects of Land's typology - the objective, the relational, and the dispositional. He believed dispositional love pertained to the orientation of the heart towards God as object. (Collins 2003; Collins 1998; Wesley 1872b; Wesley 1872z) Furthermore, God was the fountain from which love sprung, and He shed his love in human hearts through the Holy Spirit. Additionally, by this same Spirit, He transformed the human heart. Moreover, Wesley believed this radical change in humans hearts could become the Christian's characteristic disposition. In keeping with this assessment, Collins noted that any proper understanding of Wesley's views in this matter needed to keep two aspects in mind: the idea of the orientation of the heart towards God and the transformation resulting from this relationship. (Collins 2003; Collins 1998) Of course, dispositional love also possesses a relational dimension; it moves Christians to love God and to also love their neighbor as themselves.

But love also possesses dispositional aspects; it transforms individuals from the inside out. According to Wesley's purposeful list, it sets the heart aright, changes one's thinking and rightly orders one's speech and actions. For Wesley, this type of holistic transformation constituted the virtuous life. Moreover, he considered the creation of virtuous character through God's transforming love the supreme goal of the Christian life. However, by virtuous character, he did not mean one accomplished by human standards and efforts at self-discipline. He thought such virtues derived from a concern for the comfort and decency of one's present life. Instead, he conceived virtues in a radical Christian way, associating these with the life of the world to come already begun in the human soul. As expressed in the Beatitudes, the virtuous life, seemingly couched in the language of future possibility, actually comes enveloped in the present and breaks into this world's reality. Through God's love, virtues associated with His future kingdom and thus considered *not yet* became visible and efficacious in the present life of the Christian. Thus, virtues such as humility, mercy, meekness and purity of heart became realities of this present age. This virtuous state came by faith through the activity of the Holy Spirit who actualized in the believer's life, the life of the world to come. Through the Spirit's presence, believers became subject to the laws of a heavenly world and this eventuated in different values governing the Christian's present life. Thus, Wesley wrote:

> Well may a man ask his own heart, whether it is able to admit the Spirit of God. For where that divine Guest enters, the laws of another world must be observed: The body must be given up to martyrdom, or spent in the Christian warfare, as unconcernedly as if the soul were already provided of its house from heaven; the goods of this world must he parted with as freely, as if the last fire were to seize them tomorrow; our neighbor must be loved as heartily as if he were washed from all his sins, and demonstrated to be a child of God by the resurrection from the dead. The fruits of this Spirit must not be mere moral virtues calculated for the comfort and decency of the present life; but holy dispositions, suitable to the instincts of a superior life already begun. (Wesley 1872f, 569)

As noted here, he saw the Holy Spirit playing the central role in making holy dispositions possible. (Wesley 1872f) Of course, since grace was also cooperant, the Spirit's action did not nullify human action in working out what God had worked in. However, God's work through the Holy Spirit played the initiative and pivotal role in forming holy dispositions. Furthermore, lying at the core of these renewed dispositions was the love of God made real in us through the Holy Spirit. For Wesley, this perfection of love meant that the virtues that existed in Christ became resident in the

Christian's life. (Wesley 1872a; Wesley 1872f; Wesley 1872i) This idea clearly appeared in Wesley's sermon, *The Circumcision of the Heart*. In it, he described circumcision of the heart in terms of the virtuous life. Circumcision of the heart involved for him: "... that habitual disposition of soul which, in the sacred writings, is termed holiness; and which directly implies, the being cleansed from sin, "from all filthiness both of flesh and spirit;" and, by consequence, the being endued with those virtues which were also in Christ Jesus; the being so "renewed in the spirit of our mind," as to be "perfect as our Father in heaven is perfect." (Wesley 1872a, 283)

But as one might observe here, Wesley firmly connected dispositions to the soul, the seat of human will and volition. (Wesley 1872u; Wesley 1872v) Being made holy meant that one's soul or heart was so moved by this new reality in such a way that love shaped the inward disposition of the Christian. This shaping made loving relationships the normal way of being for the Christian so transformed. Moreover, having one's heart circumcised meant a reorientation away from the creature and towards the creator. This indwelling love and reoriented stance became the characteristic way of being, described as a "habitual disposition of the soul." Wesley placed such emphasis on the soul or heart because he believed it lay at the very core of true religion. (Wesley 1872o; Wesley 1872p; Wesley 1872r; Wesley 1872v) He held tightly to this conviction, convinced that this reflected the scriptural view; namely that the heart served as the locus of God's activity in humans. Moreover, he also held to the primacy of the right heart. Some have used the term *Orthokardia* to describe this emphasis in Wesley. (Collins 1998; Land 1993; Leffel 2007; Strawn and Leffel 2001) This term underscores the necessity of the changed heart for the right functioning of the mind, sometimes referred to as *orthodoxy*, or right belief. (Clapper 1985a; Wesley 1997) However, although the right mind does include components of right belief, the term goes beyond this in Wesley. He associated right thinking with having the mind of Christ. Furthermore, he included in the latter term the idea of thinking as Christ thought and walking in the way he walked, demonstrated by the fruit of the Spirit. (Wesley 1872a; Wesley 1872i; Wesley 1872m; Wesley 1872q) These inward changes in heart and mind then give rise to right words and actions (*orthopraxis*). Tomas Špidlík also affirmed this central and critical role of the heart. In *The Art of Purifying the Heart*, quoting from the Russian spiritual writer, Theophan the Recluse, he wrote: "Our heart is truly the root and center of life. It reveals if a person's state is good or evil and incites the other forces to action and, after they have carried out their work, it receives within itself the results of these actions to strengthen or weaken that feeling which characterizes a person's permanent disposition. It seems, therefore, that controlling life should be conceded to the heart." (Špidlík 2010 9) Theophan, the Recluse largely echoed the biblical writer of the book of Proverbs who cautioned: "Above all else, guard your heart, for it is the wellspring of life." (Proverbs 4:23, NIV)

In speaking about dispositions, Wesley frequently employed affectional language to describe the transformation wrought in the human heart. Most frequently, he used the terms *tempers* and *affections*. However, as argued elsewhere in this book, terms such as *designs* and *desires* also constitute affectional language. Given the previous discussion of affectional language, I will not repeat it here. Nevertheless, from the earlier discussions it seemed clear that Wesley often referred to love as a temper. Furthermore, it was for him the master temper from which all other tempers and affections flowed. (Wesley 1872g; Wesley 1872y) Moreover, he often used the word temper and disposition interchangeably, denoting these as fixed dispositions of the soul. (Collins 2003; Collins 1998) Thus, one can conclude that Wesley saw dispositional love not as some transient thing. Rather, by the Holy Spirit's continued activity in the soul, love could become a fixed posture of one's life, creating enduring virtuous character in the life of the Believer.

The Transformative Power of Dispositional Love

Perhaps the most important reason for speaking about these terms is because of the role they play in the inner transformation of the Christian. Through the presence, work and activity of the Holy Spirit, God transforms the way one relates. But beyond this relational transformation, God's love transforms the Christian dispositionally, renewing and transforming him or her at the very core of their being. As a result, one begins to exemplify the very character of God as a stable habit. Moreover, because God is by nature love, this means that Christ-like transformation largely revolves around enhancing one's capacity to love. Indeed, it involves making love the chief characteristic of one's disposition. (Leffel 2007) But love as we saw also reshapes thinking in line with the mind of Christ. (Clapper 1987; Collins 1998; Leffel 2007; Strawn and Leffel 2001) This dual transformation of heart and mind constitutes inward holiness. However, inward holiness always works its way out in outward holiness, demonstrated in words and deeds. But even there exists mutuality in that outward holiness also shapes inward holiness. (Wesley 1872u) This is the trajectory Wesley captured in his purposeful list.

Transformation from the Inside out

Wesley provided an excellent example of this transformational path in his letter to Rev. Conyers Middleton. In one excerpt, he captured the components of the purposeful list in narrative form. Beginning with transformation in dispositional love, his narrative clearly illustrated the inside/out trajectory of Christian perfection. Although it entails a long segment, I have reproduced it here since it serves as a stunning example of his intentions. He wrote:

7. *And this universal, disinterested love is productive of all right affections.* It is fruitful of gentleness, tenderness, sweetness; of humanity, courtesy, and affability. It makes a Christian rejoice in the virtues of all, and bear a part in their happiness; at the same time that he sympathizes with their pains, and compassionates their infirmities. It creates modesty, condescension, prudence, together with calmness and evenness of temper. It is the parent of generosity, openness, and frankness, void of jealousy and suspicion. It begets candor, and willingness to believe and hope whatever is kind and friendly of every man; and invincible patience, never overcome of evil, but overcoming evil with good.

8. *The same love constrains him to converse, not only with a strict regard to truth, but with artless sincerity and genuine simplicity, as one in whom there is no guile.* And, not content with abstaining from all such expressions as are contrary to justice or truth, he endeavors to refrain from every unloving word, either to a present or of an absent person; in all his conversation aiming at this, either to improve himself in knowledge or virtue, or to make those with whom he converses some way wiser, or better, or happier than they were before.

9. *The same love is productive of all right actions.* It leads him into an earnest and steady discharge of all social offices, of whatever is due to relations of every kind; to his friends, to his country, and to any particular community, whereof he is a member. It prevents his willingly hurting or grieving any man. It guides him into an uniform practice of justice and mercy, equally extensive with the principle whence it flows. It constrains him to do all possible good, of every possible kind, to all men; and makes him invariably resolved, in every circumstance of life, to do that, and that only, to others, which, supposing he were himself in the same situation, he would desire they should do to him. (Wesley 1872d, 85-86 (Italics added))

In this excerpt, Wesley first described love as a master temper transforming other affections. This is reflected in the initial words of section seven; namely, "*And this universal, disinterested love is productive of all right affections.*" Here, he pictured a radical transformation of one's inner being in its varied aspects including in the affections and in one's mind. All these derived from the heart transformed by love. But this idea of love's fruitfulness in transforming inward attitudes appeared elsewhere. It appeared in the Sermon on the Mount, Discourse nine where he wrote: "Righteousness is the fruit of God's reigning in the heart. And what is righteousness, but love? — the love of God and of all mankind, flowing from faith in Jesus Christ, and producing humbleness of mind, meekness, gentleness, long-suffering, patience, deadness to the world; and every right disposition of heart, toward God and toward man. And by these it produces all holy actions, whatsoever are lovely or of good report; whatsoever works of faith and labor of love are acceptable to God, and profitable to man." (Wesley 1872y, 481) In this latter place, Wesley equated love with righteousness and pictured it as the by-product of God reigning in the heart; it also flowed from faith in Jesus Christ. But love's reign in the heart also transformed the interior life and produced all kind of godly fruit. Here, as in section seven of the letter, he likely envisioned the fruit of the Spirit laid out in Galatians 5: 22-23. These and other tempers served as evidence of love's inner transforming work. But beyond these named habits, he envisioned other transformations in one's tempers.

But in the excerpt of the letter to Rev. Middleton, Wesley presented us with a vital aspect of dispositional love; it is not passive but active. It acts in a variety of ways not only to transform one's inward, but also one's outward life. Accordingly, even in section seven, he discussed the various actions that result from love. He utilized several verbs to convey love's actions: verbs such as *creates, begets, constrains and makes*. At other times he employed phrases that carried the force of verbs (*is productive of, fruitful of, and the parent of*). By these, the message rings clear; disinterested love actively creates changes in our affections and our responses in the world. Transformed inner attitudes become visible in the world through words and actions. Perhaps Wesley meant to convey this same active nature of love in Discourse 9 of the Sermon on the Mount, previously referenced. In that latter place, he alluded to Philippians 4:8. The allusion suggests that holy actions are not simply worth thinking about but should be lived out in relation to others in the world.

But the movement of love from the heart into visible, action in the world also became clear when Wesley transitioned to sections eight and nine. However, in speaking about outward holiness made visible in word and action, he emphasized the same source – disinterested love. One easily detects this in the recurring phrase *the same love* in sections eight and nine. The phrase harked back to disinterested love in section seven. Thus, he began sections eight and nine by reminding the reader that the love that transforms affections and one's interior disposition is the same love that transforms word and deed. In section eight, the phrase read: "The same love constrains him to converse...." He followed this with a discussion of the ways in which love transforms speech. In addition, he noted the characteristics of this speech in relation to self and others. For Wesley, love transformed the Christian's speech so that it becomes characterized by truth, justice, simplicity and a general lack of subterfuge. But these outward qualities of speech also reflected the Christian's character denoting him or her as a "Nathaniel," in whom is no guile. Section nine reiterated the impact of dispositional love, this time in terms of action and displayed in the phrase: "The same love is productive of all right actions." Following, he discussed one's social obligations in the world. Moreover, one's actions in the world reflected not only love but also intentionality. Thus, he indicated that one's action should proceed from a pure intention whereby one did not willingly intend to hurt another. Everywhere in these sections, the message rung clear: inward attitudes of the heart, beginning in love must make themselves visible in one's word and work.

Transformation of Affections and Passions

In the referenced letter, one also discovers an implicit reference to love's ability to moderate and balance the affections and passions. Moderation of the affections appeared within section seven. Here, Wesley indicated the ways in which love transformed the affections. It produced affections characterized by habits such as gentleness, tenderness and sweetness of personality. Love also changed the passions. Passions typically refer to sudden expressions that create a kind of emotional hijack. In these situations, a person appears more prone to act by impulse and less governed by their minds. (Clapper 1985b; Collins 1998) Thus, in the letter, he depicted dispositional love giving rise to impulse control. As a result, one was less moved by sudden passions and became more tempered and moderate. What's more, this control and moderation involved the interior life and external conduct demonstrated in words and actions. Relative to the interior life, he spoke of how love contributed to "calmness and evenness of temper." Later, he referenced control of one's words; namely, refraining from unloving words and other expressions contrary to truth and justice. Finally, he implied judicious action tempered by good intentions. In these emphases, he seems to have captured Goleman's more recent emphasis on impulse control and delayed gratification as hallmarks of character. (Goleman 1995)

Even if these statements appear to infer too much from Wesley's letter, this line of thinking finds support elsewhere in his writings. In those places it appears patently clear that he saw love moderating the affections and passions and providing a degree of mastery over sudden impulse. For example, this emphasis appeared in his third discourse on the Sermon on the Mount. Speaking of those made pure in heart by love, he described them as purified "... from every unholy affection." Later, he referred to the passions noting, "They are through the power of his grace, purified from pride, by the deepest poverty of spirit; from anger, from every unkind or turbulent passion, by meekness and gentleness." (Wesley 1872t, 365) In discourse two on the Sermon on the Mount, he had made the same emphasis; while speaking of meekness, he addressed its role in balancing the affections: Meekness, according to him, "keeps clear of every extreme, whether in excess or defect. It does not destroy but balance the affections, which the God of nature never designed should be rooted out by grace, but only brought and kept under due regulations. It poises the mind aright. It holds an even scale, with regard to anger, and sorrow, and fear; reserving the mean in every circumstance of life, and not declining either to the right hand or the left." (Wesley 1872s, 348) Later, in this discourse, he specifically mentioned love's balancing of the passions in those who are meek. Here, he employed very similar language regarding the passions as he had made relative to the affections:

"They who are truly meek, can clearly discern what is evil; and they can also suffer it. They are sensible of everything of this kind, but still meekness holds the reins. They are exceeding "zealous for the Lord of Hosts;" but their zeal is always guided by knowledge, and tempered, in every thought, and word, and work, with the love of man, as well as the love of God. They do not desire to extinguish any of the passions which God has for wise ends implanted in their nature; but they have the mastery of all: They hold them all in subjection, and employ them only in subservience to those ends. And thus even the harsher and more unpleasing passions are applicable to the noblest purposes; even hatred, and anger, and fear, when engaged against sin, and regulated by faith and love, are as walls and bulwarks to the soul, so that the wicked one cannot approach to hurt it" (Wesley 1872s, 348)

According to Wesley, knowledge and love tempers zeal which is in many respects synonymous with passion. This tempering does not render zeal powerless but gives it more appropriate expression. As such, one's passion and zeal, like the affections, should not be destroyed but mastered and controlled. After all, passions and affections did not come into being by accident or human whim. Rather, they existed by divine design; God Himself placed them within humans and they can be marshaled to wise and holy ends. Like a fire, when unchecked, passions can run amok and cause deep harm. But again like fire, duly controlled, guided and mastered by divine love, affections and passions can serve the greater good and render holy service. In fact, even the harsher passions such as hatred, anger and fear can be recruited to noble ends, including playing an effective role in the struggle against sin. In Wesley's discussions one clearly discerns this regulatory function of love; love served as a control mechanism that balanced and disciplined human attitudes and reactions. Moreover, this happened without dulling the nature or wholesomeness of these intense human reactions. (Wynkoop 1972) Ultimately, love's dispositional transformation produces a mature Christian, or "a real Christian." (Collins 2003; Wesley 1872v; Wesley 1872p)

Christian Transformation through Interpersonal Relationships

But dispositional changes in all forms do not exist apart from relationship with others. In Wesley's thought, holy dispositions and changes in the affections and passions required the work of God, but also necessitated contact with others. As a result, the three sections of the letter to Rev. Middleton teemed with an emphasis on intrapersonal changes firmly tied to interpersonal contact. For Wesley, the cultivation of individual virtues was not a solitary matter; rather, nurture of the virtuous life demanded interpersonal relationships with Christians and non-Christians. Thus, he began the excerpt with a focus on affectional transformation that occurred in an interpersonal context. This extreme makeover largely equated to possessing the fruit of the Spirit. In this case, his choice of the term *is fruitful of* immediately followed by gentleness, a clear fruit of the Spirit, likely conveyed this intent. In keeping with this, he immediately addressed several other internal attitudes of the heart such as tenderness and courtesy. Later in this same paragraph, he highlighted habits such as modesty, prudence, calmness and evenness of temper. In addition to the fruit of the Spirit, he might also have envisaged the virtues; several of the named qualities like prudence and self-control (calmness, evenness of temper) directly relates to the virtues, particularly the moral and intellectual virtues. (Sire 2000) But even when one engaged in outward actions such as speech, one remained critically aware of its potential intrapersonal impact; it can influence one's interior being, producing knowledge or contributing to virtue.

No wonder he described the Christian faith as a social religion! (Wesley 1872s; Wesley 1872u) For him, community played an indispensable role in Christian living. (Langford 1980) In fact, Christian faith could not exist without interaction with Christians and non-Christians. (Wesley 1872u) In a similar vein, Brown, Dahl and Reuschling offered the following: "Both our sense of the self and our image of the whole and holy person are shaped and supported - or subverted and suppressed - by the social contexts in which we are located and in which we become." (Brown, Dahl, and Reuschling 2011, 2) In others words, in the crucible of relationships, especially caring ones, individuals experience the possibility of becoming holy. Wesley knew and affirmed this. He also knew relationships carried definitive benefits for transformed Christians as well as those with whom they relate.

What are the implications for dispositional changes in the Christian as it relates to interpersonal contact? First, social contact impacted the individual Christian's disposition; it fostered and enhanced character and transformation. Moreover, through contact with others, even unbelievers, one's transformed tempers become exercised. Wesley even addressed the impact of the non-Christian on a Christian in his fourth discourse on the Sermon on the Mount. The text for this sermon was Matthew 5:13-16 and pertained to the Christian being salt and light in the world. As such, the passage primarily focused on the ways in which the Christian can impact the world. However, although Wesley addressed this perspective, he also spoke to how the Christian's connection to non-Christians can facilitate transformation in the former. Thus, he wrote:

> Much more the words of our Lord; who is so far from directing us to break off all commerce with the world, that without it, according to his account of Christianity, we cannot be Christians at all. It would be easy to show, that some intercourse even with ungodly and unholy men is absolutely needful, in order to the full exertion of every temper which he has described as the way to the kingdom; that it is indispensably necessary, in order to the complete exercise of poverty of spirit, of mourning, and of every other disposition which has a place here, in the genuine religion of Jesus Christ.(Wesley 1872u, 386-387)

As seen here, such contact served to exercise and enhance godly attitudes. Specifically, Wesley resurrected the attitudes listed in the Beatitudes. Here, he named poverty of spirit and mourning. Later, he mentioned others such as meekness, mercifulness, blessing those who curse use, and praying for those who use and persecute us. But he intended more than the virtues listed in the sermon; he also envisioned other virtues consistent with a transformed heart. But without real-time and real-life contact in the world, these attitudes and tempers could not be exercised and enhanced. Contact solely with other Christians would not suffice; one also needed contact with non-believers if one would sharpen their tempers and affections. (Wesley 1872u)

Interpersonal Relationships as Feedback

Along a similar line, contact with non-believers and believers alike served as a kind of feedback system. That is, it provided a measure that permitted judgment about where one stood in relation to love and the dispositions fostered by it. For example, contact with others might help the Christian discern whether one truly acted out of love. It might also help one discern whether the dispositions consistent with love actually inhabited one's life. Likewise, contact with others helped the Christian judge the primary object of one's love; it facilitated discerning whether one had allowed others to replace God in one's affections. In Wesley's view, even the most devout believer can at times shift their love away from God as the primary object of their affection. When this happens, one is prone to make other objects the focus of one's life; one comes to love the creature more than the creator (Romans 1:25). (Wesley 1872k; Wesley 1872y) This shift might even involve legitimate love objects such as parents, child or spouse; that is, we might place these persons above our love for God, essentially replacing God with them in our affections. At other times, the Christian might find himself or herself drawn away toward inanimate objects and becoming obsessed with "the desire of the flesh," "the desire of the eye," or "the pride of life."(Wesley 1872k, 236)

Contact with others also tested love of neighbor. It helped one discern whether love truly marks those relationships or whether tempers inconsistent with love have arisen in our hearts. Thus, he wrote:

> And do we not feel other tempers, which are as contrary to the love of our neighbor as these are to the love of God? The love of our neighbor "thinketh no evil." Do not we find anything of the kind? Do we never find any *jealousies*, any *evil surmisings*, any groundless or unreasonable suspicions? He that is clear in these respects, let him cast the first stone at his neighbor. Who does not sometimes feel other tempers or inward motions, which he knows are contrary to brotherly love? If nothing of *malice*, *hatred*, or *bitterness*, is there no touch of envy; particularly toward those who enjoy

some real or supposed good, which we desire but cannot attain? Do we never find any degree of *resentment*, when we are injured or affronted; especially by those whom we peculiarly loved, and whom we had most labored to help or oblige? Does injustice or ingratitude never excite in us any desire of *revenge*? any desire of returning evil for evil, instead of "overcoming evil with good?" This also shows, how much is still in our heart, which is contrary to the love of our neighbor.(Wesley 1872k, 237-238)

Thus, social contact served as testing ground for Christian love and the tempers that arise from it. It also illuminated one's life, bringing to light the tempers that stand contrary to true brotherly love. In short, interpersonal contact revealed the true and current state of the Christian's heart. As one peruses these words from *The Repentance of Believers*, several observations become apparent. First, the words denote the possible shifting status of the believer's heart. Second, all of the words conjure up the interpersonal dimension relative to dispositional change; they all represent attitudes and behaviors that arise in interpersonal situations. Thus, Wesley mentioned negative attitudes such as jealousy, suspicion, malice, hatred and bitterness. Additionally, he mentioned other behaviors such as seeking revenge and overcoming evil with good. All these filled out his meaning of "thinketh no evil." But he also likely meant to bring two allusions to the mind of the hearer. First, because the phrase likely derived from I Corinthians 13:5, he possibly intended to bring to mind the description of love described there. In that context, the phrase stands embedded in a section outlining characteristics inconsistent with and those demonstrating love. It makes sense that he would reference this passage since his purpose captured part of Paul's intent. Second, he likely intended that the phrase would conjure up the idea of having the mind of Christ demonstrated in the fruit of the Spirit. Interestingly, in Galatians 5 where the fruit of the Spirit appear, Paul equated the call to love one's neighbor with life in the Spirit. For Paul, living the life of love means walking and being led by the Spirit. This Spirit-infused life gave rise to internal attitudes revealed in interpersonal behavior (Galatians 5:22-23). But prior to discussing these attitudes, Paul highlighted those things that were contrary to love. (Galatians 5:19-21) Not surprisingly, these characteristics largely involve interpersonal contact. The message is patently clear in all of these instances: one cannot experience dispositional transformation apart from contact with others. This was Paul's message and Wesley followed in his train.

Wesley's Intentional Methods for Interpersonal Contact

Of course, this path to holy transformation was not left to chance in the Methodist movement; at least not when it involved contact with other Christians and those desiring to work out salvation. In 1739, Wesley began the United Societies in London which he would later replicate in places like

Bristol, Kingswood and Newcastle-upon-Tyne. (Wesley 1872e) He described these societies in the following manner:

> Such a society is no other than "a company of men having the form and seeking the power of godliness, united in order to pray together, to receive the word of exhortation, and to watch over one another in love, that they may help each other to work out their salvation." (Wesley 1872e, 301)

This statement largely explicated critical membership criteria for society members; they should evidence a desire for salvation and be prepared to work hard at it. Furthermore, such godly desire necessitated three commitments from members: doing no harm and avoiding evil; doing good in all its various forms, and attending the ordinances of God. (Wesley 1872e) These purposes were partly facilitated through division into classes. About twelve persons comprised a class with one individual designated as its leader. The class leader met each person at least once a week to inquire about the state of that individual's soul. These responsibilities placed class leaders in pastoral care roles; they advised, reproved, comforted and exhorted those placed under their care. Moreover, they reported to the minister and stewards those who were infirmed or who walked disorderly and would not receive correction. Beyond these pastoral care functions, the class leader received from those under their care, any relief given for the poor. They also paid the actual monies to the stewards and provided an account of these funds. (Wesley 1872e)

Wesley's bands also supported transformation through interpersonal contact. According to him, the bands provided a place where Christians could live out the meaning of James 5:16; together they could confess faults and pray for one another for healing. (Wesley 1872l) At the least, the bands met on a weekly basis with the expressed purpose of facilitating mutual transformation. Wesley noted that the bands were designed so that Christians could "...speak each of us in order, freely and plainly, the true state of our souls, with the faults we have committed in thought, word, or deed, and the temptations we have felt, since our last meeting." (Wesley 1872l, 305) Members first shared about the state of their own soul. Following this, they queried other members about "their state, sins and temptations." The prescribed questions went beyond scratching the surface of Christian experience. Beyond questions about one's sins, experience of peace with God and having the love of God, members of the bands responded to the following:

> Has no sin, inward or outward, dominion over you?
>
> Do you desire to be told of your faults?
>
> Do you desire to be told of all your faults, and that plain and home?
>
> Do you desire that every one of us should tell you, from time to time, whatsoever is in his heart concerning you?

Consider! Do you desire we should tell you whatsoever we think, whatsoever we fear, whatsoever we hear, concerning you?

Do you desire that, in doing this, we should come as close as possible, that we should cut to the quick, and search your heart to the bottom?

Is it your desire and design to be on this, and all other occasions, entirely open, so as to speak everything that is in your heart without exception, without disguise, and without reserve? (Wesley 1872l, 306)

Beyond these searching and selective used questions, members responded to the four following questions at every meeting: 1. What known sins have you committed since our last meeting? 2. What temptations have you met with? 3. How were you delivered? 4. What have you thought, said, or done, of which you doubt whether it be sin or not? (Wesley 1872l, 306) By shaping Christian interaction in such an intentional manner, Wesley provided ample opportunity for believers to experience spiritual progress. Salvation might begin with an individual's response to God's prevenient grace. However, growth in grace largely involved a communal process. Through contact with others, "iron sharpened iron," and helped move the Christian on to Christ-like perfection. Through shaping interpersonal contact within the Methodist societies, Wesley saw to it that this important task would not be left to chance.

Dispositional Love and the Transformation of Others

So far, I have largely focused on intrapersonal and dispositional changes in Christians flowing from contact with others. But dispositional change in individual Christians always carries an interpersonal intent. Moreover, this intent involves more that transforming the quality of relationships. If it is not simply for transforming relationships, what then is its other goal? Fundamentally, God intends that Christians transformed by love help foster transformation in others. Wesley emphasized this in his fourth discourse on the Sermon on the Mount:

> "...the providence of God has so mingled you together with other men, that whatever grace you have received of God may through you be communicated to others; that every holy temper and word and work of yours may have an influence on them also. By this means a check will, in some measure, be given to the corruption which is in the world; and a small part, at least, saved from the general infection, and rendered holy and pure before God. (Wesley 1872u, 387)

As indicated here, God intended the Christian's contact with others to communicate grace. Specifically, He intended that personal transformation in inward and outward holiness stimulate and foster similar change in others. In other words, grace in the Christian begets grace in others; intrapersonal transformation begets transformed dispositions in others. As a result, such persons also become holy and pure in God's sight. In clarifying this purpose in the quotation above, Wesley invoked the purposeful list; he made reference to transformed tempers (orthokardia) leading to transformed practice in word and work (orthopraxis). Furthermore, in this same quotation, he presented the Christian's presence in the world as a check to the spreading infection of sin. This goal became accomplished directly and indirectly through the Christian's godly influence. In the first case, the Christian directly checked the spread of sin through godly being and behavior. But indirectly and through godly influence on others, the Christian fostered holy behavior, creating yet another bastion against sin.

But the Christian's presence as salt and light in the world also impacted society in other ways. These additional benefits appeared in Wesley's words to the Rev. Conyers Middleton, previously quoted. (Wesley 1872d) The world directly benefits from the Christian's transformed tempers. Dispositional love created a complex of positive qualities producing a winsomeness displayed in relationships. Specifically, disinterested love in the Christian begat "...gentleness, tenderness, sweetness; of humanity, courtesy, and affability." (Wesley 1872d, 85) In addition, it fostered characteristics such as modesty, prudence, generosity and hoping and expecting the best in others. Ultimately, it aimed to always overcome evil with good. (Wesley 1872d) In a word, God's transforming love in the Christian provides the possibility of a positive and beneficial experience when others interact with this changed individual. In a world where many appear brusque, dismissive and generally unconcerned in relationships, this winsome and caring spirit is indeed a gift to the world.

But the world also benefits from the Christian's transformed words and actions. Wesley referenced both in the previously cited excerpt from the letter to Rev. Middleton. In section 8, he spoke about the interpersonal impact of words; the Christian refrained from unloving and hurtful speech. Instead, the believer placed a premium on simplicity, justice, truth and words that stimulate virtue. The Christian remained well aware that speech seasoned with salt, possessed the ability to make others "...wiser, or better, or happier than they were before." (Wesley 1872d, 86) But these benefits did not simply pertain to worldly blessings. In fact, in speaking about an increase in wisdom, betterment and happiness, Wesley envisioned spiritual blessings. One can discern this idea from the terms employed. For example, he almost always tied happiness to holiness. True happiness sprung from the holiness of a transformed life. (Langford 1980; Wesley 1872h; Wesley 1872r; Wesley 1872z) Therefore, in wishing for a wiser, better and happier life, he primarily desired holy transformation in others.

In section 9, Wesley also spoke to the benefits for society which derived from the Christian's actions in the world. Here, he noted how disinterested love fostered care for others; it caused the believer to exhibit sympathy and compassion for others in their infirmities. But this involved more than sentimentality; rather, these sentiments precipitated action. Moved by generosity and compassion, the Christian sought to alleviate suffering in others. Moreover, the Christian engaged in an honest discharge of social responsibilities to the world and in general aimed for the uniformed practice of justice and mercy. (Wesley 1872d) Guided by the golden rule and moved by love, the Christian aimed to do all good to all persons, all the while avoiding intentional harm to others. This good includes bringing relief to the poor and a general display of charity in deeds. (Wesley 1872n; Wesley 1872r; Wesley 1872s)

But Wesley did not ascribe to a generic idea of goodness; goodness remained theological at its base and in its content. Given this understanding, he described good works as possessing several qualities: Good deeds always sprung from faith in God and in faithfulness to his commands. Additionally, it was the presence and power of the Holy Spirit that made good deeds possible. Finally, good deeds sprung from good designs and produced good ends. (Wesley 1872j, 486-560) Wesley also considered the internal and external characteristics of good works. Good deeds could only proceed from a heart made holy by God's love. This radical transformation predisposed believers to love all persons as God's creatures and to express this in loving deeds. But in the external sense, good works constituted an example of outward holiness. Given their importance, Wesley believed Christians were obligated to engage in them whenever opportunity allowed. But even in the absence of such opportunities, the Christian carried a desire to practice them. (Wesley 1872j) Through these deeds, and by the power and presence of the Spirit, the Christian could help transform others into holy followers of God.

Chapter 7
Christian Perfection and the Means of Grace

I became a Christian in a church that strongly and consistently taught Christian holiness. However, I cannot recall hearing anyone specifically mention or discuss the means of grace. The pastors admonished us to attend the services of the church, pray and read scripture. As a result, we participated in some of the ordinances. But as far as I can recall, the term itself never came up. It would not surprise me if others like me might have had this experience. Yet with Wesley, I have come to believe that any discussion of Christian perfection should include a discussion about the means of grace. But before delving too deeply into this conversation, it seems useful to pause and describe what Wesley meant by *means of grace*. Although it's easy to assume familiarity with this language, as demonstrated by my early Christian experience, this seems unwarranted; many Christians, even if they participate in God's ordinances, may remain ignorant and devoid of any understanding of the means of grace or their nature.

Wesley himself provided a rather succinct description. He wrote: "By "means of grace" I understand outward signs, words, or actions, ordained of God, and appointed for this end, to be the ordinary channels whereby he might convey to men, preventing, justifying, or sanctifying grace." (Wesley 1872f, 266) More recently, Mann described them as "... those activities which serve to actualize grace in our lives by enhancing our capacity for ever greater receptivity and responsiveness to God's call." (Mann 2006, 167) These definitions provide a glimpse in to the broad scope covered by the means of grace.

The Instituted Means of Grace

Wesley himself used the language of *instituted* and *prudential* means of grace to refer to these ordinances. By *instituted*, he meant those things clearly established in Scripture. (Wesley 1872g, 345-398) In *Minutes of*

Several Conversations Between The Rev. Mr. Wesley and Others, he provided the following statements about the instituted means of grace:

> The INSTITUTED are,
>
> (1.) Prayer; private, family, public; consisting of deprecation, petition, intercession, and thanksgiving. Do you use each of these? Do you use private prayer every morning and evening? if you can, at five in the evening; and the hour before or after morning preaching? Do you forecast daily, wherever you are, how to secure these hours? Do you avow it everywhere? Do you ask everywhere, "Have you family prayer?" Do you retire at five o'clock?
>
> (2.) Searching the Scriptures by, (i.) Reading: Constantly, some part of everyday; regularly, all the Bible in order; carefully, with the Notes; seriously, with prayer before and after; fruitfully, immediately practicing what you learn there? (ii.) Meditating: At set times? by any rule? (iii.) Hearing: Every morning? carefully; with prayer before, at, after; immediately putting in practice? Have you a New Testament always about you?
>
> (3.) The Lord's supper: Do you use this at every opportunity? With solemn prayer before; with earnest and deliberate self-devotion?
>
> (4.) Fasting: How do you fast every Friday?
>
> (5.) Christian conference: Are you convinced how important and how difficult it is to "order your conversation right?" Is it "always in grace? seasoned with salt? meet to minister grace to the hearers?" Do not you converse too long at a time? Is not an hour commonly enough? Would it not be well always to have a determinate end in view; and to pray before and after it?(Wesley 1872g, 377-378)

As noted in this section, he named five specific means of grace endorsed by Scripture. These included prayers, The Lord's Supper, fasting, Christian conferencing and reading the Scriptures. In relation to reading Scripture, he understood this to include actual reading as well as hearing and meditating on the same. (Wesley 1872f) Moreover, he sometimes referred to prayers, whether public or private, partaking of the Lord's Supper and searching the Scriptures as the chief means of grace. These he saw as the ordinary channels God used to convey grace. (Wesley 1872f) But Wesley endorsed other means of grace; he saw frequenting the house of God, that is, church attendance, as an instituted means of grace. (Wesley 1872a; Wesley 1872d) He attached great importance to this ordinance; in fact, he perceived it as so important that he exhorted attendance at the church service even when the minister was ungodly. For Wesley, any ordinance of God could transmit grace even if performed by an ungodly person. Thus, along with the Church of England, he affirmed that the unworthiness of a minister did not nullify the ordinance of God: "... because the efficacy is derived, not from him that administers, but from Him that ordains it. He does not, will not suffer his grace to be intercepted, though the messenger will not receive it himself." (Wesley 1872h, 212) He also seemed to include the covenant service among the means of grace. On January 3, 1790, he wrote in his journal: "I suppose near two thousand met at the new chapel to renew their covenant with God; a scriptural means of grace which is now almost everywhere forgotten except among the Methodists." (Wesley 1872b, 525-526)

He also considered all the ordinances mentioned above as works of piety. (Wesley 1872f) These he saw as God's normal channels for conveying grace to humans. (Wesley 1872i) But besides these, he discussed works of mercy as being real instituted means of grace. In *On Visiting the Sick*, after speaking about works of piety as means of grace, he quickly proceeded to ask: "But are they the only means of grace? Are there no other means than these, whereby God is pleased, frequently, yea, Ordinarily to convey his grace to them that either love or fear him? Surely there are works of mercy, as well as works of piety, which are real means of grace. They are more especially such to those that perform them with a single eye. And those that neglect them, do not receive the grace which otherwise they might. Yea, and they lose, by a continual neglect, the grace which they had received." (Wesley 1872i, 139) Wesley followed these words with a discussion on visiting the sick. Surprisingly, by the sick, he did not simply mean the bedridden, (although he likely did not exclude them). Rather, he meant those who were afflicted in body or mind. The latter group included those suffering from despondency and anxiety. In Wesley's view, works of mercy should extend to illnesses of both body and mind. Moreover, it should extend to all, regardless of moral or religious state; that is, it should extend to the evil and good, to those who feared God and those who did not. (Wesley 1872i) Furthermore, this type of visiting could not be done from a distance; rather, it required face-to-face visiting. Without face-to-face visitation, one lost an excellent opportunity to exercise this means of grace. But visiting did not only benefit the one suffering from illness; it also benefited the visitor. Thus, concerning those who failed to visit face to face, he remarked: "... you lose an excellent means of increasing your thankfulness to God, who saves you from this pain and sickness, and continues your health and strength; as well as of increasing your sympathy with the afflicted, your benevolence, and all social affections." (Wesley 1872i, 141)

The Prudential Means of Grace

Wesley's definition of the means of grace as God-ordained signs, words and actions largely pertained to the instituted means of grace. But he believed there existed other means that served the life of faith. He referred to these as *prudential*. By using this word, he meant that they were not ordained or instituted by Scripture. According to him, Scripture does not always provide specific but general rules; it leaves some particulars to be worked out according to common sense. (Wesley 1872k) Accordingly, prudential means of grace involved those particulars of Christian life and practice worked out on the basis of reason and experience. Because no scriptural mandate existed for these practices, he did not deem them essential. However, they permitted one "to apply the general rules given in Scripture according to particular circumstances." (Wesley 1872k, 290) Dean Blevins echoed Wesley in relation to the circumstantial nature of the prudential means of grace. He saw them as contextual in nature, varying by age, culture and person, depending on the times and circumstances. (Blevins 1997) Wesley himself described the prudential means of grace in the following language:

> "PRUDENTIAL MEANS we may use either as common Christians, as Methodists, as Preachers, or as Assistants.
>
> (1.) As common Christians. What particular rules have you in order to grow in grace? What arts of holy living?
>
> (2.) As Methodists. Do you never miss your class, or Band?
>
> (3.) As Preachers. Do you meet every society; also the Leaders and Bands, if any?
>
> (4.) As Assistants. Have you thoroughly considered your office; and do you make a conscience of executing every part of it?
>
> These means may be used without fruit: But there are some means which cannot; namely, watching, denying ourselves, taking up our cross, exercise of the presence of God.
>
> (1.) Do you steadily watch against the world, the devil, yourselves, your besetting sin?
>
> (2.) Do you deny yourself every useless pleasure of sense, imagination, honor? Are you temperate in all things? instance in food: Do you use only that kind and that degree which is best both for your body and soul? Do you see the necessity of this?
>
> (3.) Do you eat no flesh suppers? no late suppers?
>
> (4.) Do you eat no more at each meal than is necessary? Are you not heavy or drowsy after dinner?
>
> (5.) Do you use only that kind and that degree of drink which is best both for your body and soul?
>
> (6.) Do you drink water? Why not? Did you ever? Why did you leave it off? If not for health, when will you begin again? today?
>
> (7.) How often do you drink wine or ale? everyday? Do you want it?
>
> (8.) Wherein do you "take up your cross daily?" Do you cheerfully bear your cross (whatever is grievous to nature) as a gift of God, and labor to profit thereby?
>
> (9.) Do you endeavor to set God always before you; to see his eye continually fixed upon you? Never can you use these means but a blessing will ensue. And the more you use them, the more will you grow in grace." (Wesley 1872g 377-379)

This discussion contains several interesting elements worthy of note. First, one notes that Wesley recommended these means of grace for all Christians including clergy and lay. Second, it appears that prudential means of grace could be incorporated into a *rule of life*. As such, he inquired about the Christian's rules for growing in grace. By implementing such rules one would foster the holy life. Third, it appears evident that he saw participation in classes or bands as means of grace. He demonstrated this connection between the classes and bands and the means of grace elsewhere. For example, in a letter written in 1748 to Rev. Perronet, Vicar of Shoreham, Wesley described the class meetings and the bands as prudential helps. (Wesley 1872k) Fourth, it appears that he saw the prudential means of grace as rules whereby leaders within the societies might exercise their functions responsibly.

But, from Wesley's perspective, not all means of grace produced fruit. But some existed that invariably produced fruit. Among the latter, he named Christians watching, practicing self-denial, taking up the cross and practicing the presence of God. However, he did not specifically name the fruit that resulted from these. He likely intended the fruit of the Spirit. But he might also have intended fruit to mean receiving a blessing from God and further growth in grace. Thus, he specifically mentioned these latter benefits at the end of the quoted material. But instead of growing in grace, one can become stunted. From his perspective, this often occurred because one failed to practice the means of grace. But if one indeed practiced the means of grace and yet failed to grow, the lack of self-denial and taking up one's cross invariably were the main culprits. (Wesley 1872p) Wesley made this explicit assertion in *Self-Denial*. There, he wrote: "... it is always owing to the want either of self-denial, or taking up his cross, that any man does not thoroughly follow Him, is not fully a disciple of Christ." (Wesley 1872p, 131) In many respects, this connection makes sense. For Wesley, self-denial was "... the denying or refusing to follow our own will, from a conviction that the will of God is the only rule of action to us." (Wesley 1872p, 127) But over against self-denial stands its polar opposite, namely, self-will. Self-will short-circuits self-denial and actively stands in opposition to the love of God. (Wesley 1872c; Wesley 1872m; Wesley 1872n; Wesley 1872z) Thus, to live without self-denial means that one has chosen one's own path and will against the acknowledged will of God. Living out this rebellious stance hinders God's blessings, growth in grace and living fully as a disciple of Jesus Christ.

Prudential Means of Grace: Spiritual and Physical

The questions Wesley raised concerning the prudential means of grace revolved around exercising moral rectitude and engaging in habits that benefit morally and physically. From these, one clearly sees his concern for the soul and the body. Given his interest in health and the art of healing demonstrated in *Primitive Physic*, this emphasis on physical well-being should not surprise. (Wesley 1872l) However, the questions also demonstrate that he considered physical habits means of grace. This conclusion derives from several observations. First, the questions about one's physical state appeared in his queries about the prudential means of grace. Accordingly, such measures should be understood in this light. Second, he evidently saw both spiritual and physical practices as extremely important to the well-being of his helpers (and to Christians in general). This conclusion appeared even prior to the detailed discussion of the instituted and prudential means of grace described earlier. Prior to this discussion, he responded to a larger question as to whether Methodists sufficiently watched over their helpers. (Wesley 1872g) In answer, he asked several questions pertaining to both the soul and body. In relation to the soul, he asked about one's walk with God and fellowship with the Father and the Son. But alongside these, and in relation to the body, he asked about the time one rose from bed and morning and evening retirement. He concluded these initial questions by asking "Do you use all the means of grace yourself, and enforce the use of them on all other persons? (Wesley 1872g, 376) Here too, the context supports physical measures as means of grace just like spiritual activities. Third, in questions 2 and 5, Wesley inquired about the use of food and drink respectively. After question 2, pertaining to food, he asked about the kind of food and the amount consumed. In question 5, he asked about drink and in the following two questions he inquired about the use of water, wine and ale. Significantly, both opening questions about food and drink displayed the same format. In relation to food, Wesley inquired: "Do you use only that kind and that degree which is best both for your body and soul?" (Wesley 1872g, 378) Next, in relation to drink, he asked: "Do you use only that kind and that degree of drink which is best both for your body and soul?" (Wesley 1872g, 379) These questions suggest that he thought that what one ate and drank carried implications for spiritual and physical health. Finally, at the end of this whole section, Wesley offered: "Never can you use these means but a blessing will ensue. And the more you use them, the more will you grow in grace." (Wesley 1872g, 379) One can only conclude that this statement applies to all that had gone before; namely, the instituted and prudential means as well everything that pertained to soul and body.

In fact, one should see prudential means of grace as comprising a wider range of activities beyond those named. Any practice that facilitates growth in grace could by Wesley's description constitute a means of grace. His sermon *The Means of Grace* seems to include this broad definition. Here, while speaking about how God might bring a sinner to faith, he wrote: "To one who begins to feel the weight of his sins, not only hearing the word of God, but reading it too, and perhaps other serious books, may be a means of deeper conviction." (Wesley 1872f, 279) For him, God even used books beyond holy writ as a means of fostering conviction and promoting movement through the states of grace. Given this thought, one should consider such reading as a means of grace. This understanding of the means of grace fits well with the broad definition espoused by Mann. As one might recall, Mann defined means of grace as "...those activities which serve to actualize grace in our lives by enhancing our capacity for ever greater receptivity and responsiveness to God's call." (Mann 2006, 167) This definition invites us to consider a wide range of activities and practices based on reason and experiences as legitimate means of grace.

Making Null the Means of Grace

From this discussion, Wesley evidently held a high view of the means of grace. By these means, God conveyed grace. As such, he advocated participation in them whenever an opportunity availed itself. (Wesley 1872o) Furthermore, even those seekers without faith should participate in them. Rather than waiting in stillness as some advocated, the way to wait for Christ was by using all the means of grace. (Wesley 1872o) However, even in his societies, some held different views. Some held too little a view of the means of grace, even denouncing participation in them. Wesley apparently struggled with this issue in his infant societies from around 1739. An excerpt from his journal from Sunday November 4, 1739 provided a glimpse into the difficulties around this issue in the Fetter Lane Society. In the excerpt, he noted how some had intimated a lack of true faith in the women at Fetter Lane. Furthermore, they asserted that until these women received faith they should remain still. By *still,* they meant abstaining from any means of grace and in particular, the Lord's Supper. Moreover, they insisted Christ was the only means of grace; besides him, none other existed. (Wesley 1872d) Given these views, they advocated leaving off all participation in the ordinances of God.

Unfortunately, this teaching, promulgated by some Moravians especially in 1739-1740, led some astray. However, Wesley was careful not to lay the blame at the door of the Moravian Church itself. In a letter from September 8, 1746, he detailed aspects of this controversy, even noting those who had explicitly taught others to be still and ignore the ordinances of God. (Wesley 1872e) Specifically, he mentioned one Mr. Molther. On December 31, 1739, Mr. Molther had explicitly told Wesley that the way to come to faith was to remain still. This meant:

> "'Not to use (what we term) the means of grace;
> "'Not to go to church;
> "'Not to communicate;
> "'Not to fast;
> "'Not to use so much private prayer;
> "'Not to read the Scriptures;
> "'Not to do temporal good, and
> "'Not to attempt to do spiritual good.' (Wesley 1872e, 34)

From this excerpt one can note how wide a swath of territory these beliefs covered. They virtually made null and void participation in any religious means of grace whether of piety or mercy.

The Spirit and the Means of Grace

But perhaps in placing the emphasis on Christ, these persons veiled a small kernel of truth; namely, the means of grace mean nothing apart from the presence and power of God. Apart from the blood of Christ, the means of grace remain lifeless things. Without the power and presence of the Holy Spirit, they cannot convey preventing, justifying or sanctifying grace. (Wesley 1872f) In fact, from a Wesleyan perspective, any consideration of the overall concept of grace confronts us with the preeminence of divine activity. Many Wesleyans stand firm in a belief in uncreated grace. From this perspective, grace is not some created possession that God gives; rather, grace comes embodied in the gracious presence of the Holy Spirit at work in our lives. (Maddox 1994; Outler 1980) This idea of grace being embodied in the presence of the Holy Spirit helps clarify the nature of the means of grace; the means of grace draw their power and efficacy to transform lives from the activity of the Holy Spirit on account of the sacrifice of Christ (Wesley 1872f) Wesley sought to make this consistently and abundantly clear. For example, in his sermon, *The Means of Grace*, he wrote the following:

> We allow, likewise, that all outward means whatever, if separate from the Spirit of God, cannot profit at all, cannot conduce, in any degree, either to the knowledge or love of God. Without controversy, the help that is done upon earth, He doeth it himself. It is He alone who, by his own almighty power, worketh in us what is pleasing in his sight; and all outward things, unless He work in them and by them, are mere weak and beggarly elements. Whosoever, therefore, imagines there is any intrinsic power in any means whatsoever, does greatly err, not knowing the Scriptures, neither the power of God. We know that there is no inherent power in the words that are spoken in prayer, in the letter of Scripture read, the sound thereof heard, or the bread and wine received in the Lord's supper; but that it is God alone who is the Giver of every good gift, the Author of all grace; that the whole power is of Him, whereby, through any of these, there is any blessing conveyed to our souls. We know, likewise, that he is able to give the same grace, though there were no means on the face of the earth. In this sense, we may affirm, that, with regard to God, there is no such thing as means; seeing he is equally able to work whatsoever pleaseth him, by any, or by none at all. (Wesley 1872f, 267-268)

In the same sermon, he also noted: "Settle this in your heart, that the *opus operatum*, the mere *work done*, profiteth nothing; that there is no *power* to save, but in the Spirit of God, no *merit*, but in the blood of Christ;

that, consequently, even what God ordains, conveys no grace to the soul, if you trust not in Him alone. On the other hand, he that does truly trust in Him, cannot fall short of the grace of God, even though he were cut off from every outward ordinance, though he were shut up in the center of the earth." (Wesley 1872f, 281) Wesley's message rings clearly and loudly: Use all the means of grace God ordained but never forget that their efficacy depends on the presence and power of the Spirit. Wesley emphasized God's presence and power and human participation because he understood grace as cooperant. Though God provided the initiative, His activity always required a human response. (Collins 2004; Leffel 2004; Maddox 1994) One of the ways humans respond to God's grace is through participation in His ordained means of grace.

The Means of Grace and Christian Perfection

Earlier in this chapter, I noted that Wesley believed God ordained the means of grace as avenues for conveying preventing, justifying and sanctifying grace. (Wesley 1872f) As such they exist to serve God's holy purpose of developing holy character. In fact, they find their highest value when they "advance inward holiness." (Wesley 1872f) But many in Wesley's day missed this ultimate goal. As such, they considered the means ends in themselves and thereby missed God's blessings. Concomitantly, they mistakenly identified the whole of religion with doing these outward works. But even those who did not fall into this error, succumbed to equally dangerous thinking: They believed the means of grace inherently provided something that pleased God. In fact, they believed participants in the means of grace became acceptable to God, without the accompanying practice of justice, mercy and love. (Wesley 1872f) In other words, they missed the ultimate goal of religion, namely the renewal of the human heart in the very image of God. In speaking about these errors, Wesley wrote: "But in process of time, when "the love of many waxed cold," some began to mistake the means for the end, and to place religion rather in doing those outward works, than in a heart renewed after the image of God. They forgot that "the end of" every "commandment is love, out of a pure heart," with "faith unfeigned" the loving the Lord their God with all their heart, and their neighbor as themselves; and the being purified from pride, anger, and evil desire, by a "faith of the Operation of God." (Wesley 1872f, 264) In the same sermon, he cautioned believers to: "Remember also, to use all means, *as means*; as ordained, not for their own sake, but in order to the renewal of your soul in righteousness and true holiness. If, therefore, they actually tend to this, well; but if not, they are dung and dross." (Wesley 1872f, 281) In short, the means of grace only profit participants when they move them towards inward holiness. Without this, purpose, Wesley considered them an abomination to God. (Wesley 1872f)

In the quotations made in reference to the means of grace, Wesley drew a contrast between outward acts and inward holiness. The language used partly resurrects similar language found in his discussion of Christian perfection. In chapter 2, while discussing Wesley's sources, I noted that he often compared and contrasted inward and outward holiness; he identified outward holiness, cut off from inward religion of the heart, as the religion of externals. (Wesley 1872t; Wesley 1872v; Wesley 1872s) Moreover, he included the means of grace in his definition of the religion of externals; for him, external religion involved doing no harm, doing good and participating in the means of grace. (Wesley 1872t) No wonder that in discussing the means of grace, he reiterated many of the same points he made in relation to external religion; they are nothing without God and cannot profit humans anything. Nevertheless, when one's heart is right with God and one practices mercy and justice, the means of grace serve a significant role in the life of the Christian and those seeking God. In fact, for Wesley, their whole value depended on whether they served the end of religion; namely, transformation into the very image of God, having the mind of Christ and loving God and our neighbor as ourselves. (Wesley 1872f)

Wesley's sermon *On Zeal* provides an excellent image that connects Christian Perfection and the means of grace. I have endeavored to capture the image in figure 1 which appears later. In the sermon, he painted a picture of the Christian's inner being in the following language:

> In a Christian believer *love* sits upon the throne which is erected in the inmost soul; namely, love of God and man, which fills the whole heart, and reigns without a rival. In a circle near the throne are all holy tempers; — long-suffering, gentleness, meekness, fidelity, temperance; and if any other were comprised in "the mind which was in Christ Jesus." In an exterior circle are all the *works of mercy*, whether to the souls or bodies of men. By these we exercise all holy tempers; by these we continually improve them, so that all these are real means of grace, although this is not commonly adverted to. Next to these are those that are usually termed works of piety; — reading and hearing the word, public, family, private prayer, receiving the Lord's Supper, fasting or abstinence. Lastly, that his followers may the more effectually provoke one another to love, holy tempers, and good works, our blessed Lord has united them together in one body, the Church, dispersed all over the earth; a little emblem of which, of the Church universal, we have in every particular Christian congregation. (Wesley 1872j, 76-77)

Figure 1. Christian Perfection and the Means of Grace

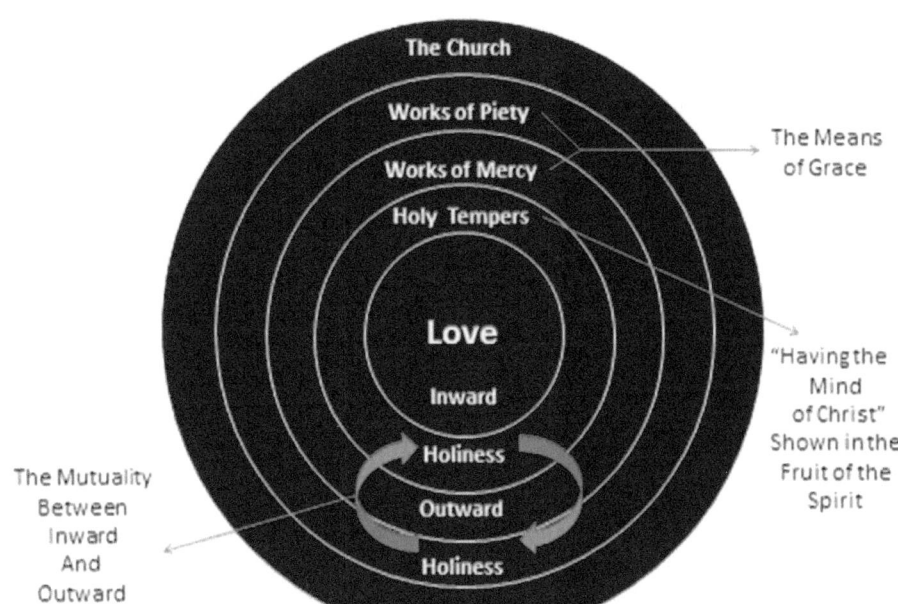

Wesley's image clearly connected Christian perfection and the means of grace. But the image also includes many noteworthy observations. One immediately discovers his central focus on love. He conceptualized this love as addressed to God and humankind and as the controlling state of one's entire being. The reference to the holy tempers that exist right next to the throne inhabited by love offers several insights. First, the image reminds one of the central role affectional language played in Wesley's understanding of Christian perfection. He conceptualized Christian perfection as involving "... the tempers of the heart, in right dispositions of mind towards God and man, producing all right words and actions." (Wesley 1872q, 205) Second, the close association between love and the holy tempers recalls love as the master temper that guides and produces all tempers. Third, his description of the holy tempers clearly associated them with the fruit of the Spirit. In naming tempers such as long-suffering, gentleness, and meekness, he seemed to have Galatians 5:22-23 in mind. But he also associated the holy tempers and the fruit of the Spirit with possessing the mind of Christ. But having the mind of Christ involved far more than the characteristics listed in Galatians. By the statement "and if any other were comprised in "the mind which was in Christ Jesus," he envisioned many other possible fruit which might characterize holy persons. For example, reviewing the kenosis passage in Philippians 2, one would conclude that the humility demonstrated by Christ would qualify as one of these holy tempers or fruit of the Spirit.

In chapter 1, I discussed Wesley's purposeful list as made visible in expanded and compacted forms. Both appear in this image. First, one finds part of the expanded purposeful list. This appears in his reference to love and to "holy tempers" that exist near the throne. Moreover, one might consider "the mind of Christ," as exemplifying right thinking at its best. Immediately following these inward dynamics, he depicted right actions in one's life and in the world. But one also sees the compacted form and its emphasis on inward and outward holiness. What's more, the description reinforced the relationship between inward and outward holiness; inward holiness, seen in love and holy tempers, always constituted the starting point for outward holiness. (Wesley 1872r) Furthermore, outward holiness showed itself through works of mercy and piety. But the relationship between inward and outward holiness involved mutuality. Just as inward holiness leads to a focus on and concern for outward holiness, engagement in the latter improves inward holiness. Wesley partly reinforced this point through a statement made about works of mercy; they serve to exercise holy tempers. He then offered that by engaging in works of mercy "... we continually improve them," namely, holy tempers. Works of mercy serve not only as a means for exercising the holy tempers, but also a path for improvement in these virtues. He likely meant that works of mercy tends to sharpen the holy tempers and to confirm one in these virtues. This stands true whether such works are performed to benefit others spiritually or physically or whether done to the souls or bodies of men.

Interestingly, in Wesley's image, he placed works of mercy prior to works of piety. Logically, since works of piety seem to exert a direct influence on inward holiness, one would expect it to come immediately after the two inner circles. Additionally, in the sermon *On Visiting the Sick*, Wesley placed priority on works of piety when he described them as the normal channels through which God conveyed His grace. (Wesley 1872i) These observations suggest works of piety likely should be considered prior to works of mercy. However, Wesley depicted works of mercy as the circle next to those indicating inward holiness. How does one explain this order? Before attempting an answer this question, one should remember that both works of piety and works of mercy serve the inward life of holiness. Just like works of piety, works of mercy improve holy tempers. As a result, Wesley likely would not have seen works of piety playing a greater role in developing holy character. Having said that, the order indicated still raises questions to which one should attempt an answer.

I suggest the following possibilities as reasons Wesley might have placed works of mercy prior to works of piety. First, properly conceived, works of piety, assume a concern for the rightness of one's interior life. However, in placing emphasis on the right heart and right affections in the image, this idea already existed in the model. Nevertheless, given the importance of works of piety he did not wish to leave it out. As a result, he placed it in the image but first chose to highlight works of mercy. Second, Wesley might have feared that a primary emphasis on works of piety might push one inward instead of outward. We well know that pious actions can sometimes become distorted and thereby fail to serve God's holy purpose of transformation. They do so when they become ends in themselves, meant to show to others how holy one is. (Wesley 1872w; Wesley 1872x; Wesley 1872y) As demonstrated in the Sermon on the Mount, even actions such as fasting and prayer can degenerate into acts that call attention to the self. But additionally, even holy persons who placed an inordinate emphasis on works of piety could potentially become too self-focused; that is, they could display a morbid concern for spiritual self-improvement above all else and thus nullify works of mercy. In *The Sermon on the Mount, Discourse 4*, Wesley partly spoke to this issue. In it, he spoke of those who wondered why Christianity should be clogged with external matters such as doing and suffering. Instead they advocated an inward communion with God without the trappings of outward works. (Wesley 1872u) Wesley described this position in the following language: "Many eminent men have spoken thus; have advised us "to cease from all outward action;" wholly to withdraw from the world; to leave the body behind us; to abstract ourselves from all sensible things; to have no concern at all about outward religion, but to work all virtues in the will; as the far more excellent way, more perceptive of the soul, as well as more acceptable to God." (Wesley 1872u, 383) Such thinking seemed to possess a gnostic tinge; it nullified legitimate concern for the body and works of mercy that attend the same. Instead, it focused on one's inward life alone. Over against such thinking, Wesley presented Christianity as a social religion requiring engagement with others. In fact, he went so far as to suggest that turning Christianity into a solitary religion would destroy it. (Wesley 1872u) As such, he could not countenance an isolated faith, totally separated from the world as was often displayed among Christian hermits. Rather, he endorsed an inward holiness in which works of mercy connected Christians to others in the world. (Wesley 1872u) Finally, and as implied above, perhaps his image was meant to reinforce the outward push of inward holiness. That is, transformation within the Christian ought to promote transformative word and action in the world. Works of mercy rather than works of piety best depicted this outward push.

The Relational Nature of the Means of Grace

Before concluding this chapter, Wesley's description of Christianity as a social religion merits some final comment as it relates to the means of grace. This description suggests the essential relational nature of the faith. This relational aspect also applies to the means of grace. It appears obvious to me that rightly practiced, works of piety can foster right relationship with God. In turn, right relationship with God can enhance relationship with others. But such thinking also applies to works of mercy. For Wesley, works of mercy constituted one of the ways in which the social nature of Christianity was worked out. Through the means of grace, especially works of mercy, Christians connect with others in the Church as well as those outside. One also encounters this relational quality in specific acts of mercy. For example, visiting the sick obviously possesses a relational quality as it can connect the visited and the visitor. But visiting the sick possesses a relational quality beyond this observation. Wesley suggested that visiting the sick served to increase one's thankfulness to God as well as one's sympathy with the afflicted. (Wesley 1872i) As such this work of mercy fosters connections with God as well as others. Following Mann's definition of the means of grace, we see another relational aspect in these ordinances; that is, they foster receptivity and responsiveness to God. (Mann 2006) But the means of grace are relational in another sense. Because we encounter the Spirit's presence in various manifestations of grace, this makes the means of grace eminently relational. This relational quality to the means of grace makes good sense when viewed in the light of Christian perfection. Christian perfection finds its ultimate expression in loving God with heart, soul and mind and our neighbor as ourselves. Given this reality, it makes sense that relational means should serve as a pathway to relational holiness.

Chapter 8

Getting it Right!

Christian Perfection from the Inside out

For the Christian, everything starts with the right heart! That's the essential message Wesley communicated in his purposeful list. From his scriptural perspective, one did not become holy by working from the outside in. One did not merely clean the outside of the platter; instead one had to open the heart to God's transformative work. Holiness in the sense in which he understood it only became possible when God worked his transformation at the very center of the human soul. Of course, as I have detailed, the right heart also gave rise to right thinking and these two constituted inward holiness. But real inward holiness always gave rise to outward holiness reflected in word and deed. This balanced perspective was pivotal to his understanding of Christian perfection. Given this understanding, he consistently communicated it in his sermons and writings. As a result, the purposeful pattern detailing the trajectory of holy transformation appeared all across his works. In fact, it was so prevalent that once one becomes aware of its presence, it's almost impossible to miss. In chapter one, I described the purposeful list as a kind of order salutis though not in the classic sense of the term. Instead, it detailed for Wesley's readers and hearers the trajectory of Christian perfection. For him, holy transformation always proceeded from the inside out. In following this line of thought, he captured the essential truth Jesus communicated in the Beatitudes and the Sermon on the Mount.

But Wesley sought to communicate another message by his purposeful list: He wanted to reinforce the truth that despite its prime importance, inward holiness required visible presence in the world through holy words and deeds. In emphasizing this truth, he addressed two errors prevalent in his day. The first error derived from those who made their boast in inward holiness. This group focused their attention on acts of piety that enhanced their supposed spotlessness. In the process, they largely disregarded the natural outgrowth of inward holiness in the world. As a result, they gave little if any attention to outward holiness. The second error belonged to those who conceived holiness only in its outward forms. Such persons thought holiness consisted entirely in doing good, avoiding harm and engaging in the ordinances of the church. From this perspective, one could live out this vision of holiness simply by doing good to one's fellow humans. Although such actions constituted valid manifestations of outward holiness, they missed an essential point; outward holiness, cut off from its internal roots of holiness was worthless as far as God was concerned. Additionally, without inward transformation, these acts stood invalid in His sight. (Wesley 1872n) Such thoughts can appear like a regurgitation of ancient history having little if any relevance to modern folk. But this simply is not the case. These errors do not simply belong to Wesley's age. Across time, and even presently, humans who carry a concern for holiness still tend to fall into these two errors. Therefore, in addressing these errors from his time, Wesley speaks across the centuries to our day.

But in laying out his emphasis, he did not intend to portray a one-directional relationship between inward and outward holiness. Valid outward expressions of holiness also impacted inward holiness. Godly words and deeds done in the world served to confirm and reinforce inward righteousness. In a sense, the relationship between inward and outward holiness mirrors that which purportedly exists between love and marriage. Some might remember the old song sung by Frank Sinatra about love and marriage. Sinatra crooned: "You can't have one without the other." Of course, given our lax commitment to marriage and new ideas about love, one could debate this axiom. But though it may no longer ring true in respect to love and marriage, it still holds true for inward and outward holiness. "You can't have one without the other." There exists a systemic and reciprocal relationship between inward and outward holiness. If one will get Christian perfection right, one needs to understand the trajectory as well as the systemic link between inward and outward holiness. Anything less makes for a mistaken notion of holiness.

In contrast to the prevalent and bifurcated views of Christian perfection, Wesley knew they belonged together. As a result, he constantly strove to strike the balance; namely, the holiness that mattered to God eschewed a bifurcation of inward and outward holiness. Moreover, rather than separate them, he brought the two together in dynamic synthesis. As displayed in the Beatitudes, transformation begins in the attitudes of the heart, but it confirmed its presence by right words and deeds in the world. Thus, Jesus tagged peacemaking and doing righteousness as the logical outcomes of having right attitudes and a pure heart. Peacemaking and doing righteousness stand as emblematic for all the words and deeds that naturally proceed from the right heart. Such a balanced vision of Christian perfection avoids a purity that maintains its pristine image by cutting itself off from the world. In essence, it avoids the religion of the Pharisees and the teachers of the law who preserved holiness by detaching themselves from their fellow human beings. In contrast, holiness looks more like that displayed by Jesus; although holy, he walked around, mingled with common folk and confirmed sinners. In the midst of sinful persons, Christ maintained His holy character and behavior. But more than this, through His holy presence, He demonstrated the power to heal and transform those he encountered. His was holiness for everyday life. It is to this same holiness that He calls all Christians.

Christian Perfection and the Practice of Ministry

The integral and reciprocal relationship between inward and outward holiness carries major implications for all Christians. Christians cannot separate holy being from holy action. In various ways, this tendency to separate the two abounds. It even exists in those who ought to know better. Here I refer to those who serve in ordained forms of ministry. We seem to constantly divorce the two. One of the ways in which we do this is by placing the emphasis on outward deeds often without a concomitant emphasis on inward transformation. Given our training, we ought to place priority on inward holiness as a precursor and necessary element for engaging in outward acts of ministry. To personalize it more, we ought to strive to live as holy persons knowing that this forms a key basis for good in the world. Of course, this does not exclude God from using the acts of one whose life is not in full accord with his vision of holiness. After all, the ultimate power to transmit grace comes not from individuals but from God through the power of the Holy Spirit. (Wesley 1872f) However, we do ministry best when such acts flow from a holy life. We encounter this truth in Matthew 7: 21-27 of the Sermon on the Mount. In this passage, Jesus responded to those who proclaimed their miraculous deeds supposedly done in God's name. In his sermon, Wesley interpreted Jesus denouncing them in the following words: "… I never knew you;" no, not then, when you were "casting out devils in my name:" Even then I did not know you as my own; for your heart was not right toward God. Ye were not yourselves meek and lowly; ye were not lovers of God, and of all mankind; ye were not renewed in the image of God; ye were not holy as I am holy. "Depart from me, ye" who, notwithstanding all this, are "workers of iniquity;" — ανομια — Ye are transgressors of my law, my law of holy and perfect love.' (Wesley 1872k, 522)

To some, this exegesis and application might seem off base. But the message appears consistent with the broader scriptural context of the Sermon on the Mount and the Beatitudes that serve as its starting point. Understood in this context, acts of ministry should be the logical outgrowth of inward holiness; that is, they ought to grow out from internal habits of the heart such as humility and purity of heart. Without them, both the doer and the works stand unacceptable in God's sight. In other words, the validity and the appropriateness of one's outward acts depend on the pure condition of one's heart. From this perspective, it was entirely possible that the best of acts, at least as appraised by humans, would still merit God's judgment. More than external deeds, God valued the condition of the heart flowing from an intimate relationship with him.

These thoughts ought to serve as an implicit warning to those of us who do ministry and those who sense a call to ministry. They ought to remind us of the true priorities in the Christian life. We live in a day that places great emphasis on performance. Church members, pastors and judicatory leaders alike sometimes seem as if they play a numbers racket; they stress visible results to such an extent as if they were the only things that matter. In other segments of the evangelical church, many place significant emphasis on miraculous deeds and various expressions of the Spirit's power. Unfortunately, these emphases sometimes take priority over establishing an intimate relationship with God and having a right heart. As such, one sometimes finds little emphasis on exemplifying the fruit of the Spirit. Moreover, the spiritual disciplines that promote intimacy with God, sometimes find little place in the life of practicing ministers and those preparing for ministry. In short, these persons sometimes substitute performance for being; they take great delight in doing big things and achieving visible results. All the while, they eschew intimacy with God and the right heart.

My colleague, Dr. Steve Stratton recently shared with me an article about divinity students at Duke Divinity School that reinforces these thoughts. In the article, Lauren Carroll indicated how knowledge and faith seemed at odds in the divinity students; academic stress and the lack of community made it difficult for divinity students to maintain spiritual vitality. In addition, these same students declared that the very study of divinity provided an added burden that forced them to grapple with their faith on a daily basis. One student expressed the dilemma well: "We are here because we want academic rigor, and that's something Duke provides... But I didn't expect my strong academic background to come at the expense of my spiritual life." (Carroll December 9, 2011) But this is not just a problem at Duke Divinity School. The same thing might be said about seminary students across the country. Students can become largely invested in academic study and even activities of ministry so as to exclude legitimate and necessary spiritual disciplines. In the process, they often neglect the cultivation of a holy heart and life as a foundation for ministry.

But such problems also exist among those who serve in ministry. Several years ago, I read *Spiritual Wholeness for Clergy*, written by a spiritual formation director and a psychologist. At the time, they operated The Barnabas Center, a recovery ministry for clergy who had fallen in various ways; some had engaged in sexual misconduct, alcohol or some other addiction. But others came because they had experienced stress and burnout. Throughout the book, the common issue that characterized their lives struck me: Each had lost touch with God; they had sacrificed intimacy with God for something less than God. (Hands and Fehr 1994) Sometimes that something involves the tasks of ministry; we sometimes give it all our attention. In short, we sacrifice intimacy for performance. One wonders if Jesus' words and Wesley's admonition does not apply in situations like these. From both sources, the message is clear: No deed in ministry, no matter how great, makes up for a lack of intimacy with God and the right heart! Of course, this is not said to minimize the importance of results. Rather, it is said to indicate the priority of the Christian life – knowing God intimately ought to be the first priority. Everything else in the Christian life flows from this reality; and in fact, it is this reality that validates all we accomplish in the world. Os Guinness described these priorities as the primary call and the secondary call. The primary call referred to the call to a relationship with God. The secondary call referred to doing something for God. (Guinness 1998) Unfortunately, many of us often get our priorities all mixed up. We place the proverbial cart before the horse, giving priority to the secondary call and sometimes neglecting the primary call altogether.

Valuing Reason and the Apprehending Faculties

Because holy transformation takes place in the soul, we ought to give attention to its various faculties as we seek holiness of heart and life. What does appropriate attention to these areas look like? I think it means that we gratefully receive these powers as God-given gifts without undervaluing or overvaluing them. Wesley made this point particularly in relation to reason. (Wesley 1872a) Some persons tended to undervalue reason whereas others overvalued it. From Wesley's perspective, both extremes posed problems. Rather, one should take a balanced perspective valuing reason but never making it more than it was designed to be. I suppose Wesley chose to illustrate reason because this is the faculty that most often lies open to these errors. The reader might have encountered Christians who see reason as antithetical to faith and the Christian life. These persons sometimes query and possibly judge harshly those who aspire to gain a seminary education. They do so because they picture seminary as a place where faith goes to die; in such cases, seminary gets reinterpreted as cemetery. In short, they see little value in reason. The idea that reason could be an intellectual virtue is anathema to them. Wesley's criticism of folk like this makes good sense. As seen in his criticism of William Law, setting aside reason can lead to unholy alliances. Thus, Wesley wrote: "And I fear they who stop the workings of their reason, lie the more open to the workings of their imagination." (Wesley 1872c, 581)

But you might also have encountered those who make reason a panacea. In fact, such folk tend to value reason above everything else. For such folk, reason becomes the ultimate basis for everything they believe and do. Quite frankly, I have seen both types of persons who bifurcate head and heart even among seminary students. The first group spiritualizes everything and avoids reason as if it was a dirty word. They eschew diligent study and effort because they see these as unimportant and even detrimental to the spiritual life. Some even give the tendency a weird spiritual twist. My dear departed friend, Dr. Harold Burgess once told me about a student who avoided study as though it was a scourge. When Dr. Burgess asked him about his misguided stance in relation to an upcoming exam, the student responded: "Jesus is in me and He knows everything, He will give me everything I need to do well on the exam." Talk about spiritualizing a lazy attitude and disdain for study! The second group disdains spirituality and seems to believe that a seminary education simply exists to enlarge their reason and mind. As such, they trivialize any emphasis on spiritual disciplines believing them to be a waste of time. I actually had a student once enunciate this very stance to me; that student cared nothing about spiritual disciplines and forming Christian character. According to that individual, the academic life was the major draw for attending seminary.

Thomas A Kempis provided a rather sobering thought about the latter stance. He believed that the effort to pattern one's life after Christ carried greater import than the capacity to reason and understand. Accordingly, he wrote:

> What good does it do to speak learnedly about the Trinity if, lacking humility, you displease the Trinity? Indeed it is not learning that makes a man holy and just, but a virtuous life makes him pleasing to God. I would rather feel contrition than know how to define it. For what would it profit us to know the whole Bible by heart and the principles of all the philosophers if we live without grace and the love of God? Vanity of vanities and all is vanity, except to love God and serve Him alone. (A Kempis 1997, 11)

In fact, A Kempis believed that without a corresponding increase in holiness, greater knowledge and understanding brought greater judgment. (A Kempis 1997) John Bunyan evidently held a similar view. In *The Pilgrim's Progress*, Bunyan depicted a scene between Faith and Talkative. In it, Faith asked Talkative about those things that provided proof that a work of grace had been enacted in the human heart. Having already provided an initial answer, Faith requested a second proof. Talkative immediately pointed to great knowledge about Gospel mysteries. In response, Faith indicated that the statement was false "...for knowledge, great knowledge, may be obtained in the mysteries of the Gospel, and yet no work of grace in the soul (1 Cor. 13). Yea, if a man have all knowledge, he may yet be nothing, and so consequently be no child of God." (Bunyan 1985, 90) However, Faith also proceeded to validate knowledge to some degree; the heart needed knowledge and without it, it was nothing. In fleshing out this perspective, Faith pointed to two types of knowledge: A speculative knowledge and one attended by the grace of faith and love. Thus, Bunyan placed the following words in Faith's mouth: "There is, therefore, knowledge and knowledge. Knowledge that resteth in the bare speculation of things; and knowledge that is accompanied with the grace of faith and love; which puts a man upon doing even the will of God from the heart: the first of these will serve the talker; but without the other the true Christian is not content. "Give me understanding, and I shall keep Thy law; yea, I shall observe it with my whole heart." (Bunyan 1985, 90-91)

Both A Kempis and Bunyan struck a balanced perspective in relation to knowledge. At the same time, they clearly emphasized the right heart above the right head. Wesley also offered a similar balanced perspective: Namely, accept reason for what is – a gift of God to be embraced, but not overvalued. When we take the balance perspective, we begin to use reason to think for the glory of God (Sire 2000). Reason becomes a servant intended for God's glory and a way of serving ourselves and humanity. It ceases to be a master dictating all of life. Rather, it exists fundamentally to help us apprehend true reality and to transform us into holy creatures. But these realities also extend to the other apprehending faculties of the soul. Just as we endeavor to take a balanced attitude toward reason, we ought to do the same in relation to the other apprehending faculties of the soul. We ought to appropriately value memory and imagination while endeavoring to live by a conscience void of offense towards God and man. Indeed, we ought to appropriately value all the faculties of the soul, seeing all as eminently serving the divine purpose of holy transformation.

Using Liberty for Holy Transformation

How do these truths apply to liberty? As previously discussed, liberty involved for Wesley the power of self-direction. (Wesley 1872d; Wesley 1872g; Wesley 1872j) Applied to Christian perfection, this means that we cannot shirk responsibility for our spiritual lives and the great goal of becoming holy. Although others can travel with us on the journey, we cannot delegate responsibility for holy transformation to another human, no matter how close. We have to take responsibility for the cultivation of our interior lives. Of course, this perspective makes primary space for God's initiating work in our lives. Only God can begin the work of holy transformation in our lives. However, because Wesleyans believe in cooperant grace, we also believe that we must respond to the grace initiated by God. Furthermore, because, God is the one who grants us liberty, He will not force us to become holy persons. For example, although God wills that we give ourselves entirely to Him, He will not force us. We must choose to bring our will in alignment with His will. It is then that we truly become the living and holy sacrifices that God intended.

In his letter to the Galatians, Paul himself had much to say about liberty as it related to holy transformation. In Galatians 5: 13-18, he wrote: "You, my brothers and sisters, were called to be free. But do not use your freedom to indulge the flesh; rather, serve one another humbly in love. For the entire law is fulfilled in keeping this one command: "Love your neighbor as yourself." If you bite and devour each other, watch out or you will be destroyed by each other. So I say, walk by the Spirit, and you will not gratify the desires of the flesh. For the flesh desires what is contrary to the Spirit, and the Spirit what is contrary to the flesh. They are in conflict with each other, so that you are not to do whatever you want. But if you are led by the Spirit, you are not under the law." (NIV) In these verses Paul affirmed the role of liberty in living a godly life. One can choose to live according to the dictates of the flesh. But one can also choose to live according to the Spirit and as a consequence, experience the holy life. In short one can choose to live in or out of step with the Spirit (Galatians 5: 25).

In fact, in his understanding of Christian perfection as involving loving relationships, Paul indicated that we are free to choose the way of love. We can choose to love others as we love ourselves; we can devote attention to learning to love ourselves and then respond to others in similar fashion. But as implied in some places, our capacity to love sometimes becomes circumscribed by past experiences and anxieties about the future. In this latter regard, Emil Brunner has provided me useful insights about love and its relationship to the past and the future. In his book *Faith, Hope and Love* Brunner related these biblical concepts to time. In his discussion, he related faith to the past and hope to the future. He related love, the third member of the trilogy, to the present. From his perspective, we are called to love but we can only live out love in the present. (Brunner 1956) But chains from the past and fears of the future stymie love in the present. We can sometimes allow the past to bind us through guilt and or brokenness and find ourselves without a faith to set us free. We can also become stymied by fears of the future that riddles us with anxiety. Thus bounded by the past and anxiety-ridden by the future, we sometimes find it difficult to love in the moment as we ought. This might hold true even though we know that God calls us to love and provides the means to make it presently possible. What choices exist for such situations? Of course, we can choose to remain as we are, bounded by fear from the past and the future. But we can also choose to break the bonds of fear and help free ourselves to love. This might involve choosing activities that release us from a fear driven life that stymies love. At the same time, we might also choose to actively participate in those things that enlarge our capacity to love freely in the present. Even though God sheds His love abroad in our hearts, we still must choose to live it out. God will not do such things for us. He endows us with freedom of self-direction so we can enlarge our capacities to be and to love.

But we can use liberty in other ways as a path to transformation; we can choose to engage in the means of grace that advance the holy life. The works of piety can become transformative disciplines helping to mold us into the image of Christ. When we truly understand that we possess liberty even in relation to the spiritual disciplines, this knowledge can foster a different attitude towards them. When they appear imposed from without, they can become onerous burdens merely endured. However, when we freely choose them, they can become free of care and satisfying endeavors.

As a result, we might even come to think and feel differently about institutional policies and admonitions to cultivate the disciplines. We might stop perceiving them as uncaring demands and rules imposed from without; rather, they might become caring invitations to choose paths of holy transformation. But this way of thinking also applies to works of mercy done to others. Although these means of grace primarily has others in view, this does not mean that intrapersonal transformation cannot occur in those who do them. As indicated in the previous chapter, engaging others also tends to have personal impact. For one, it can become a means of exercising outwardly the holiness made real in us. But besides this, helping others also tends to shape us directly, refining us inwardly and fortifying us in holy habits.

But beyond choosing to participate in the means of grace, we can also freely choose to participate in relationships that foster holiness in ourselves and in others. In fact, David Benner sees transformation as one of the major purposes of relationships. In keeping with this, he suggested that significant progress on the transformational journey derives from spiritual friendship relationships. Accordingly, he noted: "Spiritual friends nurture the development of each other's souls. Their love for each other translates into the desire that the other settle for nothing less that becoming all that he or she was intended to be." (Benner 2002, 16) It is this interest that makes spiritual friends, soul friends. Thus, he offered: "Soul friends become spiritual friends when they seek to help each other attend and respond to God." (Benner 2002, 16)

Surrendering the Will

We also must learn to know and value the will. Knowing and valuing the will means that we understand its spiritual purpose; it attunes us to God's will when we surrender it. As Oswald Chambers aptly noted: ""Surrender is not the surrender of the external life, but of the will; when that is done, all is done." (Chambers 1963, September 13) Chambers is absolutely right! The will serves as the motivating center of the soul and largely determines where we place our allegiances. As Wesley indicated, God gave the human will so that one would use it freely to follow His will and purposes. (Wesley 1872i; Wesley 1872q) But with the fall of humanity came the possibility of following one's own path in contradiction to God's path. This engendered a battle of wills; it pitted human wills directly in opposition to doing the will of God. Thus the eternally relevant question is: will we follow our own dictates or will we choose to follow God's plan? Evidently, in such considerations, liberty always comes in play. As much as we might sometimes like God to bend us unwilling to His will, He will not do it. He asks us to come and freely choose to live according to His will. Unfortunately, many persons choose to follow their own path instead of God's. As indicated elsewhere, this brings its own baggage; we become filled with pride, idolatry and a host of negative attitudes that serve as self-will's companion. But still more baggage remains; this stance in life also connects to loving the world, the flesh and the devil along with the cumbersome, destructive bondage they bring.

So what does over-valuing the will mean in this context? I think it means that we value our own chosen path as more necessary and more valid than God's path. We think we know ourselves better than God does. As such, we think that we can more clearly chart out the right course for ourselves, even in opposition to God's. Even in born-again believers, the stubborn proclamation of our rights and the active determination to run our own lives sometimes remain actively alive. But along with these comes an exercise in rebellion. For following our own paths often puts us in active rebellion against God. This might even be true when our wills seem in accord with what God intended. Here the rebellion might entail pursuing *our will, our way* even when God might desire to achieve the same end in a different way. When I contemplate this matter, I cannot help but think of some of the Old Testament stories involving the Patriarch Abraham and his family. Clearly, God intended to build Abraham a line through Isaac as he had promised. But the promise of a son seemed too long in coming. Convinced by Sarah, Abraham chose to pursue the path to a son through Hagar. A lot of bitterness has ensued from that decision! One might even think of Jacob who was the line through which God planned to fulfill His promise to Abraham. But Jacob chose scheming, lying and extorting birthrights and blessings. He got many of the things God intended but in his own way and cunning deceit. This too proved disastrous with ensuing negative consequences.

So what then is the appropriate stance in relation to the will? Clearly from the previous discussions, there exists but one choice - aligning our wills with God's. As demonstrated in Jesus' life, it meant coming to the place where He responded honestly and fully: "Not my will, but yours be done." I recall a similar critical decision point in my life in regard to the will. Very early in my Christian walk, it became apparent that God had placed a call on my life. My initial understanding of the call involved faithfully responding to God and going off to Bible College. I was pretty sure this involved the will of God for me. But I had my own plan and will; I wanted to become a lawyer. I had harbored the dream from a very young age. Moreover, the dream seemed to lie within easy reach. I had already been accepted provisionally to the local university's law program pending my high school results. The dream was so close I could almost touch it! Why give this up to go out like Abraham not knowing where and to what end I was going. I wish I could say that I immediately made the right choice; that is, to follow my clear understanding of God's will for me at the time. But I didn't. I actively fought with God over the decision for about a year and a half. It was only in a moment of desperation, fearing being lost that I finally yielded completely. I have never regretted the decision! One of my daily short prayers to God still remains, "Lord, not my will but yours be done!" I sometimes clearly know what that prayer means. But at other times, I have no clue what it might mean. I only know that for all of my life, in whatever matter, I want to remain fully yield to God.

Actually, when we fully yield, God does some marvelous and unexpected things with us. When I left Barbados to go to Bible College in a neighboring island, a close friend told me I was throwing my life away. Such surrender of our wills rarely makes sense to believers much less non-believers. Perhaps that individual was right! Perhaps I was throwing away my life. But in throwing it away, I found so much more! God returned to me a much more fulfilling life. Furthermore, going off to Bible College did not stymie my usefulness to the kingdom. Instead, it broadened my horizons and provided greater and wider opportunities to serve the kingdom. But more important than all of this has been the joy and security in knowing that I am following His will. But lest you misunderstand me, the joy has not excluded difficult periods; it has not always been a bed of roses and rising to heaven on a flowery bed of ease. There have often been difficult days. But through all circumstances, the sense that God is with me as He was with Joseph has always remained. This is the peace and joy amidst struggles that comes from fully yielding to the will of God.

I am not sure what inspired Leila Norris to write the words to the hymn, *Sweet Will of God*. I suspect that like Francis Havergal's hymn *Take my Life and Let it be*, the hymn was birthed from some personal experience. Judging by the words of the opening lines to the hymn, I suspect it involved some personal situation that tested the surrender of her will to God's. Furthermore, I suspect she knew that the choice involved deciding who would control her life – herself or God. Thus, she penned the words to the hymn:

> My stubborn will at last hath yielded;
> I would be Thine, and Thine alone;
> And this the prayer my lips are bringing,
> Lord, let in me Thy will be done.
>
> *Refrain:*
> Sweet will of God, still fold me closer,
> Till I am wholly lost in Thee.
>
> I'm tired of sin, footsore and weary,
> The darksome path hath dreary grown;
> But now a light has ris'n to cheer me;
> I find in Thee my Star, my Sun.
>
> Thy precious will, O conqu'ring Savior,
> Doth now embrace and compass me;
> All discords hushed, my peace a river,
> My soul, a prisoned bird set free.

> Shut in with Thee, O Lord, forever,
> My wayward feet no more to roam;
> What pow'r from Thee my soul can sever?
> The center of God's will my home. (Norris 1900)

The first verse of the hymn captured the choice we all encounter at sometime in our Christian journey. Will we remain stubbornly tied to our own way or will we yield our wills to God's will? The verse did not picture this as an easy choice or one that happens quickly. We are often a lot like the early Israelites; we stubbornly cling to our plans for our lives, even when they clearly are not working. I suspect we think we know ourselves better than God does. Inwardly, we somehow think that this judgment about ourselves will eventually prove itself true. So in stubbornness we fight God all the way so that we might cling to our misshapen plans for our lives. Getting beyond our stubborn wills often comes painfully slow. I know it was painfully slow for me as I struggled for well over a year to maintain my chosen path instead of God's. Yet all during this time, I continued my spiritual disciplines. Mine was not an outwardly visible rebellion. Yet I somehow knew that in my heart, there existed rebellion. In many ways, I was caught between wanting to maintain my path but still keep my relationship with God. I wanted God on my terms. Of course, it didn't work! God never comes on our terms but on His own! If we will continue to walk with Him in unbroken communion, surrender to His will must become a reality.

In the succeeding verses of the hymn following her proffered surrender, Norris presented vivid images of the transformation that takes place in a life fully yielded up to God. In verse two she wrote of a light that came to dispel her wearisome darkness. Like Bunyan's *A Pilgrim's Progress*, it roused images of one who struggled under a heavy weigh to sin, too burdensome to bear. Freedom only came at the foot of the cross where in surrender to God, her burdens rolled away. But Norris also pictured the peace that comes to a life fully yielded to God. She experienced peace like a river that enveloped her soul. In the embrace of Christ, her soul found unending peace. In contrast, prior to her surrender she had experienced only discord. She had felt like a bird caged by bars of its own making. Now yielded to God, her soul found flight; she could mount up with wings like the high-flying eagle, soaring on the thermals of God's grace. In the final verse, she resurrected the earlier image of a wearisome wanderer from verse two. The image seems to conjure up for me the picture of the prodigal son from Luke 15. He had wandered far, moved by his own lust to pursue his will in rebellion to his father's. He had pursued the lust of the flesh, the lust of the eyes and the pride of life. But what had he gained? Only degradation, debauchery and a little drowned in the gutter of life. I don't suspect that this was Norris' dilemma. But even if the circumstances remained drastically different, the result is eerily similar; no one enhances life by seeking one's own way and will. The outcome is typically the same – wandering, lost, directionless. Amidst the lostness of the final verse, glimmers of hope shined through – but all birthed in full surrender. Instead of a directionless life, with no stability, Norris pictured a stability and security centered in being at home in God's will. Yielding to God's will was by Wesley's account, the soul's intended home.

Norris' varied images, positive and negative, reinforce for me a reality that comes from surrendering to God. I suspect that many of us think that yielding to God will cause us to lose control of life. Along with that, we might think that in losing control, life will become disordered guided by the whims of a fickle and uncaring God. That's what many would have us believe. Did not Satan imply to Eve that she could have so much more, if she followed her own way? The temptation promised much but actually only delivered deformation. Actually, the opposite is true. Left to pursue our own paths and guided by our own will, the only possible life is a disordered life, focused on false objects: disordered feelings, ravaged self images, fractured relationships, divorce from God's companionship and ultimately death. Instead, surrender to the will of God orders life in varied ways: ordered affections and passions, a true sense of our identity in God, and the possibility of right relationships with God, ourselves and others.

Reframing and Reshaping the Religious Affections

In chapter 4, I indicated that the religious affections flow from the will of the soul. This intimate connection means that along with wrestling with and appropriately valuing the will, we will also come to value our affectional and emotional life. I don't know about you, but earlier in my Christian life, I believed becoming more holy would entail doing away with the harsher emotions. Put another way and using Wesley's language, I subconsciously believed God wished to extinguish the passions and affections. I unconsciously subscribed to a theory of circumscribed or diminished affectional life and emotionality. I no longer believe that! Instead I believe the opposite. I now believe that holiness actually works to expand the capacity and use of all of one's affections and passions in an appropriate manner. These affections and passions bring vibrancy and color to our lives. What's more, they remain vital to the life of holiness. As I have read Wesley's writings in this area, I have found an appropriate rationale and language for describing this different way of thinking about the affections and emotional life.

Relative to a rationale, I believe that as evidenced in creation, God created humans as goodly creatures. In addition, he endowed them with faculties that were essentially good. Thus, in His description of Adam at creation, Wesley pointed to the power and goodness of his varied faculties. In reference to the will, he pointed to its lack of bias; it unerringly conformed itself to God's will. Given the will's commitment to God's will, Wesley also embraced the goodness of the passions and affections. Thus, he wrote: "... but all his passions and affections were regular, being steadily and uniformly guided by the dictates of his unerring understanding; embracing nothing but good, and every good in proportion to its degree of intrinsic goodness." (Wesley 1872d, 274) However, with the fall, all of these faculties, together with the religious affections became disordered. In becoming alienated from God, these good powers now became employed for wrong purposes. Rather than being used to enhance human life, the perverted use of the faculties and the affections diminished life. What's more, concomitantly, these faculties and affections came to be employed in service to the Devil.

But of course, that which became disordered through rebellion against God can become ordered when given over to Him. By aligning our wills with God's will, we create space where all the faculties of the soul can be reordered and put to their intended use and transformative purposes. This ordering also applies to our affections. All the components of affectional life can become ordered and regulated. When so regulated, all the affections and passions become means through which God can accomplished holy ends. Wesley certainly believed this. In fact, he believed God desired the full engagement of our affections. Without the engagement of the affections, we become "stocks and stones," impervious to the normal feelings God intended humans to experience. But God does not desire that we become wooden and without appropriate feelings. He desires that we become fully alive. This vibrant life becomes impossible in persons whose affections have been extinguished. (Wesley 1872e) Instead of extinguishing the affections and passions, God wishes to bring them under the regulation of faith and love through the power of the Holy Spirit. (Wesley 1872l) This perspective on the affections and passions rang clear in Wesley. In Discourse two on the Sermon on the Mount, he produced a definitive statement on the goodness of the passions (and by implication, the affections). Here, he also noted God's desired plan to regulate rather than extinguish the affections. I previously quoted this passage in chapter six, but it seems worthwhile to reproduce it here again:

> "They who are truly meek, can clearly discern what is evil; and they can also suffer it. They are sensible of everything of this kind, but still meekness holds the reins. They are exceeding "zealous for the Lord of Hosts;" but their zeal is always guided by knowledge, and tempered, in every thought, and word, and work, with the love of man, as well as the love of God. *They do not desire to extinguish any of the passions which God has for wise ends implanted in their nature; but they have the mastery of all: They hold them all in subjection, and employ them only in subservience to those ends. And thus even the harsher and more unpleasing passions are applicable to the noblest purposes; even hatred, and anger, and fear, when engaged against sin, and regulated by faith and love, are as walls and bulwarks to the soul, so that the wicked one cannot approach to hurt it*" (Wesley 1872l, 348 (italics added))

But Wesley also believed normal human emotions carried implications for the soul and the affections. For example, he believed that varied and legitimate feelings such as sorrow and grief could overshadow the soul and color the affections. When this occurred, the result inevitably became visible in behaviors and even in physical functioning. But such afflictions yet served a holy purpose; they helped advance holiness of heart and life. Through afflictions and accompanying emotions of varied kind, God advances the believer in holiness. This He accomplishes through the Holy Spirit who uses such occasions to purify the believer. (Wesley 1872e) This transformation by the Spirit entails a two-fold process. In the first, the Holy Spirit uses difficult circumstances and consequent emotions to purify the believer. The Spirit uses these circumstances and emotional turmoil to cleanse the believer from self-will, pride, unbridled passion, love of the world and in general from evil affections. In the second part of the process, the Holy Spirit uses afflictions like sorrow to begin the work of holy transformation. Through such circumstances, He creates in the believer, holy habits of the heart. Thus, Wesley wrote: "Beside that, sanctified afflictions have, through the grace of God, an immediate and direct tendency to holiness. Through the operation of his Spirit, they humble, more and more, and abase the soul before God. They calm and meeken our turbulent spirit, tame the fierceness of our nature, soften our obstinacy and self-will, crucify us to the world, and bring us to expect all our strength from, and to seek all our happiness in, God." (Wesley 1872e, 121) Given these perspectives on the affections and the role of emotions in the life of the believer, we err greatly when we despise the affections and our emotional life.

Previously, I mentioned that Wesley also gave me a language for understanding the appropriate use of our affectional life. This language involves the use of the words *ordered* and *regulated* that stand in stark contrast to being *disordered* and *unregulated*. Wesley believed that the latter options constituted the only possibilities when our wills stand in rebellion against the will of God. However, he believed that when we surrender our wills to God, He begins to order and regulate all of life. I have found this idea of an ordered and regulated life a helpful way of thinking about a life transformed by God. I suppose the term *ordered* partly appeals to me because of my role as a psychologist. In my field, I often encounter the opposite since much of our work focuses on disorder; psychologists and other mental health clinicians most often treat mental disorders. Such disorders revolve around behavioral or psychological indications in an individual and are associated with distress and impairment in several areas of functioning. What's more such distress or impairment usually revolves around suffering and the possibility of death, pain, additional disability or some loss of freedom. (American Psychiatric Association 2000) This is the stuff we deal with on a regular basis. Of course, the positive psychology movement now suggests that this ought not to be the only focus; rather, it suggests psychology ought to focus on strength and virtue. This entails a return to two of psychology's original missions: Facilitating more productive and fulfilling humans lives and nurturing human talent once identified. (Seligman and Csikszenmihalyi 2000) Accordingly, such proponents suggest a new message and mission for psychology:

> ... our message is to remind our field that psychology is the not just the study of pathology, weakness, and damage; it is also the study of strength and virtue. Treatment is not just fixing what is broken; it is nurturing what is best. Psychology is not just a branch of medicine concerned with illness or health; it is much larger. It is about work, education, insight, love, growth and play." (Seligman and Csikszenmihalyi 2000, 7)

But despite such calls, many of us still major in disorder – disordered individuals, disordered relationships and disordered lives. How much better it would be to focus on order rather than disorder! I do not say this to eliminate any consideration of disorder; Instead, I do so to suggest that that which gives order merits closer and keener consideration. I think it is to order that the positive psychologists beckon when they invite us to focus on strengths and virtue. However, such calls to virtue can sometimes appear nebulous. Virtue requires a standard by which one can decide what is really virtuous and best. I am not sure that positive psychology provides such a standard.

But God does provide such standards by which one can judge virtuous. In fact, His true purpose is to create virtuous persons. Fundamentally, this involves creating persons whose lives are ordered instead of disordered. Through His transformation in the human soul God seeks to create order everywhere, just like He did at creation. One fundamental area in which God seeks to bring order is within our tempers, affections and passions. He wishes to regulate these affections and passions by the power of faith and love poured into us by the Holy Spirit. When the affections and passions become so ordered, they begin to function as God intended. God begins to transform them to such a degree that they can become habituated tempers of the heart reflecting a standing way of being. But the ordered life God envisions for us extends beyond the religious affections. Living our lives under the reign of God has the potential to bring all of life under due regulation. We can have an ordered sense of identity whereby we make realistic assessments about ourselves, based on God's criteria. Relationships with ourselves and with others can also become ordered. In all of this, there lies a strange irony. We often think that by controlling our own lives and living by our own will, we will produce an ordered life. Yet, by pursuing this path, we normally bring a great deal of disorder to our lives. Paradoxically, life becomes ordered when we live under the rule of God.

Cultivating Love

But life also becomes ordered when God's love reigns in our lives. Love's reign orders our relationships with God, ourselves and others. Ordered love also becomes the wellspring of other holy tempers and affections. (Wesley 1872o) Of course, this transformation in love centrally stems from God's work in the human heart through the Holy Spirit. (Romans 5:5) But even here, there exists a place for us to cooperantly respond. This means we have a role to play in enhancing and living out love. Since love cannot be coerced from anyone, we must choose to love. (Wynkoop 1972) Choosing to love only becomes real when we exercise liberty or agency. Deliberate choice helps actualize our ability to love our neighbors or even ourselves. We even see this idea implicit in the words of Jesus. We see it in the Sermon on the Mount when Jesus called His disciples to a new way of love; instead of hating their enemies as was commonly endorsed, He called them to love. (Matthew 5:43-44) It's also present in the Great Commandment. Jesus enjoined a thoroughgoing love for God with a concomitant love to neighbor-as-self. (Matthew 22: 37-39) But even though Jesus commanded it, the hearers had a choice; instead of following His command, they could choose to hate their neighbors. Loving in the way God intended involved a choice only they could make; no one could coerce them or us to love. In fact, this idea that love involves choice appears across many pages of Scripture. However, for brevity's sake I choose to mention one key passage. This passage is Paul's famous declaration on love in I Corinthians 13. In it, he extolled the virtue of love and then described it's nature. Immediately following this passage, Paul called his readers to "Follow the way of love." (I Corinthians 14:1, NIV) In this command, there exists the implicit message that one can choose to follow another way. However, Paul desired they chose to follow the path of love he had laid out in chapter 13. Love always involves choice.

In fact, according to previous insights portrayed in chapter five, one can choose to love even when one does not feel loving. As the reader might recall, Leffel drew a distinction between the action tendency of love and the phenomenological experience of feeling loving. (Leffel 2007) Christian love gives rise to loving behaviors. However, this does not mean that loving feelings always accompany loving behaviors; in short, one can act out of love, without necessarily experiencing loving feelings in that moment. When Jesus commanded that we love our enemies, I rather doubt he envisioned having loving and warm fuzzy feelings towards them. But even in the absence of these feelings, one can choose to act out of love. One can act like God who impartially sends His rain and sun without condition. He calls us to be like that even to our enemies. As such, we can do loving deeds towards such persons. We can even pray for them. In the process, we might notice a strange paradox; we might actually develop great compassion and positive feelings towards our enemies. Moreover, this loving transformation might occur even if our enemies still maintain their hateful stance towards us.

As strange as it sounds, the choice to love begins with our choice to love God. But we do not start the movement; any choice to love God stems from His initiating love towards us. But in loving God, we must also choose to love ourselves and our neighbors. For Christians, one of the most difficult parts of this equation is learning to love ourselves. This partly derives from a Christian culture that seems to make self-hatred a virtue. As such, it indicates to many persons, sometimes against our better instincts, that we ought not to love ourselves. But this difficulty or inability to adequately love ourselves sometimes derives from deep wounds from the past. These ancient wounds sometimes stymie our ability to lovingly relate to ourselves in the present. (Brunner 1956) In the therapy room some individuals sometimes betray a deep hatred for themselves. Often, this derived from growing up in homes and institutions where one could only gain love if one measured up to conditions of worth; that is, one could experience momentary times when one felt loved but only if some externally imposed standard was met. Those standards often involved such things as getting good grades or exemplifying good behavior. Love for self does not grow very well under conditions of worth. Such conditions more likely foster perfectionism – measuring up as a basis for receiving momentary love and affection. But even if love is offered under these conditions, it is not love for persons because of who they are; it is a love that springs from what they do. No wonder this kind of momentary love quickly dissipates when the standard is met! Any recurrence and hints of rekindled love awaits another instance of measuring up; in the interim, love received remains a distant memory. Living under conditions of worth rarely produces an authentic love for self.

In fact, such conditions more likely envelopes us in fear; fears from the past combined with a yearning to be love. But the fears also involve the future; we might fear that given past experiences, we will never find love in the future. Gripped by these fears of the past and anxieties of the future, we find it almost impossible to lovingly relate in the present. (Brunner 1956) Even the most sincere believer might find it difficult to lovingly relate to God. After all, God looks too much like the parent or the authority figure who only loved if certain conditions were met. We might find it difficult to love ourselves, deeming ourselves thoroughly unlovable and unworthy of love. Of course, because love for self constitutes a prerequisite for loving others, these difficulties makes loving others rather difficult. (Lindstrom 1980) Along with this difficulty in loving, there often also coexists a lack of empathy for others and the inability to be gracious with others. This is no great surprise! A lack of self-empathy and the inability to extend grace to ourselves often carry interpersonal consequences: It's almost impossible to do for others what we cannot do for ourselves.

So what can one do to cultivate love in such circumstances? Following Wesley's intentional methods for transformation, one can choose to engage in community. I do not mean to communicate that this is an easy task. We might yet approach it with a great deal of trepidation and fearfulness. However, participation in community can offer tremendous benefits; it can become a place that provides a corrective emotional experience. Here, we can discover a love that goes beyond conditions of worth. In fact, we might discover that it provides a place where we are accepted and loved unconditionally. This unconditional love can facilitate coming out of our shells even if done slowly and cautiously. With each expression of love and acceptance, we might even learn to accept and reveal who we truly are. In short, community might become a looking glass where in the context of relationships, we come to perceive ourselves more accurately than before. Love received from others might even help objectify our sense of worth so that we come to love ourselves in an acceptable manner. Furthermore, a community characterized by love might help us to form a more accurate view of the love God has for us. But it might also serve to counteract faulty views about God; in the symbolic love of others who love us unconditionally, we might come to perceive God as the loving father He is. This new perception can foster more loving and intimate relationship with Him. But in such contexts, we can also come to honestly and openly love others. In short, a community might become a place where love and its role in relationships become radically redefined and corrected. It might also become a place where we choose, even if slowly and hesitantly, to move away from fear. Here, we might actually learn not to fear and how to love. (Cozolino 2006a; Cozolino 2006b)

But besides this avenue of social contact, there exists other options for cultivating the ability to love. Though I might appear somewhat self-serving in this regard, I wish to focus on therapeutic activities which can further the work of love and holy transformation. Several persons have suggested that counseling and therapy can influence and deepen the affections and tempers. (Stevens 2006; Strawn 2004; Tjeltveit 2006) This influence and deepening also applies to the master temper of love. What's more, counseling, psychotherapy and various therapeutic activities can also address the relational barriers that inhibit the growth of love. (Headley October 5, 2010) In this regard and in keeping with Wesley, one can consider these activities means of grace. As such, psychotherapeutic activities when done from a Christian perspective might serve spiritual formation. Furthermore, although some might debate it, these activities might form one spiritually even when the practice is not explicitly Christian. Psychotherapy can serve this role because it "... creates and maintains a relational space, addresses interpersonal fears, and fosters love for others in an atmosphere of love." (Watson 2000, 290) I would add that psychotherapy can also foster a love of self that opens wide the gate for loving others. Ultimately, psychotherapy and related activities help foster in individuals the capacity to love. (Watson 2000) But they also facilitate love through weakening or removing the barriers that impede love. Driven by fear and anxiety, these barriers might dictate who we love, when we love, to what extent and under what circumstances. All of these considerations serve to limit our capacity to love. What's more, few of us come to adulthood without being impacted in some of these ways, whether unintentional or intentional; most, if not all of us, have had experiences that hinder, obstruct or detract from fully engaging in relationships deeply characterized by love. Engaging and addressing these issues can remove the barriers. When this occurs, it creates the possibility of new growth in love. But whatever path we choose, by choosing to love consistently, even when difficult, we help foster that habit within ourselves; love then becomes a standing temper, a habitual disposition what deeply characterizes who we are.

In chapters four and five, I devoted some attention to describing three aspects of the religious affections: the objective, the relational and the dispositional. I also indicated that these three applied to love. Without traversing this entire ground once more, it seems wise to briefly speak about these in relation to cultivating love. From the objective perspective, the love that transforms is a love where God serves as both the subject (the spring) as well as the object of love. In the latter regard, we best cultivate love when we make God the principal focus of our attention. Making Him the singular focus of our attentions fosters holy transformation. Unfortunately, we often allow other things to capture our heart. Some of these things, though legitimate, become disordered when they become the principle focus of our attention. How many persons are they who allow legitimate appetites to grasp their focus and attention so as to lead their hearts astray? Even within the Christian community there are rising reports of believers becoming hooked on pornography and other habits that tease legitimate God-given appetites. Unfortunately, the habits invariably leave us deformed rather than transformed. Such habits do not contribute to the holy transformation God requires for us. But compelled and deeply drawn by such habits, such persons actively resist anything that looks like rules. After all, rules might help draw them away from the objects of their affections. Personally, I have no problem with good rules. To me, good rules serve as boundaries for our protection and wellbeing; they set limits that keep humans from shaming, deforming and destroying themselves. Good rules also precipitate self-awareness that can inspire choice. In turn, making responsible choices invariably plays a major role in who we become. H. Richard Niebuhr said as much when he reminded us that: "We come to self-awareness if not to self-existence in the midst of mores, of commandments and rules, Thou shalts and Thou shalt nots, of direction and permission." (Niebuhr 1963, 52) But if one yet despises rules, perhaps one will do: *Never allow any person or thing other than God to become the primary object of your affection.*

But as I have repeatedly stressed, love also involves relationships. Principally, we should aspire to relate to God above all else. In this sense, every other relationship is secondary. That's why making other objects the principal focus of our attention involves a kind of idolatry. But giving God his rightful place in our lives inevitably leads to loving others. St. John put it well when he reminded us: "Whoever claims to love God yet hates a brother or sister is a liar. For whoever does not love their brother and sister, whom they have seen, cannot love God, whom they have not seen. And he has given us this command: Anyone who loves God must also love their brother and sister." (1 John 4:20-21, NIV) In other words, love of God is inextricably bound up with loving others. Christianity is eminently a social religion that binds believer to believer and believers to the world. (Wesley 1872m) But even this love recognizes priorities; it starts with attending to our nearest neighbors before wending its way into the world. (Wesley 1872b; Wesley 1872p) How many of us, whether in the ordained ministry or not, ignore the duty we owe to ourselves and our families. I have heard countless stories of believers and ministers who ignored themselves and their families in their drive to save the world. These persons placed the great focus on others to the detriment of themselves and families. It is not that the world doesn't matter. It's a matter of priorities: Disinterested love owed to all starts at home, even while it seeks to make itself visible in the larger world.

Finally, the love that God desires to cultivate in us is dispositional in nature; it aims to transform us at the core of our being making us into the very likeness of Christ. It aims to go so deeply as to transforms our very character. In fact, what God really desires is to make His pure love the chief characteristic of our being. He desires to deeply embed His love within us so that it naturally flows out in every area of our lives. To speak in this manner is really to come full circle and again resurrect images of Wesley's purposeful list. Wesley began his list with an emphasis on the right heart and right thinking. It is within these interior places that God aims to transform us.

But one can also think of dispositional transformation in terms of the virtues. Holy transformation or Christian perfection involves embracing and becoming a person of virtuous character. This means that we intentionally work to cultivate the virtues in our lives. Following a classic definition of the virtues, Sire described the virtues as theological, moral, and intellectual. The theological virtues involve charity, faith and hope. These virtues have God as their object and God himself infuses these with humans. To a large extent, when I speak of the inculcation of love with humans, I largely have these virtues in mind. But one cannot help cultivate these moral virtues without relinquishing vice and along with it the love of the world, the flesh and the devil. However, the other virtues also have a legitimate role in the life of the Christian. The moral virtues that involve prudence, justice, fortitude and temperance only become real in the

Christian through habitual exercise. But I think these also connect to the fruit of the Spirit, especially when one notes the presence of temperance (self-control). Finally, the intellectual include prudence, science, wisdom and art. These virtues become real through the use of the faculties of the soul, particularly the apprehending faculties. (Sire 2000) Thus, although I have implicitly given primary emphasis to the moral virtues, one ought not to ignore these other categories. All of these virtues ought to become the aspirations of one who embraces the holy life.

Practicing the Means of Grace

Finally, becoming holy persons requires participation in the means of grace. Not surprisingly, the means of grace possess a vital connection to love. The means of grace serve as a path for exercising and enhancing love and the holy tempers and affections it engenders. (Wesley 1872h) Wesley especially attached such purposes to the works of mercy. Works of mercy in all their forms serve to accomplish these holy purposes within the believer. Thus, even though we participate in works of mercy to benefit the souls and bodies of our neighbors, this does not mean no personal benefits accrue to the believer. They all serve to confirm us in love. Additionally, they serve to exercise and improve us in the fruit of the Spirit and contribute to more fully embracing the mind of Christ. (Wesley 1872h) But these benefits also apply to works of piety. Spiritual disciplines like reading Scripture, church attendance, participation in the Lord's Supper, prayer and fasting all serve to foster holy transformation. One of the ways in which the disciplines foster transformation is through liberating us from our fears and our stubborn determination to pursue our own interests. But the disciplines also place us before God so He can transform us. (Foster 1993) They allow for focused concentration on God as divine object. Through such focus, with "unveiled faces," God can transform us more and more into His likeness. Ruth Haley Barton affirmed a similar stance. For her, spiritual transformation primarily concerns choosing a way of life that opens us up to God's presence. Being opened up, God can then transform us at the deepest levels of our being. (Barton 2006)

This being the case, how does one explain the hesitation and sometimes, the refusal to participate in the means of grace? I suspect the reasons are numerous: busyness, benign neglect, disdain for the disciplines and the like. But whatever the reasons, many sincere believers neglect the spiritual disciplines. I often encounter persons training for ministry for whom the means of grace lie rather low in their list of priorities. Strangely enough, this even exists in those who claim great intimacy with God. Sometime ago, my colleague, Dr. Steve Stratton shared information on the Spiritual Transformation Inventory that I and many others found puzzling. Among other things, this instrument focuses on issues related to intimacy with God as well as participation in the disciplines. Students at Asbury Theological

Seminary take the instrument on two occasions: on entry and prior to graduation. What proved so puzzling for us was the contrast between reported intimacy with God and participation in the spiritual disciplines. Incoming students reported a strong sense of intimacy with God. However, they also reported low participation in the spiritual disciplines. (Stratton January 24, 2013) This data seemed to suggest a bifurcation between intimacy with God and the disciplines that foster relationship with Him. The data raises many questions in my mind. What was the nature of the intimacy being reported? To what degree was the intimacy primarily perceived in terms of *feeling* close to God? How much did this reported intimacy foster transformation in those who reported it? But more pertinent, what kind of intimacy with God is there that is not linked to the disciplines that place us in His presence? I am not sure of the answers to the previous questions. However, I think I know the answer to the last one. There is no real, transforming intimacy with God apart from opening up to Him through the disciplines. If we really desire for God to transform us from the inside out we will have to make place for all the means of grace.

Postscript

John Wesley described himself as a man of one book. However, this is only true if one considers the statement from a distinct perspective: Wesley committed himself deeply to the truth of Scripture and maintained this stance throughout his life. With this as the firm ground on which he stood, he read and wrote on a wide variety of topics. He demonstrated keen interest in the various writings and theories of his day, reading and interacting with various findings. When I read Wesley, I am amazed to discover the varied topics on which he wrote. Besides his scriptural sermons and writings, he wrote on mental health, science, politics, physical health and a range of other topics. Thereby, he demonstrated breadth and depth of interest coupled with keen insight. Besides being a man of the Church, he was a man of the world, if you will, a man of science who exhibited curiosity and keen observational skills. Because of these enduring traits, I think he would have reveled in the discoveries of neuroscience. I think he would have loved reading and investigating the latest findings, especially those that provided new insights into love. After all, his theology was centered on love. As such, I think he would show keen interest in the insights and observations made below by my friend and colleague, Dr. Steve Stratton.

Anthony Headley

Thinking Ahead: The Neuroscience of Wesley's Dispositional Love

Stephen P. Stratton, PhD
Professor of Counseling and Pastoral Care
Asbury Theological Seminary

John Wesley's theology about the growth of love is a balanced one. Looking across the previous chapters, we find that his view regarding the transformed heart, established in dispositional love, holds in tension a number of elements of human functioning that must remain in relation to one another. Lesser accounts often emphasize one aspect of humanity over another and tend to miss the messy but creative synthesis birthed in the tension. Less balanced perspectives tend to view love as a cognitive act of the will instead of an emotional expression related to will, but not both. Poorly integrated love may be interpreted as only a conscious choice, failing to take into account the nuisance of less conscious mindsets that include untidy predisposing motivations. Love with less balance can also become a single and solitary intrapersonal perspective, avoidant of the real world influences associated with interpersonal embeddedness. Moreover, love may be viewed as simply a spiritual process that is somehow higher and separate from an embodied approach, often seen as inherently carnal and creaturely. Wesley appears unwilling to engage in this kind of artificial bifurcation of human functioning, because he is not only systematic in his thinking but also experiential in his expression. For Wesley, there seems to be no right theology that is impractical, and there is no practical theology that lacks the inherent balance found in Scripture followed by reason, tradition, and experience. His theology is "fleshed out" so it can be "lived out." Wesley was a man of head, heart, and body – all were considered in the invitation to love.

Wesley's Radical Plan

Wesley's "fleshed out" and "lived out" theology of love, represented in the previous pages of this book, makes the connection to modern day behavioral sciences hard to avoid. This is not to say that Wesley was aware of the integrative foundation he was laying for the future. He was an inspired man of his day, but still a person of his age. He was certainly not able to glimpse the advances related to brain and relational research today. But in retrospect, he proposed embodied and embedded directions that continue to prove helpful for human functioning. He was a keen observer of the inner experience of human beings, and he was an innovative social architect of personal and corporate transformation. Without a precise understanding of all that he was doing, Wesley created a heart-renewal movement that appears directly connected to the growth of what we now call, the social brain. Grounded in a relational view of God and human persons, Wesley's method preemptively and fortuitously launched a radical plan that rested on principles of neural growth and neural change. In other words, Wesley's approach was inadvertently designed to grow brains managed by love instead of brains managed by fear.

In *The Neuroscience of Human Relationships* Louis Cozolino suggests from a brain-based perspective that personal and relational health is associated with learning to love and learning not to fear. (Cozolino 2006) This kind of healing "brain change" sounds amazingly reminiscent of the admonition in I John that perfect love casts out fear (4:18). For Cozolino, Wesley, and the Apostle John, the growth of dispositional love puts fear in its place. A mind centered on love reduces the domination of fear-related processes. A dispositionally loving brain is noted for its balance and integration, both qualities that get lost in a dispositionally fearful brain. Cozolino reports,

> [T]he experience of love . . . .greatly decreases activation of the [brain-based] fear systems . . . .Love is a relief from scanning the outer world for threat and our inner worlds for shame. Love turns off the alarm, cancels our insurance, and frees us from worry. (Cozolino 2006, 316)

Wesley's perspective grows from his biblically based assumption that human beings were made for a "Community of Love." Love was and is the natural habitat for men and women. It is where living is balanced and integrated. To extend the metaphor of the above quote from Cozolino, in a loving brain the hyper-alert sirens are silenced, and the self-protective weaponry can be laid aside when persons live in the confidence of loving attachments. Previous chapters on Wesley's thinking implicitly reinforce the idea that when persons grow in love, self can be viewed more accurately, and others can be seen in a realistic way, neither tainted by fearful reactivity. Nothing, even the Fall, has changed the fact that humans were and are made to live in the security of loving relationships with God and others. God's commands in Scripture for persons to love one another would be less than unkind; they would indeed be evil if such admonitions were not related to human design. Wesley's approach affirms this theological understanding – God commands love because it is characteristic of divine and human persons. Humans were made for love by Love. Dispositional fear works against design.

Growing Love in Community

Wesley's methods are intended to move us into loving communion where, incidentally, we have the best conditions for growing brains less dominated by fear. It is no mistake that Wesley wanted people to learn to love in "bands." Although he did not know explicitly that he was promoting brain change, he gravitated toward a model that had the potential of promoting secure attachments and non-shaming social engagements. Embedded in safe contexts, persons metaphorically became "naked and unashamed" (Genesis 2:25) as they were made to be. They were encouraged in a predictable communal setting to be open and vulnerable for their sake and others. Each "class meeting" became a holding environment where appropriate support and strategic challenge was not only permissible but also expected. A regular "dose" of connectedness and belonging from the communal method not only provided a less fearful context while meeting together, but it also increased the chances of generalizing such security to life beyond the band. (Wampold and Budge 2012)

These "holy clubs" became places where institutional and prudential habits were encouraged and practiced together. As considered in earlier chapters, these "means of grace" made space for the God of securing love to be present in the midst of a fallen and fearful world. When functioning well, a shared lifestyle and mindset grew within the community that inoculated one another against anxiety. Members were literally practicing security while being exposed to situations that provoked fear and self-protection. Situations that once reinforced fear were gradually associated with God's presence. This replacement of fear with love is the formula for intrapersonal and interpersonal transformation facilitated by principles of neuronal growth and change.

Learning not to Fear

Interpersonal neurobiologists suggest that the secure relationships, such as those one might find in Wesley's bands, could be seen as a hot house for growing loving brains over fearful ones. (Cozolino 2010; Siegel 2012b) Sociological research provides convincing evidence that emotional qualities, such as happiness and dysphoria, tends to cluster in social networks. (Christakis and Fowler 2009) Why not love? When brains come in contact in the context of safety and security, the activation of fear circuitry is usually reduced, while systems that are associated with love are increasingly stimulated. Growth in love requires repetitive calming of fear and persistent attention to love across real life situations. In the process, neurons grow to support dispositional love, while fear-based arousal patterns and memories are re-conditioned as well. Love and fear do indeed appear to be related, as the Apostle John proposed. Responding with love in the moment is directly connected to the development of lifestyles and mindsets that challenge fears. Moreover, it could be said that to grow a disposition of love, persons must develop practical plans (or holy habits) that are directly targeting their own unique way of fearing.

In *The Emotional Brain*, Joseph LeDoux summarizes the basic neuroscience literature to date to explain how fearful brains work. (LeDoux 1998) His description helps to clarify the relationship between fear and love. Whether the result of the Fall or God's created design, it is clear that increasing fear will trump attempts to create the conditions for love. Fear-based circuitry, centered in the brain's limbic system, operates faster than conscious reasoning and appears to be nearly automatic. A self-absorbed focus feels inevitable to persons perceiving some sort of threat. When human beings are faced with a threatening situation, the brain works by promoting survival first and foremost. Very simply, in milliseconds the limbic system of the brain perceives threat and demands fight, flight, or freeze before any real analysis of the circumstances can be effectively made. Frightened brains put love and other states on hold for later moments when that car is not so close or that growling dog is put on a leash. As neurobiologist Robert Sapolosky points out, such a system works well when threats are imminent, realistic, and short-lived. (Sapolsky 2004) Problems however begin to arise when fear-based living becomes the rule and not the exception. The body is never off alert and seldom balanced. The brain's functioning is no longer integrated; it is dominated by the body's emergency protection systems.

Wesley appears to have built his innovative transformational approach on the recognition that although humans are made for love, they now live in a fallen world that is invasively fear promoting. His practical theology is based on the idea of creating the conditions for love in the midst of a fearing culture. Intentional or not, renewing a love-based image of God in all human persons is strategically associated with growing secure relationships to God and others that persists in fearful moments. Based on the description of Wesley's thought in previous chapters, this process is not a call to general piety; it is more strategic. Reminiscent of Jesus' admonition in Luke 9:23-24, Wesley essentially calls for persons (1) to "deny" the entrenched self-protective and fear-based strategies upon which personal security relies, (2) to "take up" the task of living moment to moment without those self-absorbing strategies, and (3) to "follow" in a trusted relational journey with God.

Learning to Love

When a God-follower faces fear, intentional awareness of God and/or a trustworthy Christian community becomes the vitalizing force for the whole transformative process. A sustained, deliberate focus on particular sources of security makes the difference. Fear is not suppressed; instead, the conditions for love are intentionally selected where once they had been overlooked and forgotten. Developing a loving brain from a neuroscientific perspective ultimately comes down to "directed attention." Paying attention to and remaining attuned to love shapes the experience of the moment, restoring balance and integrated functioning. It is literally brain changing.

Interpersonal neurobiologists provide help in understanding the indispensable role of the "following" step, mentioned above (3), when it comes to learning not to fear. Any movement toward integrative states related to love and away from more fearful states is motivated by brain-based patterns that have been encoded from previous experiences with others. (Siegel 1999; Siegel 2012a) In essence, decisions about what is safe and/or approachable and what is unsafe and should be avoided grow from past episodes of "following" significant others. Those episodes, depending on time and intensity, progressively become embodied expectations about how self has to negotiate in a fearful world. The predictions that follow from such expectations enhance survival by promoting blazingly fast extrapolations from that which was learned in the past to the present. Those remembered experiences form the basis for an efficient life-management approach that is unconscious as well as conscious. Learning to love and learning not to fear must take into account memory at both levels.

Embodied and Embedded Love

Human memory certainly refers to that which can be intentionally recalled, consciously analyzed, and purposely structured, but it is also much deeper and more profound. Balancing this more explicit organization is an implicit version, related to that which Christopher Bollas creatively calls "unthought knowns." (Bollas C. 1987) Those are aspects of previous experiences that are encoded in memory but are not directly recalled or analyzed. They form the basis for that which is "assumed" about self and the world, and they tend to prime any conscious interpretation of what is happening in life. Some call these less conscious priming processes, "procedural memory," because they allow persons to know how to act without having to deliberately think through each aspect of the task. It can be an activity as simple as tying shoes, or it may be as complicated as handling an angry relative. The procedures that reduced fear in the past are initiated based on the felt-connection with the present moment. Again, this "fast" habituated mode of operating happens so quickly that human beings are often unconsciously primed for prescribed "protective" reactions before they "slowly" decide what actually fits the moment. The fast system is more related to minimizing fears than any well-considered and contextualized plan.

The growth of a dispositionally loving brain from a dispositionally fearing brain involves the adaptation of memory at the known and "unknown" levels. In actuality, it means a new kind of balance for slow and fast memory systems, respectively. It requires transformation in the way persons think and feel at known and unknown levels of human functioning. Cozolino explains,

> Getting past our fears and phobias does not entail forgetting to be afraid; rather, the extinction of fears presents new learning organized by our slow systems . . . .In other words, extinction learning represents the formation of new neural associations that somehow keep the memory stored in [limbic brain structures] from triggering the sympathetic nervous system.(Cozolino 2010, 254)

Notice that balanced and integrated brain change does not make fears go away. The goal is new learning through securing relational experiences that eventually make it less likely for the sympathetic nervous system and adrenal glands to be triggered by older patterns. The neural and hormonal systems are the ones that initiate the fight, flight, or freezes responses in the human body. Once those processes are initiated, the slow memory systems that support new learning are pushed aside for more efficient procedural crisis management. The hijacking of the brain for these remembered procedures from the past decreases the probability of more balanced and integrated loving responses that fit the relational context. The embodied brain opts for speed, not accuracy or contextualization, when facing the perceived needs of the moment.

If there is to be any balance, the time for new learning organized by the slow systems is before acute stressors occur. Then, the way persons have "slowly" and repetitively practiced thinking and feeling are more likely to remain present when "fast" responding is initiated. Over time, the practices that a person holds in place become the perceived reality that holds them in a fearful moment. Those habits truly become "means of grace." A revised version of a fearful brain requires this new approach to living – one that practices disciplined and integrated living with secure others across social situations and across time. The aim is to form new neural connections and revise old ones that support a sense of security, no matter what circumstances the person encounters. Slow and fast memory systems are gradually integrated, slowly adapting that which is known and unknown. Learning to love dispositionally means that persons remember in a new way. New and even healing social experiences are engaged, and old memories are revised in light of new learning. Habitually paying attention to and remaining attuned to love shapes the experience of the moment, restoring balance and integrated functioning. Over time, what captures a person's attention eventually captivates that person's brain and body.

Overcoming Immunity to Change

Robert Kegan is a pioneering developmental psychologist whose work has led him from researching theories about meaning-making across the lifespan into the practical engagement of fear in the corporate world. (Kegan 1982) Getting entrepreneurial women and men to consider their fears is not always a welcome task in the business sector, but it has very practical advantages. The creative engagement of fear has helped Kegan and his colleague, Lisa Lahey to understand why there is such a gap between a CEO's, for example, highest values and convictions and the way that CEO may actually live out those ideals in the organization. (Kegan and Lahey 2001; Kegan and Lahey 2009) Kegan and Lahey explain that it is not an issue of willpower or even motivation that seems to hinder the achievement of genuinely valued commitments. It is typically not a problem of skill or lack of applicable planning. For the areas that seem "immune to change," it is a more fundamental protective mechanism that competes with those true convictions. (Kegan and Lahey 2001)

Persons want their ideals *plus* they want to be free from fears. They absolutely want what they value, but they also desperately need to be safe and secure. Kegan and Lahey describe how most persons have their foot on "the gas" toward their ideals, while at the same time having their other foot on "the brake" to manage core fears that have developed over the years. (Kegan and Lahey 2009, 40) Ultimately, survival-based fears trump on-going resolutions for sincere adaptive change. Unthought knowns compete with more conscious commitments to be persons who are dedicated to, say, love.

Kegan and Lahey report,

> At the simplest level, any particular expression of the immunity to change provides us a picture of how we are systematically working against the very goal we genuinely want to achieve. But this dynamic equilibrium is preventing much more than progress on a single goal. It is maintaining a given place on the continuum of mental complexity (Kegan and Lahey 2009, 47)

From the preceding chapters, Wesley would certainly agree. Intentional or not, his approach appears to be less a call to perform certain loving actions and more a call to be a certain kind of person. Members of Wesley's bands were not learning a formula for being "nice" people instead of being fearful people. Like his Master and for the sake of his Master, Wesley seems to be developing a person who can act out of increased mental complexity that supports well-considered love and not reactive fears. Such persons are growing to see God, themselves, and a fallen world in a qualitatively different way. They appear to be cultivating a bigger picture of how to live with God and others in a fearful culture – less reacting and more reflecting. These persons are not smarter or even more creative, but they are growing more complex brains that can see and feel threats to fear, but they can also see opportunities to love. Dispositionally loving persons see both but are training to choose love long before they are even faced with the choice.

How does this happen? Wesley's innovative transformational strategies impact the embedded and embodied brain. His sanctifying approach creates the opportunities for fast and slow systems to be integrated. Learning to love in this Wesleyan model means training not to fear long before a person is faced with inevitable threats in this fearing culture. This training for Wesley occurs primarily in social contexts where security is practiced with partners who integrate tender and tough love. This process results in practical conditions for members to be "one as the Father and the Son are one" (John 17:21). An intrapersonal oneness creates the opportunity for an interpersonal oneness. It is an emotional as well as a cognitive exchange. The integration of head, heart, and body creates a balance where support and challenge are operative. The final goal is personal and corporate transformation – that the world may see and want, too. Wesley, the practical theologian, can still teach us a thing or two about learning to love.

References

Chapter 1: Christian Perfection and Wesley's Purposeful List

Baker, Frank. 1970. *John wesley and the church of england*. London: Epworth Press.

Clapper, Gregory S. 1987. Finding a place for emotions in christian theology. *Christian Century*: 409-410.

_____. 1985a. John wesley on religious affections: His views on experience and emotion and their role in the christian life and theology.Emory, Department of Theological Studies/Division of Philosphy.

_____. 1985b. True religion" and the affections : A study of john wesley's abridgement of jonathan edwards's treatise on religious affections. *Wesleyan Theology Today*: 416-423.

_____. 1984. True religion" and the affections : A study of john wesley's abridgement of jonathan edward's treatise on religious affections. *Wesleyan Theological Journal* 19, no. 2: 77-89.

Collins, Kenneth J. 2004. The promise of john wesley's theology for the 21st. century. *The Asbury Theological Journal* 59, no. 2: 171-180.

_____. 2003. *John wesley: A theological journey*. Nashville, TN: Abingdon Press.

_____. 1998. Wesley's topography of the heart: Dispositions, tempers, and affections. *Methodist History* 36, no. 3: 162-175.

Headley, Anthony J. 2010 Wesleyan theology: Its relevance for christian ministry. Asbury Theological Seminary.

Land, Steven J. 1993. *Pentecostal spirituality: A passion for the kingdom*. Sheffield, England: Sheffield Academic Press.

Leffel, G. Michael. 2007. Emotion and transformation in the relational spirituality paradigm part 3. A moral motive analysis. *Journal of Psychology and Theology* 35, no. 4: 298-316.

Maddox, Randy. 1994. *Responsible grace*. Nashville, TN: Kingswood Books.

Smith, Timothy L. 1982. A chronological list of wesley's sermons and doctrinal essays. *Wesleyan Theological Journal* 17, no. 2: 88-110.

Wesley, John. 1872a. *An extract of the rev. mr. john wesley's journal from august 12, 1738, to november 1, 1739*. The works of john wesley. Ed. Thomas Jackson. Vol. 1. Grand Rapids, Michigan: Baker Book House.

_____. 1872b. The good steward. In *The works of john wesley*, ed. Thomas Jackson. Vol. 6, 160-173. Grand Rapids, Michigan: Baker Book House.

_____. 1872c. The great assize. In *The works of john wesley*, ed. Thomas Jackson. Vol. 5, 249-263. Grand Rapids, Michigan: Baker Book House.

_____. 1872d. The new birth. In *The works of john wesley*, ed. Thomas Jackson. Vol. 6, 83-95. Grand Rapids, Michigan: Baker Book House.

_____. 1872e. On predestination. In *The works of john wesley*, ed. Thomas Jackson. Vol. 6, 254-260. Grand Rapids, Michigan: Baker Book House.

_____. 1872f. *A plain account of christian perfection*. The works of john wesley. Ed. Thomas Jackson. Vol. 11. Grand Rapids, Michigan: Baker Book House.

_____. 1872g. The repentance of believers. In *The works of john wesley*, ed. Thomas Jackson. 1872nd ed. Vol. 5, 234-248. Grand Rapids, Michigan: Baker Book House.

_____. 1872h. The righteousness of faith. In *The works of john wesley*, ed. Thomas Jackson. Vol. 5, 133-145. Grand Rapids, Michigan: Baker Book House.

_____. 1872i. The spirit of bondage and of adoption. In *The works of john wesley*, ed. Thomas Jackson. Vol. 5, 169-182. Grand Rapids, Michigan: Baker Book House.

_____. 1872j. Upon our lord's sermon on the mount, discourse 1. In *The works of john wesley*, ed. Thomas Jackson. Vol. 5, 331-346. Grand Rapids, Michigan: Baker Book House.

_____. 1872k. Upon our lord's sermon on the mount, discourse 10. In *The works of john wesley*. Vol. 5, 487-498. Grand Rapids, Michigan: Baker Book House.

_____. 1872l. Upon our lord's sermon on the mount, discourse 2. In *The works of john wesley*, ed. Thomas Jackson. Vol. 5, 347-363. Grand Rapids, Michigan: Baker Book House.

_____. 1872m. Upon our lord's sermon on the mount, discourse 4. In *The works of john wesley*, ed. Thomas Jackson. Vol. 5, 382-398. Grand Rapids, Michigan: Baker Book House.

_____. 1872n. Upon our lord's sermon on the mount, discourse 5. In *The works of john wesley*, ed. Thomas Jackson. Vol. 5, 399-416. Grand Rapids, Michigan: Baker Book House.

_____. 1872o. Upon our lord's sermon on the mount, discourse 7. In *The works of john wesley*, ed. Thomas Jackson. Vol. 5, 435-452. Grand Rapids, Michigan: Baker Book House.

_____. 1872p. Upon our lord's sermon on the mount, discourse 8. In *The works of john wesley*, ed. Thomas Jackson. Vol. 5, 453-470. Grand Rapids, Michigan: Baker Book House.

_____. 1872q. Upon our lord's sermon on the mount, discourse 9. In *The works of john wesley*, ed. Thomas Jackson. Vol. 5, 471-486. Grand Rapids, Michigan: Baker Book House.

_____. 1872r. The witness of our own spirit. In *The works of john wesley*, ed. Thomas Jackson. Vol. 5, 209-219. Grand Rapids, Michigan: Baker Book House.

Chapter 2: Wesley's Sources for Christian Perfection

Baker, Frank. 1970. *John wesley and the church of england*. London: Epworth Press.

Clapper, Gregory S. 1987. Finding a place for emotions in christian theology. *Christian Century*: 409-410.

_____. 1985a. John wesley on religious affections: His views on experience and emotion and their role in the christian life and theology. Emory, Department of Theological Studies/Division of Philosophy.

_____. 1985b. True religion" and the affections : A study of john wesley's abridgement of jonathan edwards's treatise on religious affections. *Wesleyan Theology Today*: 416-423.

_____. 1984. True religion" and the affections : A study of john wesley's abridgement of jonathan edward's treatise on religious affections. *Wesleyan Theological Journal* 19, no. 2: 77-89.

Collins, Kenneth J. 2004. The promise of john wesley's theology for the 21st. century. *The Asbury Theological Journal* 59, no. 2: 171-180.

_____. 2003. *John wesley: A theological journey*. Nashville, TN: Abingdon Press.

_____. 1998. Wesley's topography of the heart: Dispositions, tempers, and affections. *Methodist History* 36, no. 3: 162-175.

_____. 1989. *Wesley on salvation: A study in the standard sermons*. Grand Rapids: Francis Asbury Press.

Curnock, Nehemiah. 1909. *The journal of the rev. john wesley, A.M.* London: Charles H. Kelly.

Edwards, Maldwyn Lloyd. 1961. *Sons to samuel*. London: Epworth Press.

Headley, Anthony J. 2010. *Family crucible: The influence of family dynamics in the life and ministry of john wesley*. Eugene, Oregon: Wipf and Stock.

Heitzenrater, Richard P. 1984. *The elusive mr. wesley*. Nashville: Abingdon Press.

Langford, Thomas A. 1980. John wesley's doctrine of sanctification. *Bulletin of the United Church of Canada Committee on Archives and History* 29, : 63-73.

Law, William. 1997a. *A serious call to a devout and holy life*. 5th ed. Vol. 9. Albany, Oregon: Ages Software.

———. 1997b. *The spirit of love*. Vol. 9. Albany, Oregon: Ages Software.

Leffel, G. Michael. 2007. Emotion and transformation in the relational spirituality paradigm part 3. A moral motive analysis. *Journal of Psychology and Theology* 35, no. 4: 298-316.

Lindstrom, Harald. 1980. *Wesley and sanctification*. Wilmore, KY: Francis Asbury Publishing Company.

Maddox, Randy. 1994. *Responsible grace*. Nashville, TN: Kingswood Books.

Mann, Mark H. 2006. *Perfecting grace: Holiness, human being, and the sciences*. New York: T and T Clark International.

Outler, Albert Cook. 1980. John wesley's interest in the early fathers of the church. *Bulletin of the United Church of Canada Committee on Archives and History* 29, : 5-17.

———. 1964. *John wesley*. New York: Oxford University Press.

Smith, Timothy L. 1982. A chronological list of wesley's sermons and doctrinal essays. *Wesleyan Theological Journal* 17, no. 2: 88-110.

Strawn, Brad, D. 2004. Restoring moral affections of heart: How does psychotherapy heal. *Journal of Psychology and Christianity* 23, no. 2: 140-148.

Wesley, John. 1872a. Brief thoughts on christian perfection. In *The works of john wesley*, ed. Thomas Jackson. Vol. 11, 523-524. Grand Rapids, Michigan: Baker Book House.

———. 1872b. The end of christ's coming. In *The works of john wesley*, ed. Thomas Jackson. Vol. 6, 300-310. Grand Rapids, Michigan: Baker Book House.

———. 1872c. Farther thoughts on separation from the church. In *The works of john wesley*, ed. Thomas Jackson. Vol. 13, 337-339. Grand Rapids, Michigan: Baker Book House.

———. 1872d. The law established through faith, discourse 2. In *The works of john wesley*, ed. Thomas Jackson, 557-566. Grand Rapids, Michigan: Baker Book House.

———. 1872e. Of evil angels. In *The works of john wesley*, ed. Thomas Jackson. Vol. 6, 411-422. Grand Rapids, Michigan: Baker Book House.

———. 1872f. Of good angels. In *The works of john wesley*, ed. Thomas Jackson. Vol. 6, 401-410. Grand Rapids, Michigan: Baker Book House.

———. 1872g. On predestination. In *The works of john wesley*, ed. Thomas Jackson. Vol. 6, 254-260. Grand Rapids, Michigan: Baker Book House.

———. 1872h. *A plain account of christian perfection*. The works of john wesley. Ed. Thomas Jackson. Vol. 11. Grand Rapids, Michigan: Baker Book House.

———. 1872i. Upon our lord's sermon on the mount, discourse 1. In *The works of john wesley*, ed. Thomas Jackson. Vol. 5, 331-346. Grand Rapids, Michigan: Baker Book House.

_____. 1872j. Upon our lord's sermon on the mount, discourse 10. In *The works of john wesley*. Vol. 5, 487-498. Grand Rapids, Michigan: Baker Book House.

_____. 1872k. Upon our lord's sermon on the mount, discourse 11. In *The works of john wesley*, ed. Thomas Jackson. Vol. 5, 499-507. Grand Rapids, Michigan: Baker Book House.

_____. 1872l. Upon our lord's sermon on the mount, discourse 12. In *The works of john wesley*, ed. Thomas Jackson. Vol. 5, 508-518. Grand Rapids, Michigan: Baker Book House.

_____. 1872m. Upon our lord's sermon on the mount, discourse 13. In *The works of john wesley*, ed. Thomas Jackson. Vol. 5, 519-529. Grand Rapids, Michigan: Baker Book House.

_____. 1872n. Upon our lord's sermon on the mount, discourse 2. In *The works of john wesley*, ed. Thomas Jackson. Vol. 5, 347-363. Grand Rapids, Michigan: Baker Book House.

_____. 1872o. Upon our lord's sermon on the mount, discourse 3. In *The works of john wesley*, ed. Thomas Jackson. Vol. 5, 364-381. Grand Rapids, Michigan: Baker Book House.

_____. 1872p. Upon our lord's sermon on the mount, discourse 4. In *The works of john wesley*, ed. Thomas Jackson. Vol. 5, 382-398. Grand Rapids, Michigan: Baker Book House.

_____. 1872q. Upon our lord's sermon on the mount, discourse 5. In *The works of john wesley*, ed. Thomas Jackson. Vol. 5, 399-416. Grand Rapids, Michigan: Baker Book House.

_____. 1872r. Upon our lord's sermon on the mount, discourse 6. In *The works of john wesley*, ed. Thomas Jackson. Vol. 5, 417-434. Grand Rapids, Michigan: Baker Book House.

_____. 1872s. Upon our lord's sermon on the mount, discourse 7. In *The works of john wesley*, ed. Thomas Jackson. Vol. 5, 435-452. Grand Rapids, Michigan: Baker Book House.

_____. 1872t. Upon our lord's sermon on the mount, discourse 8. In *The works of john wesley*, ed. Thomas Jackson. Vol. 5, 453-470. Grand Rapids, Michigan: Baker Book House.

_____. 1872u. Upon our lord's sermon on the mount, discourse 9. In *The works of john wesley*, ed. Thomas Jackson. Vol. 5, 471-486. Grand Rapids, Michigan: Baker Book House.

_____. 1872v. The witness of our own spirit. In *The works of john wesley*, ed. Thomas Jackson. Vol. 5, 209-219. Grand Rapids, Michigan: Baker Book House.

_____. 1872w. The witness of the spirit, discourse 2. In *The works of john wesley*, ed. Thomas Jackson. Vol. 5, 196-208. Grand Rapids, Michigan: Baker Book House.

Chapter 3: Mapping the Soul: Liberty and the Apprehending Faculty of the Soul

Aquinas, Thomas. 1997. Summa theologica. In , ed. Version 5.0. Version 5.0 ed. Vol. 1. Albany, Oregon: Ages Software.

Beecher, Henry, Ward. 1995. The power of imagination. In *Developing A christian imagination: An interpretive anthology*, ed. Warren Wiersbe W., 215-221. Wheaton, Illinois: Victor Books.

Benner, David G. 2002. *Sacred companions: The gift of spiritual friendship and direction*. Downers Grove, Illinois: Intervarsity Press.

_____. 1998. *Care of souls: Revisioning christian nurture and counsel*. Grand Rapids, Michigan: Baker Books.

_____. 1988. *Psychotherapy and the spiritual quest*. Grand Rapids, Michigan: Baker Publishing Group.

Clapper, Gregory S. 1985. True religion" and the affections : A study of john wesley's abridgement of jonathan edwards's treatise on religious affections. *Wesleyan Theology Today*: 416-423.

Collins, Kenneth J. 1998. Wesley's topography of the heart: Dispositions, tempers, and affections. *Methodist History* 36, no. 3: 162-175.

_____. 1989. *Wesley on salvation: A study in the standard sermons*. Grand Rapids: Francis Asbury Press.

Defoe, Daniel. (On) the education of women. Fordham University. http://www.fordham.edu/halsall/mod/1719defoe-women.asp (accessed June/26, 2012).

Edwards, Jonathan. 1997. *A treatise concerning religious affections*. Vol. 2. Albany, OR: Ages Software.

Foster, Richard. 1993. *Celebration of discipline*. San Francisco: Harper.

Hands, Donald, R. and Wayne Fehr L. 1994. *Spiritual wholeness for clergy: A new psychology of intimacy with god, self and others*. Washington, D.C.: Alban Institute.

Headley, Anthony J. Summer, 1997. Wesley on depression. *The Asbury Herald*,.

Hurlbut, William and Paul Kalanithi. 2001. Evolutionary theory and the emergence of moral nature. *Journal of Psychology and Theology* 29, no. 4: 330-339.

Kaplan, Harold I. and Benjamin Sadock. 1991. *Synopsis of psychiatry*. Sixth ed. Baltimore, Maryland: Williams and Wilkins.

Land, Steven J. 1993. *Pentecostal spirituality: A passion for the kingdom*. Sheffield, England: Sheffield Academic Press.

Langford, Thomas A. 1980. John wesley's doctrine of justification by faith. *Bulletin of the United Church of Canada Committee on Archives and History* 29, : 47-62.

Lazarus, Arnold, A. 1989. *The practice of multimodal therapy*. Baltimore, Maryland: John Hopkins University Press.

Leffel, G. Michael. 2004. Prevenient grace and the re-enchantment of nature: Towards a wesleyan theology of psychotherapy and spiritual formation. *Journal of Psychology and Christianity* 23, no. 2: 130-139.

Maddox, Randy. 1994. *Responsible grace*. Nashville, TN: Kingswood Books.

Myers, Benjamin. 2006. Prevenient grace and conversion in paradise lost. *Milton Quarterly* 40, no. 1: 20-35.

Outler, Albert Cook. 1980. John wesley's interest in the early fathers of the church. *Bulletin of the United Church of Canada Committee on Archives and History* 29, : 5-17.

Richardson, Mary Sue. 2012. Counseling for work and relationships. *The Counseling Psychologist* 40, no. 2: 191-242.

Shapiro, David. 2000. *Dynamics of character: Self-regulation in psychopathology*. New York: Basic Books.

Sire, James W. 2000. *Habits of the mind: Intellectual life as a christian calling*. Downers Grove, IL: Intervarsity Press.

Strawn, Brad,D. 2004. Restoring moral affections of heart: How does psychotherapy heal. *Journal of Psychology and Christianity* 23, no. 2: 140-148.

Strawn, Brad and G. Michael Leffel. 2001. John wesley's orthokardia and harry guntrip's 'heart of the personal': Convergent aims and complementary practices in psychotherapy and spiritual formation. *Journal of Psychology and Christianity* 20, no. 4: 351-359.

Tjeltveit, Alan C. 2006. Psychology's love-hate relationship with love: Critiques, affirmations, and christian responses. *Journal of Psychology and Theology* 34, no. 1: 8-22.

Tozer, A. W. 1995. The value of a sanctified imagination. In *Developing a christian imagination: An intepretive anthology*, ed. Warren Wiersbe W., 211-214. Wheaton, Illinois: Victor Books.

Wesley Center Online. 2009. *The sermons of john wesley 1872 edition, chronologically ordered*Wesley Center for Applied Theology: Northwestern Nazarene University.

Wesley, John. 1872a. The almost christian. In *The works of john wesley*, ed. Thomas Jackson. Vol. 5, 81-89. Grand Rapids, Michigan: Baker Book House.

_____. 1872b. The case of reason impartially considered. In *The works of john wesley*, ed. Thomas Jackson. Vol. 6, 389-400. Grand Rapids, Michigan: Baker Book House.

_____. 1872c. Christian perfection. In *The works of john wesley*, ed. Thomas Jackson. Vol. 6, 13-36. Grand Rapids, Michigan: Baker Book House.

_____. 1872d. The end of christ's coming. In *The works of john wesley*, ed. Thomas Jackson. Vol. 6, 300-310. Grand Rapids, Michigan: Baker Book House.

_____. 1872e. An extract of A letter to the rev. mr. law occasioned by some of his late writings. In *The works of john wesley*, ed. Thomas Jackson. Vol. 9, 536-587. Grand Rapids, Michigan: Baker Book House.

_____. 1872f. A farther appeal to men of reason and religion, part 1. In *The works of john wesley*, ed. Thomas Jackson. Vol. 8, 55-157. Grand Rapids, Michigan: Baker Book House.

_____. 1872g. The first fruits of the spirit. In *The works of john wesley*, ed. Thomas Jackson. Vol. 5, 157-168. Grand Rapids, Michigan: Baker Book House.

_____. 1872h. The general deliverance. In *The works of john wesley*, ed. Thomas Jackson. Vol. 6, 272-284. Grand Rapids, Michigan: Baker Book House.

_____. 1872i. The good steward. In *The works of john wesley*, ed. Thomas Jackson. Vol. 6, 160-173. Grand Rapids, Michigan: Baker Book House.

_____. 1872j. Heaviness through manifold temptations. In *The works of john wesley*, ed. Thomas Jackson. Vol. 6, 111-123. Grand Rapids, Michigan: Baker Book House.

_____. 1872k. The important question. In *The works of john wesley*, ed. Thomas Jackson. Vol. 6, 545-558. Grand Rapids, Michigan: Baker Book House.

_____. 1872l. In what sense we are to leave the world. In *The works of john wesley*, ed. Thomas Jackson. Vol. 6, 514-525. Grand Rapids, Michigan: Baker Book House.

_____. 1872m. The journal of john wesley. In *The works of john wesley*, ed. Thomas Jackson. Vol. 1. Grand Rapids, Michigan: Baker Book House.

_____. 1872n. Justification by faith. Chap. 5, In *The works of john wesley*, ed. Thomas Jackson. Vol. 5, 120-132. Grand Rapids, MI: Baker Book House.

_____. 1872o. A letter to his brother charles, june 25, 1746. In *The works of john wesley*, ed. Thomas Jackson. Vol. 12, 88-99. Grand Rapids, Michigan: Baker Book House.

_____. 1872p. The new birth. In *The works of john wesley*, ed. Thomas Jackson. Vol. 6, 83-95. Grand Rapids, Michigan: Baker Book House.

_____. 1872q. On divine providence. In *The works of john wesley*, ed. Thomas Jackson. Vol. 6, 350-362. Grand Rapids, Michigan: Baker Book House.

_____. 1872r. On perfection. In *The works of john wesley*, ed. Thomas Jackson. Vol. 6, 455-469. Grand Rapids, Michigan: Baker Book House.

_____. 1872s. On the fall of man. In *The works of john wesley*, ed. Thomas Jackson. Vol. 6, 244-253. Grand Rapids, Michigan: Baker Book House.

_____. 1872t. Original sin. In *The works of john wesley*, ed. Thomas Jackson. Vol. 6, 71-82. Grand Rapids, Michigan: Baker Book House.

_____. 1872u. The original, nature, property and use of the law. In *The works of john wesley*. Vol. 5, 530-543. Grand Rapids, Michigan: Baker Book House.

_____. 1872v. Part 7: The doctrine of original sin. In *The works of john wesley*, ed. Thomas Jackson. Vol. 9, 496-533. Grand Rapids, Michigan: Baker Book House.

_____. 1872w. The repentance of believers. In *The works of john wesley*, ed. Thomas Jackson. Vol. 5, 234-248. Grand Rapids, Michigan: Baker Book House.

_____. 1872x. The righteousness of faith. In *The works of john wesley*, ed. Thomas Jackson. Vol. 5, 133-145. Grand Rapids, Michigan: Baker Book House.

_____. 1872y. The scripture way of salvation. In *The works of john wesley*, ed. Thomas Jackson. Vol. 6, 59-70. Grand Rapids, Michigan: Baker Book House.

_____. 1872z. Spiritual idolatry. In *The works of john wesley*, ed. Thomas Jackson. Vol. 6, 482-497. Grand Rapids, Michigan: Baker Book House.

_____. 1872aa. Thoughts on memory. In *The works of john wesley*, ed. Thomas Jackson. Vol. 13, 573. Grand Rapids, Michigan: Baker Book House.

_____. 1872ab. Thoughts on nervous disorders: Particularly that which is usually termed lowness of spirits. In *The works of john wesley*, ed. Thomas Jackson. Vol. 11, 603-608. Grand Rapids, Michigan: Baker Book House.

_____. 1872ac. Thoughts upon necessity. In *The works of john wesley*, ed. Thomas Jackson. Vol. 10, 541-559. Grand Rapids, Michigan: Baker Book House.

_____. 1872ad. Upon our lord's sermon on the mount, discourse 10. In *The works of john wesley*. Vol. 5, 487-498. Grand Rapids, Michigan: Baker Book House.

_____. 1872ae. Upon our lord's sermon on the mount, discourse 9. In *The works of john wesley*, ed. Thomas Jackson. Vol. 5, 471-486. Grand Rapids, Michigan: Baker Book House.

_____. 1872af. Wandering thoughts. In *The works of john wesley*, ed. Thomas Jackson. Vol. 6, 37-46. Grand Rapids, Michigan: Baker Book House.

_____. 1872ag. What is man? In *The works of john wesley*, ed. Thomas Jackson. Vol. 7, 254-260. Grand Rapids, Michigan: Baker Book House.

_____. 1872ah. The witness of our own spirit. In *The works of john wesley*, ed. Thomas Jackson. Vol. 5, 209-219. Grand Rapids, Michigan: Baker Book House.

Wynkoop, Mildred Bangs. 1972. *A theology of love*. Kansas City, MO: Beacon Hill Press.

Chapter 4: Mapping the Soul: The Will and the Religious Affections

American Psychiatric Association. 2000. *Diagnostic and statistical manual of mental disorders: Text revision, DSM-IV-TR*. Fourth ed. Washington, DC: American Psychiatric Association.

Bailey, Albert, Edward. 1950. *The gospel in hymns: Backgrounds and interpretations*. New York: Charles Scribner's Sons.

Chambers, Oswald. 1963. *My utmost for his highest.* Westwood, NJ: Barbour and Company, Inc.

Clairvaux, Bernard, Of. 1997. *On loving god.* The master christian library. Version 5 ed. Albany, OR: Ages Software.

Clapper, Gregory S. 1987. Finding a place for emotions in christian theology. *Christian Century*: 409-410.

———. 1985a. John wesley on religious affections: His views on experience and emotion and their role in the christian life and theology. Emory, Department of Theological Studies/Division of Philosophy.

———. 1985b. True religion" and the affections : A study of john wesley's abridgement of jonathan edwards's treatise on religious affections. *Wesleyan Theology Today*: 416-423.

———. 1984. True religion" and the affections : A study of john wesley's abridgement of jonathan edward's treatise on religious affections. *Wesleyan Theological Journal* 19, no. 2: 77-89.

Collins, Kenneth J. 2004. The promise of john wesley's theology for the 21st. century. *The Asbury Theological Journal* 59, no. 2: 171-180.

———. 2003. *John wesley: A theological journey.* Nashville, TN: Abingdon Press.

———. 1998. Wesley's topography of the heart: Dispositions, tempers, and affections. *Methodist History* 36, no. 3: 162-175.

Edwards, Jonathan. 1997. *A treatise concerning religious affections.* Vol. 2. Albany, OR: Ages Software.

Goleman, Daniel. 1995. *Emotional intelligence.* New York: Bantam Books.

Hurlbut, William and Paul Kalanithi. 2001. Evolutionary theory and the emergence of moral nature. *Journal of Psychology and Theology* 29, no. 4: 330-339.

Kilian, Marcus K. and Stephen Parker. 2001. A wesleyan spirituality: Implications for clinical practice. *Psychology and Theology* 29, no. 1: 72-80.

Law, William. 1997. *A serious call to a devout and holy life.* 5th ed. Vol. 9. Albany, Oregon: Ages Software.

Leffel, G. Michael. 2007. Emotion and transformation in the relational spirituality paradigm part 3. A moral motive analysis. *Journal of Psychology and Theology* 35, no. 4: 298-316.

Lillenas, Publishing. 1972. *Worship in song.* Kansas City, Missouri: Lillenas Publishing Company.

Maddox, Randy. 1998. Reconnecting the means to the end: A wesleyan prescription for the holiness movement. *Wesleyan Theological Journal* 33, no. 2: 29-66.

———. 1994. *Responsible grace.* Nashville, TN: Kingswood Books.

Nolfi, George. 2011. *The adjustment bureau.*

Špidlík, Tomáš. 2010. *The art of purifying the heart.* Miami: Convivium Press.

Wesley, John. 1997. *John wesley notes on the whole bible: The new testament*. Version 2.0 ed. Albany, Oregon: Sages Software.

_____. 1872a. A caution against bigotry. In *The works of john wesley*, ed. Thomas Jackson. Vol. 6, 580-594. Grand Rapids, Michigan: Baker Book House.

_____. 1872b. The end of christ's coming. In *The works of john wesley*, ed. Thomas Jackson. Vol. 6, 300-310. Grand Rapids, Michigan: Baker Book House.

_____. 1872c. An extract of A letter to the rev. mr. law occasioned by some of his late writings. In *The works of john wesley*, ed. Thomas Jackson. Vol. 9, 536-587. Grand Rapids, Michigan: Baker Book House.

_____. 1872d. The general deliverance. In *The works of john wesley*, ed. Thomas Jackson. Vol. 6, 272-284. Grand Rapids, Michigan: Baker Book House.

_____. 1872e. The general spread of the gospel. In *The works of john wesley*, ed. Thomas Jackson. Vol. 6, 311-322. Grand Rapids, Michigan: Baker Book House.

_____. 1872f. The great assize. In *The works of john wesley*, ed. Thomas Jackson. Vol. 5, 249-263. Grand Rapids, Michigan: Baker Book House.

_____. 1872g. Heaviness through manifold temptations. In *The works of john wesley*, ed. Thomas Jackson. Vol. 6, 111-123. Grand Rapids, Michigan: Baker Book House.

_____. 1872h. A letter to the reverend dr. conyers middleton: Occasioned by his late "free inquiry.". In *The works of john wesley*, ed. Thomas Jackson. Vol. 10, 11-97. Grand Rapids, Michigan: Baker Book House.

_____. 1872i. The new birth. In *The works of john wesley*, ed. Thomas Jackson. Vol. 6, 83-95. Grand Rapids, Michigan: Baker Book House.

_____. 1872j. Of evil angels. In *The works of john wesley*, ed. Thomas Jackson. Vol. 6, 411-422. Grand Rapids, Michigan: Baker Book House.

_____. 1872k. Of good angels. In *The works of john wesley*, ed. Thomas Jackson. Vol. 6, 401-410. Grand Rapids, Michigan: Baker Book House.

_____. 1872l. On perfection. In *The works of john wesley*, ed. Thomas Jackson. Vol. 6, 455-469. Grand Rapids, Michigan: Baker Book House.

_____. 1872m. On sin in believers. In , ed. Thomas Jackson. Vol. 5, 220-233. Grand Rapids, Michigan: Baker Book House.

_____. 1872n. On the fall of man. In *The works of john wesley*, ed. Thomas Jackson. Vol. 6, 244-253. Grand Rapids, Michigan: Baker Book House.

_____. 1872o. Original sin. In *The works of john wesley*, ed. Thomas Jackson. Vol. 6, 71-82. Grand Rapids, Michigan: Baker Book House.

_____. 1872p. Part 7: The doctrine of original sin. In *The works of john wesley*, ed. Thomas Jackson. Vol. 9, 496-533. Grand Rapids, Michigan: Baker Book House.

_____. 1872q. The repentance of believers. In *The works of john wesley*, ed. Thomas Jackson. Vol. 5, 234-248. Grand Rapids, Michigan: Baker Book House.

_____. 1872r. The righteousness of faith. In *The works of john wesley*, ed. Thomas Jackson. Vol. 5, 133-145. Grand Rapids, Michigan: Baker Book House.

_____. 1872s. The spirit of bondage and of adoption. In *The works of john wesley*, ed. Thomas Jackson. Vol. 5, 169-182. Grand Rapids, Michigan: Baker Book House.

_____. 1872t. Thoughts upon necessity. In *The works of john wesley*, ed. Thomas Jackson. Vol. 10, 541-559. Grand Rapids, Michigan: Baker Book House.

_____. 1872u. Upon our lord's sermon on the mount, discourse 2. In *The works of john wesley*, ed. Thomas Jackson. Vol. 5, 347-363. Grand Rapids, Michigan: Baker Book House.

_____. 1872v. Upon our lord's sermon on the mount, discourse 6. In *The works of john wesley*, ed. Thomas Jackson. Vol. 5, 417-434. Grand Rapids, Michigan: Baker Book House.

_____. 1872w. Upon our lord's sermon on the mount, discourse 7. In *The works of john wesley*, ed. Thomas Jackson. Vol. 5, 435-452. Grand Rapids, Michigan: Baker Book House.

_____. 1872x. Upon our lord's sermon on the mount, discourse 9. In *The works of john wesley*, ed. Thomas Jackson. Vol. 5, 471-486. Grand Rapids, Michigan: Baker Book House.

_____. 1872y. Wandering thoughts. In *The works of john wesley*, ed. Thomas Jackson. Vol. 6, 37-46. Grand Rapids, Michigan: Baker Book House.

_____. 1872z. The way to the kingdom. In *The works of john wesley*, ed. Thomas Jackson. Vol. 5, 146-156. Grand Rapids, Michigan: Baker Book House.

_____. 1872aa. What is man? In *The works of john wesley*, ed. Thomas Jackson. Vol. 7, 254-260. Grand Rapids, Michigan: Baker Book House.

_____. 1872ab. What is man? In *The works of john wesley*, ed. Thomas Jackson. Vol. 7, 194-201. Grand Rapids, Michigan: Baker Book House.

_____. 1872ac. *The works of john wesley: Journals 1735-1745*. Ed. Thomas Jackson. Vol. 1. Grand Rapids: Baker Book House.

Chapter 5: Relational Love and Christian Perfection

Bang Wynkoop, Mildred. 1975. John wesley - mentor or guru. *Wesleyan Theological Journal* 10, no. Spring: 5-5-14.

Clairvaux, Bernard, Of. 1997. *On loving god*. The master christian library. Version 5 ed. Albany, OR: Ages Software.

Clapper, Gregory S. 1984. True religion" and the affections : A study of john wesley's abridgement of jonathan edward's treatise on religious affections. *Wesleyan Theological Journal* 19, no. 2: 77-89.

Collins, Kenneth J. 1989. *Wesley on salvation: A study in the standard sermons*. Grand Rapids: Francis Asbury Press.

Headley, Anthony J. 2006. *Created for responsibility*. Anderson, IN: Bristol House Ltd.
Kilian, Marcus K. and Stephen Parker. 2001. A wesleyan spirituality: Implications for clinical practice. *Psychology and Theology* 29, no. 1: 72-80.
Land, Steven J. 1993. *Pentecostal spirituality: A passion for the kingdom*. Sheffield, England: Sheffield Academic Press.
Leffel, G. Michael. 2004. Prevenient grace and the re-enchantment of nature: Towards a wesleyan theology of psychotherapy and spiritual formation. *Journal of Psychology and Christianity* 23, no. 2: 130-139.
Lindstrom, Harald. 1980. *Wesley and sanctification*. Wilmore, KY: Francis Asbury Publishing Company.
Maddox, Randy. 1994. *Responsible grace*. Nashville, TN: Kingswood Books.
Myers, Benjamin. 2006. Prevenient grace and conversion in paradise lost. *Milton Quarterly* 40, no. 1: 20-35.
Olthuis, James H. 2006. With-ing: A psychotherapy of love. *Journal of Psychology and Christianity* 34, no. 1: 66-77.
Oord, Thomas and Michael Lodahl. 2005. *Relational holiness*. Kansas City, MO: Beacon Hill Press.
Richardson, Mary Sue. 2012. Counseling for work and relationships. *The Counseling Psychologist* 40, no. 2: 191-242.
Smith, Timothy L. 1982. A chronological list of wesley's sermons and doctrinal essays. *Wesleyan Theological Journal* 17, no. 2: 88-110.
Špidlík, Tomáš. 2010. *The art of purifying the heart*. Miami: Convivium Press.
Tjeltveit, Alan C. 2006a. Psychology returns to love --of god and neighbor-as-self: Introduction to the special issue. *Journal of Psychology and Theology* 34, no. 1: 3-7.
_____. 2006b. Psychology's love-hate relationship with love: Critiques, affirmations, and christian responses. *Journal of Psychology and Theology* 34, no. 1: 8-22.
Watson, Robert, A. 2000. Towards union in love: The contemplative spiritual tradition and contemporary psychoanalytic theory in the formation of persons. *Journal of Psychology and Theology* 28, no. 4: 282-282-292.
Wesley, John. 1997. *John wesley notes on the whole bible: The new testament*. Version 2.0 ed. Albany, Oregon: Sages Software.
_____. 1872a. The case of reason impartially considered. In *The works of john wesley*, ed. Thomas Jackson. Vol. 6, 389-400. Grand Rapids, Michigan: Baker Book House.
_____. 1872b. Catholic spirit. In *The works of john wesley*, ed. Thomas Jackson. Vol. 5, 595-607. Grand Rapids, Michigan: Baker Book House.
_____. 1872c. A collection of forms of prayers for every day in the week, sunday morning. In *The works of john wesley*, ed. Thomas Jackson. Vol. 11, 232-277.

_____. 1872d. The duty of reproving our neighbor. In *The works of john wesley*, ed. Thomas Jackson. Vol. 6, 331-339. Grand Rapids, Michigan: Baker Book House.

_____. 1872e. *An earnest appeal to men of reason and religion.* The works of john wesley. Ed. Thomas Jackson. Vol. 8. Grand Rapids, Michigan: Baker Book House.

_____. 1872f. The end of christ's coming. In *The works of john wesley*, ed. Thomas Jackson. Vol. 6, 300-310. Grand Rapids, Michigan: Baker Book House.

_____. 1872g. A farther appeal to men of reason and religion, part 2. In *The works of john wesley*, ed. Thomas Jackson. Vol. 8, 158-226. Grand Rapids, Michigan: Baker Book House.

_____. 1872h. The first fruits of the spirit. In *The works of john wesley*, ed. Thomas Jackson. Vol. 5, 157-168. Grand Rapids, Michigan: Baker Book House.

_____. 1872i. The general deliverance. In *The works of john wesley*, ed. Thomas Jackson. Vol. 6, 272-284. Grand Rapids, Michigan: Baker Book House.

_____. 1872j. Letter to a sister – miss furly, ST. IVES, *September* 15, 1762. In *The works of john wesley*, ed. Thomas Jackson. Vol. 12, 239-240. Grand Rapids, Michigan: Baker Book House.

_____. 1872k. A letter to the reverend dr. conyers middleton: Occasioned by his late "free inquiry.". In *The works of john wesley*, ed. Thomas Jackson. Vol. 10, 11-97. Grand Rapids, Michigan: Baker Book House.

_____. 1872l. The new birth. In *The works of john wesley*, ed. Thomas Jackson. Vol. 6, 83-95. Grand Rapids, Michigan: Baker Book House.

_____. 1872m. Of evil angels. In *The works of john wesley*, ed. Thomas Jackson. Vol. 6, 411-422. Grand Rapids, Michigan: Baker Book House.

_____. 1872n. Of good angels. In *The works of john wesley*, ed. Thomas Jackson. Vol. 6, 401-410. Grand Rapids, Michigan: Baker Book House.

_____. 1872o. On divine providence. In *The works of john wesley*, ed. Thomas Jackson. Vol. 6, 350-362. Grand Rapids, Michigan: Baker Book House.

_____. 1872p. On perfection. In *The works of john wesley*, ed. Thomas Jackson. Vol. 6, 455-469. Grand Rapids, Michigan: Baker Book House.

_____. 1872q. On riches. In *The works of john wesley*, ed. Thomas Jackson. Vol. 7, 244-253. Grand Rapids, Michigan: Baker Book House.

_____. 1872r. On the death of the rev. mr. george whitefield. In *The works of john wesley*, ed. Thomas Jackson. Vol. 6, 194-209. Grand Rapids, Michigan: Baker Book House.

_____. 1872s. On the fall of man. In *The works of john wesley*, ed. Thomas Jackson. Vol. 6, 244-253. Grand Rapids, Michigan: Baker Book House.

———. 1872t. *A plain account of christian perfection.* The works of john wesley. Ed. Thomas Jackson. Vol. 11. Grand Rapids, Michigan: Baker Book House.

———. 1872u. A second letter to the author of "the enthusiasm of methodists and papists compared" to the right reverend lord bishop of exeter. In *The works of john wesley*, ed. Thomas Jackson. Vol. 9, 23-29. Grand Rapids, Michigan: Baker Book House.

———. 1872v. A short address to the inhabitants of ireland occasioned by some late occurrences. In *The works of john wesley*, ed. Thomas Jackson. Vol. 9, 203-208. Grand Rapids, Michigan: Baker Book House.

———. 1872w. The unity of the divine being. In *The works of john wesley*, ed. Thomas Jackson. Vol. 7, 298-307. Grand Rapids, Michigan: Baker Book House.

———. 1872x. Upon our lord's sermon on the mount, discourse 1. In *The works of john wesley*, ed. Thomas Jackson. Vol. 5, 331-346. Grand Rapids, Michigan: Baker Book House.

———. 1872y. Upon our lord's sermon on the mount, discourse 10. In *The works of john wesley*. Vol. 5, 487-498. Grand Rapids, Michigan: Baker Book House.

———. 1872z. Upon our lord's sermon on the mount, discourse 11. In *The works of john wesley*, ed. Thomas Jackson. Vol. 5, 499-507. Grand Rapids, Michigan: Baker Book House.

———. 1872aa. Upon our lord's sermon on the mount, discourse 13. In *The works of john wesley*, ed. Thomas Jackson. Vol. 5, 519-529. Grand Rapids, Michigan: Baker Book House.

———. 1872ab. Upon our lord's sermon on the mount, discourse 2. In *The works of john wesley*, ed. Thomas Jackson. Vol. 5, 347-363. Grand Rapids, Michigan: Baker Book House.

———. 1872ac. Upon our lord's sermon on the mount, discourse 3. In *The works of john wesley*, ed. Thomas Jackson. Vol. 5, 364-381. Grand Rapids, Michigan: Baker Book House.

———. 1872ad. Upon our lord's sermon on the mount, discourse 4. In *The works of john wesley*, ed. Thomas Jackson. Vol. 5, 382-398. Grand Rapids, Michigan: Baker Book House.

———. 1872ae. Upon our lord's sermon on the mount, discourse 5. In *The works of john wesley*, ed. Thomas Jackson. Vol. 5, 399-416. Grand Rapids, Michigan: Baker Book House.

———. 1872af. Upon our lord's sermon on the mount, discourse 7. In *The works of john wesley*, ed. Thomas Jackson. Vol. 5, 435-452. Grand Rapids, Michigan: Baker Book House.

———. 1872ag. Upon our lord's sermon on the mount, discourse 8. In *The works of john wesley*, ed. Thomas Jackson. Vol. 5, 453-470. Grand Rapids, Michigan: Baker Book House.

_____. 1872ah. Upon our lord's sermon on the mount, discourse 9. In *The works of john wesley*, ed. Thomas Jackson. Vol. 5, 471-486. Grand Rapids, Michigan: Baker Book House.

_____. 1872ai. The use of money. In *The works of john wesley*, ed. Thomas Jackson. Vol. 6, 147-159. Grand Rapids, Michigan: Baker Book House.

_____. 1872aj. The way to the kingdom. In *The works of john wesley*, ed. Thomas Jackson. Vol. 5, 146-156. Grand Rapids, Michigan: Baker Book House.

Wesley, John. 1872ak. Circumcision of the heart. Chap. 5, In *The works of john wesley*, ed. Thomas Jackson, 282-292. Grand Rapids: Baker Book House.

_____. 1872al. The scripture way of salvation. In *The works of john wesley*, ed. Thomas Jackson. Vol. 6, 59-70. Grand Rapids, Michigan: Baker Book House.

Wynkoop, Mildred Bangs. 1972. *A theology of love*. Kansas City, MO: Beacon Hill Press.

Chapter 6: Objective, Dispositional Love and Christian Perfection

American Psychiatric Association. 2000. *Diagnostic and statistical manual of mental disorders: Text revision, DSM-IV-TR*. Fourth ed. Washington, DC: American Psychiatric Association.

Brown, Jeannine K., Carla M. Dahl, and Wyndy Corbin Reuschling. 2011. *Becoming whole and holy: An integrative conversation about christian formation*. Grand Rapids, Michigan: Baker Academic.

Brown, William P. 1996. *Character in crisis: A fresh approach to the wisdom literature of the old testament*. Grand Rapids, Michigan: William B. Eerdmans.

Clapper, Gregory S. 1987. Finding a place for emotions in christian theology. *Christian Century*: 409-410.

_____. 1985a. John wesley on religious affections: His views on experience and emotion and their role in the christian life and theology. Emory, Department of Theological Studies/Division of Philosophy.

_____. 1985b. True religion" and the affections : A study of john wesley's abridgement of jonathan edwards's treatise on religious affections. *Wesleyan Theology Today*: 416-423.

_____. 1984. True religion" and the affections : A study of john wesley's abridgement of jonathan edward's treatise on religious affections. *Wesleyan Theological Journal* 19, no. 2: 77-89.

Collins, Kenneth J. 2003. *John wesley: A theological journey*. Nashville, TN: Abingdon Press.

_____. 1998. Wesley's topography of the heart: Dispositions, tempers, and affections. *Methodist History* 36, no. 3: 162-175.

Edwards, Jonathan. 1997. *A treatise concerning religious affections.* Vol. 2. Albany, OR: Ages Software.
Goleman, Daniel. 1995. *Emotional intelligence.* New York: Bantam Books.
Headley, Anthony J. 2006. *Created for responsibility.* Anderson, IN: Bristol House Ltd.
Kaplan, Harold I. and Benjamin Sadock. 1991. *Synopsis of psychiatry.* Sixth ed. Baltimore, Maryland: Williams and Wilkins.
Kilian, Marcus K. and Stephen Parker. 2001. A wesleyan spirituality: Implications for clinical practice. *Psychology and Theology* 29, no. 1: 72-80.
Land, Steven J. 1993. *Pentecostal spirituality: A passion for the kingdom.* Sheffield, England: Sheffield Academic Press.
Langford, Thomas A. 1980. John wesley's doctrine of sanctification. *Bulletin of the United Church of Canada Committee on Archives and History* 29, : 63-73.
Leffel, G. Michael. 2007. Emotion and transformation in the relational spirituality paradigm part 3. A moral motive analysis. *Journal of Psychology and Theology* 35, no. 4: 298-316.
Mann, Mark H. 2006. *Perfecting grace: Holiness, human being, and the sciences.* New York: T and T Clark International.
Maxmen, Jerrold S. and Nicholas G. Ward. 1995. *Essential psychopathology and its treatment.* Second ed. New York: W. W. Norton and Company.
Shapiro, David. 2000. *Dynamics of character: Self-regulation in psychopathology.* New York: Basic Books.
Sire, James W. 2000. *Habits of the mind: Intellectual life as a christian calling.* Downers Grove, IL: Intervarsity Press.
Špidlík, Tomáš. 2010. *The art of purifying the heart.* Miami: Convivium Press.
Strawn, Brad and G. Michael Leffel. 2001. John wesley's orthokardia and harry guntrip's 'heart of the personal': Convergent aims and complementary practices in psychotherapy and spiritual formation. *Journal of Psychology and Christianity* 20, no. 4: 351-359.
Wesley, John. 1997. *John wesley notes on the whole bible: The new testament.* Version 2.0 ed. Albany, Oregon: Sages Software.
_____. 1872a. Circumcision of the heart. In *The works of john wesley,* ed. Thomas Jackson. Vol. 5, 282-292. Grand Rapids: Baker Book House.
_____. 1872b. The end of christ's coming. In *The works of john wesley,* ed. Thomas Jackson. Vol. 6, 300-310. Grand Rapids, Michigan: Baker Book House.
_____. 1872c. The law established through faith, discourse 2. In *The works of john wesley,* ed. Thomas Jackson, 557-566. Grand Rapids, Michigan: Baker Book House.
_____. 1872d. A letter to the reverend dr. conyers middleton: Occasioned by his late "free inquiry.". In *The works of john wesley,* ed. Thomas Jackson. Vol. 10, 11-97. Grand Rapids, Michigan: Baker Book House.

———. 1872e. The nature, design, and general rules of the united societies. In *The works of john wesley*, ed. Thomas Jackson. Vol. 8, 301-304. Grand Rapids, Michigan: Baker Book House.

———. 1872f. *On grieving the holy spirit.* The works of john wesley. Ed. Thomas Jackson. Vol. 7. Grand Rapids, Michigan: Baker Book House.

———. 1872g. On predestination. In *The works of john wesley*, ed. Thomas Jackson. Vol. 6, 254-260. Grand Rapids, Michigan: Baker Book House.

———. 1872h. On sin in believers. In , ed. Thomas Jackson. Vol. 5, 220-233. Grand Rapids, Michigan: Baker Book House.

———. 1872i. *A plain account of christian perfection.* The works of john wesley. Ed. Thomas Jackson. Vol. 11. Grand Rapids, Michigan: Baker Book House.

———. 1872j. The principles of A methodist further explained. In *The works of john wesley*, ed. Thomas Jackson, 486-560. Grand Rapids, Michigan: Baker Book House.

———. 1872k. The repentance of believers. In *The works of john wesley*, ed. Thomas Jackson. 1872nd ed. Vol. 5, 234-248. Grand Rapids, Michigan: Baker Book House.

———. 1872l. Rules of the band-societies. In *The works of john wesley*, ed. Thomas Jackson. Vol. 8, 305-308. Grand Rapids, Michigan: Baker Book House.

———. 1872m. Scriptural christianity. In *The works of john wesley*, ed. Thomas Jackson. Vol. 5, 103-119. Grand Rapids, Michigan: Baker Book House.

———. 1872n. A short address to the inhabitants of ireland occasioned by some late occurrences. In *The works of john wesley*, ed. Thomas Jackson. Vol. 9, 203-208. Grand Rapids, Michigan: Baker Book House.

———. 1872o. The spirit of bondage and of adoption. In *The works of john wesley*, ed. Thomas Jackson. Vol. 5, 169-182. Grand Rapids, Michigan: Baker Book House.

———. 1872p. Upon our lord's sermon on the mount, discourse 10. In *The works of john wesley*. Vol. 5, 487-498. Grand Rapids, Michigan: Baker Book House.

———. 1872q. Upon our lord's sermon on the mount, discourse 12. In *The works of john wesley*, ed. Thomas Jackson. Vol. 5, 508-518. Grand Rapids, Michigan: Baker Book House.

———. 1872r. Upon our lord's sermon on the mount, discourse 13. In *The works of john wesley*, ed. Thomas Jackson. Vol. 5, 519-529. Grand Rapids, Michigan: Baker Book House.

———. 1872s. Upon our lord's sermon on the mount, discourse 2. In *The works of john wesley*, ed. Thomas Jackson. Vol. 5, 347-363. Grand Rapids, Michigan: Baker Book House.

———. 1872t. Upon our lord's sermon on the mount, discourse 3. In *The works of john wesley*, ed. Thomas Jackson. Vol. 5, 364-381. Grand Rapids, Michigan: Baker Book House.

_____. 1872u. Upon our lord's sermon on the mount, discourse 4. In *The works of john wesley*, ed. Thomas Jackson. Vol. 5, 382-398. Grand Rapids, Michigan: Baker Book House.

_____. 1872v. Upon our lord's sermon on the mount, discourse 6. In *The works of john wesley*, ed. Thomas Jackson. Vol. 5, 417-434. Grand Rapids, Michigan: Baker Book House.

_____. 1872w. Upon our lord's sermon on the mount, discourse 7. In *The works of john wesley*, ed. Thomas Jackson. Vol. 5, 435-452. Grand Rapids, Michigan: Baker Book House.

_____. 1872x. Upon our lord's sermon on the mount, discourse 8. In *The works of john wesley*, ed. Thomas Jackson. Vol. 5, 453-470. Grand Rapids, Michigan: Baker Book House.

_____. 1872y. Upon our lord's sermon on the mount, discourse 9. In *The works of john wesley*, ed. Thomas Jackson. Vol. 5, 471-486. Grand Rapids, Michigan: Baker Book House.

_____. 1872z. The way to the kingdom. In *The works of john wesley*, ed. Thomas Jackson. Vol. 5, 146-156. Grand Rapids, Michigan: Baker Book House.

Wynkoop, Mildred Bangs. 1972. *A theology of love*. Kansas City, MO: Beacon Hill Press.

Chapter 7: Christian Perfection and the Means of Grace

Blevins, Dean G. 1997. The means of grace: Toward a wesleyan praxis of spiritual formation. *Wesleyan Theological Journal* 32, no. 1: 69-83.

Collins, Kenneth J. 2004. The promise of john wesley's theology for the 21st. century. *The Asbury Theological Journal* 59, no. 2: 171-180.

Leffel, G. Michael. 2004. Prevenient grace and the re-enchantment of nature: Towards a wesleyan theology of psychotherapy and spiritual formation. *Journal of Psychology and Christianity* 23, no. 2: 130-139.

Maddox, Randy. 1994. *Responsible grace*. Nashville, TN: Kingswood Books.

Mann, Mark H. 2006. *Perfecting grace: Holiness, human being, and the sciences*. New York: T and T Clark International.

Outler, Albert Cook. 1980. John wesley's interest in the early fathers of the church. *Bulletin of the United Church of Canada Committee on Archives and History* 29, : 5-17.

Wesley, John. 1872a. The almost christian. In *The works of john wesley*, ed. Thomas Jackson. Vol. 5, 81-89. Grand Rapids, Michigan: Baker Book House.

_____. 1872b. An extract of the rev. mr. john wesley's journal, june 29, 1786 to october 24, 1790, number 21. In *The works of john wesley*, ed. Thomas Jackson. Vol. 4. Grand Rapids, Michigan: Baker Book House.

_____. 1872c. The first fruits of the spirit. In *The works of john wesley*, ed. Thomas Jackson. Vol. 5, 157-168. Grand Rapids, Michigan: Baker Book House.

_____. 1872d. Journal from november 1, 1739 to september 3, 1741. In *The works of john wesley*, ed. Thomas Jackson. Vol. 1. Grand Rapids, Michigan: Baker Book House.

_____. 1872e. A letter written on september 8, 1746, the journal of john wesley, 1745 to 1760. In *The works of john wesley*, ed. Thomas Jackson. Vol. 2. Grand Rapids, Michigan: Baker Book House.

_____. 1872f. The means of grace. In *The works of john wesley*, ed. Thomas Jackson. Vol. 5, 264-281. Grand Rapids, Michigan: Baker Book House.

_____. 1872g. Minutes of several conversations between the rev. mr. wesley and others; from the year 1744 to the year 1789. In *The works of john wesley*, ed. Thomas Jackson. Vol. 8, 345-398. Grand Rapids, Michigan: Baker Book House.

_____. 1872h. On attending the church service. In *The works of john wesley*, ed. Thomas Jackson. Vol. 7, 202-213. Grand Rapids, Michigan: Baker Book House.

_____. 1872i. *On visiting the sick*. The works of john wesley. Ed. Thomas Jackson. Vol. 7. Grand Rapids, Michigan: Baker Book House.

_____. 1872j. On zeal. In *The works of john wesley*, ed. Thomas Jackson. Vol. 7, 73-83. Grand Rapids, Michigan: Baker Book House.

_____. 1872k. A plain account of the people called methodists in a letter to the rev. mr. perronet, vicar of shoreham, in kent, written in the year 1748. In *The works of john wesley*, ed. Thomas Jackson. Vol. 8, 278. Grand Rapids: Baker Book House.

_____. 1872l. Primitive physic: Or, an easy and natural method of curing most diseases. In *The works of john wesley*, ed. Thomas Jackson. Vol. 14, 421-434. Grand Rapids, Michigan: Baker Book House.

_____. 1872m. The repentance of believers. In *The works of john wesley*, ed. Thomas Jackson. Vol. 5, 234-248. Grand Rapids, Michigan: Baker Book House.

_____. 1872n. The righteousness of faith. In *The works of john wesley*, ed. Thomas Jackson. Vol. 5, 133-145. Grand Rapids, Michigan: Baker Book House.

_____. 1872o. *A second letter to the author of "the enthusiasm of methodists and papists compared."*. The works of john wesley. Ed. Thomas Jackson. Vol. 9. Grand Rapids, Michigan: Baker Book House.

_____. 1872p. Self-denial. In *The works of john wesley*, ed. Thomas Jackson. Vol. 6, 124-135. Grand Rapids, Michigan: Baker Book House.

_____. 1872q. A short address to the inhabitants of ireland occasioned by some late occurrences. In *The works of john wesley*, ed. Thomas Jackson. Vol. 9, 203-208. Grand Rapids, Michigan: Baker Book House.

_____. 1872r. Upon our lord's sermon on the mount, discourse 1. In *The works of john wesley*, ed. Thomas Jackson. Vol. 5, 331-346. Grand Rapids, Michigan: Baker Book House.

_____. 1872s. Upon our lord's sermon on the mount, discourse 13. In *The works of john wesley*, ed. Thomas Jackson. Vol. 5, 519-529. Grand Rapids, Michigan: Baker Book House.

_____. 1872t. Upon our lord's sermon on the mount, discourse 2. In *The works of john wesley*, ed. Thomas Jackson. Vol. 5, 347-363. Grand Rapids, Michigan: Baker Book House.

_____. 1872u. Upon our lord's sermon on the mount, discourse 4. In *The works of john wesley*, ed. Thomas Jackson. Vol. 5, 382-398. Grand Rapids, Michigan: Baker Book House.

_____. 1872v. Upon our lord's sermon on the mount, discourse 5. In *The works of john wesley*, ed. Thomas Jackson. Vol. 5, 399-416. Grand Rapids, Michigan: Baker Book House.

_____. 1872w. Upon our lord's sermon on the mount, discourse 6. In *The works of john wesley*, ed. Thomas Jackson. Vol. 5, 417-434. Grand Rapids, Michigan: Baker Book House.

_____. 1872x. Upon our lord's sermon on the mount, discourse 7. In *The works of john wesley*, ed. Thomas Jackson. Vol. 5, 435-452. Grand Rapids, Michigan: Baker Book House.

_____. 1872y. Upon our lord's sermon on the mount, discourse 8. In *The works of john wesley*, ed. Thomas Jackson. Vol. 5, 453-470. Grand Rapids, Michigan: Baker Book House.

_____. 1872z. Upon our lord's sermon on the mount, discourse 9. In *The works of john wesley*, ed. Thomas Jackson. Vol. 5, 471-486. Grand Rapids, Michigan: Baker Book House.

Chapter 8: Getting It Right!

A Kempis, Thomas. 1997. *The imitation of christ*. Version 2.0 ed. Albany, OR: Books for the Ages: Ages Software.

American Psychiatric Association. 2000. *Diagnostic and statistical manual of mental disorders: Text revision, DSM-IV-TR*. Fourth ed. Washington, DC: American Psychiatric Association.

Barton, Ruth Haley. 2006. *Sacred rhythms: Arranging our lives for spiritual transformation*. Downers Grove, IL: Intervarsity Press.

Benner, David G. 2002. *Sacred companions: The gift of spiritual friendship and direction*. Downers Grove, Illinois: Intervarsity Press.

Brunner, Emil. 1956. *Faith, hope and love*. Philadelphia: Westminster Press.

Bunyan, John. 1985. *The pilgrim's progress*. Uhrichsville, Ohio: Barbour Publishing, Inc.

Carroll, Lauren. December 9, 2011. Students flounder at divinity school. *The Duke Chronicle*.

Chambers, Oswald. 1963. *My utmost for his highest.* Westwood, NJ: Barbour and Company, Inc.

Cozolino, Louis. 2006a. *The neuroscience of human relationships.* W. W. Norton and Company.

———. 2006b. *The neuroscience of human relationships: Attachment and the developing social brain.* New York: W.W. Norton.

Foster, Richard. 1993. *Celebration of discipline.* San Francisco: Harper.

Guinness, Os. 1998. *The call: Finding and fulfilling the central purpose of your life.* Waco, TX: Word.

Hands, Donald, R. and Wayne Fehr L. 1994. *Spiritual wholeness for clergy: A new psychology of intimacy with god, self and others.* Washington, D.C.: Alban Institute.

Headley, Anthony J. October 5, 2010Wesleyan theology: Its relevance for christian ministry. Asbury Theological Seminary, .

Leffel, G. Michael. 2007. Emotion and transformation in the relational spirituality paradigm part 3. A moral motive analysis. *Journal of Psychology and Theology* 35, no. 4: 298-316.

Lindstrom, Harald. 1980. *Wesley and sanctification.* Wilmore, KY: Francis Asbury Publishing Company.

Niebuhr, H. Richard. 1963. *The responsible self.* New York: Harper and Row.

Norris, Leila N. 1900. *Sweet will of god.*

Seligman, Martin and Mihaly Csikszenmihalyi. 2000. Positive psychology: An introduction. *American Psychologist* 55, no. 1: 5.

Sire, James W. 2000. *Habits of the mind: Intellectual life as a christian calling.* Downers Grove, IL: Intervarsity Press.

Stevens, Bruce, A. 2006. "Love supreme": On spiritual experience and change in personality structure. *Journal of Psychology and Theology* 34, no. 4: 318.

Stratton, Stephen. January 24, 2013. Asbury Theological Seminary: .

Strawn, Brad,D. 2004. Restoring moral affections of heart: How does psychotherapy heal. *Journal of Psychology and Christianity* 23, no. 2: 140-148.

Tjeltveit, Alan C. 2006. Psychology returns to love --of god and neighbor-as-self: Introduction to the special issue. *Journal of Psychology and Theology* 34, no. 1: 3-7.

Watson, Robert, A. 2000. Towards union in love: The contemplative spiritual tradition and contemporary psychoanalytic theory in the formation of persons. *Journal of Psychology and Theology* 28, no. 4: 282-282-292.

Wesley, John. 1872a. The case of reason impartially considered. In *The works of john wesley,* ed. Thomas Jackson. Vol. 6, 389-400. Grand Rapids, Michigan: Baker Book House.

_____. 1872b. The duty of reproving our neighbor. In *The works of john wesley*, ed. Thomas Jackson. Vol. 6, 331-339. Grand Rapids, Michigan: Baker Book House.

_____. 1872c. An extract of A letter to the rev. mr. law occasioned by some of his late writings. In *The works of john wesley*, ed. Thomas Jackson. Vol. 9, 536-587. Grand Rapids, Michigan: Baker Book House.

_____. 1872d. The general deliverance. In *The works of john wesley*, ed. Thomas Jackson. Vol. 6, 272-284. Grand Rapids, Michigan: Baker Book House.

_____. 1872e. Heaviness through manifold temptations. In *The works of john wesley*, ed. Thomas Jackson. Vol. 6, 111-123. Grand Rapids, Michigan: Baker Book House.

_____. 1872f. On attending the church service. In *The works of john wesley*, ed. Thomas Jackson. Vol. 7, 202-213. Grand Rapids, Michigan: Baker Book House.

_____. 1872g. On the fall of man. In *The works of john wesley*, ed. Thomas Jackson. Vol. 6, 244-253. Grand Rapids, Michigan: Baker Book House.

_____. 1872h. On zeal. In *The works of john wesley*, ed. Thomas Jackson. Vol. 7, 73-83. Grand Rapids, Michigan: Baker Book House.

_____. 1872i. Part 7: The doctrine of original sin. In *The works of john wesley*, ed. Thomas Jackson. Vol. 9, 496-533. Grand Rapids, Michigan: Baker Book House.

_____. 1872j. The spirit of bondage and of adoption. In *The works of john wesley*, ed. Thomas Jackson. Vol. 5, 169-182. Grand Rapids, Michigan: Baker Book House.

_____. 1872k. Upon our lord's sermon on the mount, discourse 13. In *The works of john wesley*, ed. Thomas Jackson. Vol. 5, 519-529. Grand Rapids, Michigan: Baker Book House.

_____. 1872l. Upon our lord's sermon on the mount, discourse 2. In *The works of john wesley*, ed. Thomas Jackson. Vol. 5, 347-363. Grand Rapids, Michigan: Baker Book House.

_____. 1872m. Upon our lord's sermon on the mount, discourse 4. In *The works of john wesley*, ed. Thomas Jackson. Vol. 5, 382-398. Grand Rapids, Michigan: Baker Book House.

_____. 1872n. Upon our lord's sermon on the mount, discourse 5. In *The works of john wesley*, ed. Thomas Jackson. Vol. 5, 399-416. Grand Rapids, Michigan: Baker Book House.

_____. 1872o. Upon our lord's sermon on the mount, discourse 9. In *The works of john wesley*, ed. Thomas Jackson. Vol. 5, 471-486. Grand Rapids, Michigan: Baker Book House.

_____. 1872p. The use of money. In *The works of john wesley*, ed. Thomas Jackson. Vol. 6, 147-159. Grand Rapids, Michigan: Baker Book House.

_____. 1872q. The way to the kingdom. In *The works of john wesley*, ed. Thomas Jackson. Vol. 5, 146-156. Grand Rapids, Michigan: Baker Book House.

Wynkoop, Mildred Bangs. 1972. *A theology of love.* Kansas City, MO: Beacon Hill Press.

Postscript: Thinking Ahead: The Neuroscience of Wesley's Dispositional Love –
Stephen P. Stratton

Bollas C. 1987. *The shadow of the object: Psychoanalysis of the unthought known.* New York: Columbia University Press.

Christakis, N. A. and J. H. Fowler. 2009. *Connected: How your friends' friends' friends affect everything you feel, think, and do.* New York: Little, Brown and Co.

Cozolino, Louis. 2010. *The neuroscience of psychotherapy: Healing the social brain.* 2nd. ed. New York: W. W. Norton.

_____. 2006. *The neuroscience of human relationships.* W. W. Norton and Company.

Kegan, R. 1982. *The evolving self: Problems and process in human development.* Cambridge, MA: Harvard University Press.

Kegan, R. and L. L. Lahey. 2009. *Immunity to change: How to overcome it and unlock the potential in yourself and your organization.* Boston: Harvard Business Press.

_____. 2001. *How the way we talk can change the way we work: Seven languages for transformation.* San Francisco: Jossey-Bass.

LeDoux, J. 1998. *The emotional brain: The mysterious underpinnings of emotional life.* New York: Touchstone.

Sapolsky, R. M. 2004. *Why zebras don't get ulcers.* Third ed. New York: Holt, Henry & Company.

Siegel, D. J. 2012a. *The developing mind: How relationships and the brain interact to shape who we are.* Second ed. New York: Guilford.

_____. 2012b. *Pocket guide to interpersonal neurobiology: An integrative handbook of the mind.* New York: Norton.

_____. 1999. *The developing mind: How relationships and the brain interact to shape who we are.* First ed. New York: Guilford.

Wampold, B. E. and S. L. Budge. 2012. The relationship -- and its relationship to common and specific factors of psychotherapy. *The Counseling Psychologist* 40, no. 4: 601-623.

www.ingramcontent.com/pod-product-compliance
Lightning Source LLC
Chambersburg PA
CBHW021841220426
43663CB00005B/350